Lullaby by the River

Temperance Johnson

Contents

Chapter One	1
Chapter Two	12
Chapter Three	25
Chapter Four	38
Chapter Five	54
Chapter Six	65
Chapter Seven	78
Chapter Eight	90
Chapter Nine	104
Chapter Ten	111
Chapter Eleven	124
Chapter Twelve	132
Chapter Thirteen	144
Chapter Fourteen	150
Chapter Fifteen	159
Chapter Sixteen	181
Chapter Seventeen	194
Chapter Eighteen	214
Chapter Nineteen	226
Chapter Twenty	236
Chapter Twenty-One	247
Chapter Twenty-Two	259
Chapter Twenty-Three	265
Chapter Twenty-Four	277
Chapter Twenty-Five	285
Chapter Twenty-Six	295
Chapter Twenty-Seven	305
Chapter Twenty-Eight	313
Chapter Twenty-Nine	317
Chapter Thirty	322

Chapter Thirty-One	333
Chapter Thirty-Two	339
Acknowledgments	345

To my bestie, Sarah, for all of your support and encouragement with this story. I couldn't imagine doing it without you. You are inspiring with how much you have overcome! Never forget that. Love you, Princess.

Lullaby by the River by Temperance Johnson

Copyright © 2024 by Temperance Johnson. All rights reserved.

Content editing by: Jessica Hamm

Cover Design by: Hannah Linder

Book Interior Formatting by: Temperance Johnson

Available in print and ebook format on amazon.com and other platforms

All Scripture references taken from the King James Version. Public domain.

All rights reserved. Non-commercial interests may reproduce portions of this book without the express written permission of the author, provided the text does not exceed 500 words. Commercial interests: No part of this publication may be reproduced in any form, stored in a retrieval system, or transmitted in any form by any means—electronic, photocopy, recording, or otherwise—without prior written permission of the author, except as provided by the United States of America copyright law.

This is a work of fiction. Names, characters, and incidents are all products of the author's imagination or are used for fictional purposes. Any mentioned brand names, places, and trademarks remain the property of their respective owners, bear no association with the author or the publisher, and are used for fictional purposes only. Any similarities to individuals living or dead is purely coincidental.

Published in the United States of America.

Chapter One

Priscilla looked down from the loft of the barn. Not that far. The spring Kentucky grass was just starting to green up as it moved in the wind. The sun beamed down on her like it brought promise of a new day, but she only felt despair. She smelled the cows she had just milked that morning.

If she did this, she would never milk them again. She didn't know if the fall would kill her or just cause an injury. What would her family think when they found her? Would she be in a wheelchair for the rest of her life if she lived?

If she was in a wheelchair, maybe *he* wouldn't want her anymore. Would she go to hell for committing the unforgivable sin? And what of her child? Maybe *he* would take the child if she could not care for him or her.

Stepping closer to the edge, she looked down again. She didn't see another way out. Putting her hand on her stomach, she covered her baby.

"I can't put you through living with him," she whispered.

Closing her eyes, about to jump, she was suddenly pulled roughly backward onto hay. Frowning and dizzy, she blinked.

She looked up to see Danny Taylor glaring at her and breathing hard. "What would make you do that?" He looked at her stomach. "And to your child?"

She sat up and crossed her arms. "I won't let this child grow up with a father like that. I can't live another day with him. I can't have more children with him. I don't see another way out."

She sobbed, feeling dirty and so filthy in front of Danny. He was her friend, and with his father being the bishop, she wasn't surprised he was here. She had almost expected him to come now when she needed him most. He always helped everyone. Especially women in the community.

Danny just stood there and let her cry. Then he finally said, "There has to be another way."

Priscilla couldn't take the pain anymore. She moved over to the ladder and climbed down. As Danny followed her, she got on her pony despite being short and petite and ran. She knew she could fall with the way she was riding and hurt the baby, but she just wanted away from her problems. Of her future.

She could hear Danny riding up behind her. His horse, Spirit, was much taller and faster than her pony.

He stopped her pony by grabbing the reins, dismounted, and pulled her off. Then caught her in his arms. Trees surrounded them in the small wooded area.

She hit him. Taking her fists at his chest, he didn't stop the blows, just held her as she sobbed. Finally, she leaned against a tree and threw up, feeling even more shame.

After wiping her mouth, she rested against the cool

bark, not looking at him. The wind had been light with spring warmth and a cloud covered the once shining sun, but it looked like it might rain now. Maybe a curse for what she was about to do.

Danny moved in front of her. His deep blue eyes now looked worried about her. "I might know of a way to protect you and the baby."

She didn't want to look at him but couldn't pull her gaze from him. There was hope with him. She just moaned.

"Marry me?" he said simply.

She looked at him then. Her eyes went wide. Marry him? She did care for him and had even loved him at one time.

But to marry him now?

She knew many girls in her community adored him, but he was not a good Amish boy. He wore shiny black cowboy boots all the time. His blond, curly hair reached to his shoulders. Many of the girls said he would leave the Amish, and she knew personally they were right. He would leave; it was a matter of time. His leaving was why she stopped courting him and then made the worst decision of her life.

But leaving the Amish and marrying him didn't sound worse than marrying a rapist and staying. What if she went to hell for leaving the Amish with him? But wouldn't living with her abuser be a hell? She would lose her family if she left the Amish, but maybe she could convince Danny to stay?

Yes, that was it. She could convince him to stay. He was sweet, as everyone knew, and she could show how great it would be to stay. That had to be better than living with *that man*. Her stomach flipped and felt in such knots.

She nearly threw up again, but she finally cried, "Yes. I will marry you." She wiped her eyes. "Yes."

Danny was happy Priscilla said yes, his eyes softened, but he didn't plan to ask her like this. He wanted to touch her cheek. But he was also sad he couldn't offer her more. A home or family like she wanted. He wanted to tell her he loved her, but she already knew he did. She was pale but her expression also looked firm. Her blonde, curly hair was pulled back in a kapp, and those blue beautiful eyes were sorrowful. She was short and petite. This was the woman he knew and loved.

"Thank you for accepting." He didn't know what else to say.

"What will the bishop, your Datt, say?" she asked quietly.

He frowned and swore. "I don't care. We will say anything to get by him."

Her eyes got wide.

"Pardon me."

"What if the bishop says our marriage is wrong?" She bit her lip. "Especially since I've been courting another."

"It doesn't matter. He isn't God."

Her eyes were so innocent. "If the bishop doesn't tell us how to live, who will?"

"God."

She looked at him with no understanding. He had joined the church a year or so ago. If a rebel like him had joined the church, then maybe he wouldn't leave the Amish. Joining the church was a major step.

"You already joined the church, that will help," her eyes widened, still trying to figure out why he joined. It was one of many things he never told her. She might as well get used to that in their marriage.

He smiled at her, his white teeth shining. "I can see I have shocked you. A bad boy like me joined the Amish church."

She nodded shyly.

"Even though I joined, I want to follow God more than the church."

She just blinked and nodded. It was obvious she had no understanding of what he meant. Could he marry a girl who didn't share his passion for Christ? Who understood nothing of faith? Looking at her flat stomach, her baby, he knew he was doing the right thing. He already loved her so much. He couldn't lose her again?

He ran a hand over his face. She had a lot to learn. Things would differ from now on. First, she would learn to have a voice. Find her voice. He should be honest with her about what their future looked like. Well, most of it.

"You know one day I will leave the Amish. Probably before the… the baby is born," he said gently. But his eyes showed how serious he was. His tense body showed how he didn't want to leave but had too.

She shrugged. "Of course, I know."

But then she narrowed her eyes at him, thinking of why they stopped courting. She knew he was thinking of the same thing. That day in the barn when they said goodbye. The kisses. She shook her head.

"But I don't want to go to hell if we leave or my baby to go…" she didn't say it. Couldn't say it.

He knew she believed her baby may end up in hell being born in the world.

"That is a lie. You will not go to hell by leaving the Amish," he sighed. "It's too hard to explain now, but you are a believer, right?"

She nodded.

"That is what will get you to heaven."

She blinked, not understanding. They were silent for a bit as the wind picked up and the rain seemed to be in the air. The horses just stood there like they were trained.

Then she looked away. "Can I ask one thing?"

He nodded and smiled. She was speaking up. "Anything?"

She looked down. "We don't share a...a bed till the baby is born."

Her face was pale with fear, guilt, and shame.

His face turned bright red.

"Mmm yes." He stepped closer. "I will never hurt you." He looked down, probably remembering the same thing she just had. "You know, when you ask me to stop or not do anything, I will always listen."

She looked at him, not believing a word of it. He had stopped kissing her in the past when she asked, but now she was too afraid that in marriage he had rights to her. Her body was his now. He could do what he wanted, no matter what she said.

But at least he promised and that was something. By his red face, she could tell he had never been with a woman. But if he hadn't been with a woman, why would he want her? She had been so used up now. It wasn't like before, and he knew that.

Which made her feel more guilty.

Guilty because she knew he deserved better than what she had to offer, and a child who wasn't his.

∼

The next day, Danny got up enough courage to go to his closest friend. He walked into his boss's office without knocking. Not like him at all. He was glad his boss was his English dad.

Stan looked up in surprise, but then recovered with a small smile and acted like nothing was wrong. He was glad Stan was alone.

"Sorry, I should have knocked," he muttered and dropped dejectedly into a chair. His hair was messy from him running his hands through it. He sighed.

"What is wrong, Daniel? I have never seen you like this," Stan said.

"I am getting married on Sunday to an Amish girl. And I am marrying her when I don't agree with the faith. But not much more than that," he ran a hand through his hair.

Stan stood up, walking over to the edge of the desk. "Now, why don't you slow down and tell me what happened?" He paused. "It's about Priscilla?"

He nodded and told him what had happened. Stan knew Danny loved Priscilla. When he finished, he was tired. He could work hours with no rest, but this situation was making him exhausted.

"I didn't go there ready to propose, but it was the first thing that came to my mind. I just don't want her hurt by James again. I know she won't take outside help. So, I just asked her and she said yes almost right away. I want to marry her, but I hate that she has to be forced into marriage. I know she is afraid. Very scared," he sighed.

Stan stood there, his hand on his chin as he thought it out. Then nodded. "You're probably right. She is terrified of marrying James. But she ain't afraid of marrying you, or she wouldn't have said yes. She is probably pretty nervous. But can you marry an Amish girl? Even if you love her?"

Danny stood up and started to pace the floor.

"That is what I am worried about. I want a woman who can tell me what she is thinking. Someone who will tell me no. Someone to strengthen my faith," he sat back down, hard. "Someone who will stand up for her faith, our kids, and me. But I also want Priscilla. I still love her, even though she has changed."

"Those are big concerns and good questions. Have you prayed about it?"

He nodded.

Stan stayed silent for a moment then asked, "Have you noticed the change in her the past few months?"

"I have seen the change in her, yes. She started seeing James right after we broke up. I feel like she did it to get back at me." If he hadn't messed it up with her, she wouldn't have gotten hurt. Be with child. Another man's child. "I think James had been dating other girls, too. All young. I think soon after she started dating him, he started hurting her. Priscilla was so innocent and happy before. So pretty. She was always shy but friendly. Then she became withdrawn and more controlled, like so many Amish girls who are bundling bedroom dating." He slammed his fist into his other hand. Bundling was spending together in bed all night fully clothed. Too often sexual abuse or sexual activity took place. "And the hardest thing is, I can't take James to court for what he did, even if he forced her and is older."

Stan frowned, knowing that was true. "He will probably continue to do this to others."

Danny glared and then sighed knowing anger never did any good. He ran a hand through his long hair. "I hate cutting it."

His hair had been his way to rebel, just a bit. He looked

at Stan. "What is she going to do when she finds out I am going to be a cop in a couple of months?"

"That is a big question, son. You don't want to start your marriage dishonestly."

"I don't. But if I tell her I am living a double life, will she still marry me? Or will she hate me? We broke up because of how much I like the world," Danny wanted Stan to give him the answers. He had been both his boss and his English father, a man who had half-raised him from age ten.

"I don't know what I would do. From what you tell me, she is shy. She probably won't understand your job, but when you tell her, tell her from your heart. Give yourself up for her. She needs it. How strong is her faith?"

Danny gave him a sad smile. "Not strong. She doubts. She has only been a believer for a year."

"Start there." He crossed his arms. "But you need to remember to accept her for who she is. Don't expect her to have your faith. You have been on this journey for many years. You have seen the truth she hasn't seen or doesn't know. Her faith is almost like a child. Show her unconditional love and grace through your own faith."

Danny's burden lightened. He would enjoy showing her what his English parents had shown him. He already loved her so much. That part would be easy. He respected her will and who she had been in the past. Would he ever see her that way again?

"I will. Maybe it will make up for…" he didn't finish. Couldn't finish.

His family. The one that carried his blood should be here. They should be here for this day. But they wouldn't be. Ever.

Stan shook his head. "Don't put Priscilla in their shadows. It will fail. That is not right for her or you. Just treat her like herself. God has been working on this, for sure."

Danny smiled.

"I think so too. She is one beautiful lady. Those curls," he muttered.

Though Stan had never seen them. No one had but him.

Stan chuckled.

"It helps to find one's spouse attractive," he paused. "Pam and I would like to meet her soon."

Danny grinned. "I would like that. I rented a dawdy's house. It's small. So I need stuff in it and to have it cleaned up, but I don't have the time. And I don't want Priscilla to have to do it before the wedding. She is so nervous."

"I will get Pam and the girls over there. Pam will buy what it needs and we will pay for it."

Danny raised an eyebrow.

Stan grinned. "It will be part of my wedding gift, and I will take it from the mission. Priscilla is a victim. She deserves better things."

The mission was what Stan ran, and it helped girls like Priscilla in her situation. Danny had worked there since being an adult.

Danny nodded. "She sure does."

They remained silent, contemplating. Then Stan said in his deep, gentle voice, "Daniel, I am talking to you as a married man. You will need to respect all of Priscilla, even where she comes from."

Danny wrinkled his forehead, and he looked confused. "What do you mean?"

"She is her own person. She has experienced hurt, and her voice has not been heard in this situation." He paused. "Think of her like a wounded sparrow you might have helped as a kid. She has had no voice for so long that it would be easy to step on her voice. To not see her needs because she won't share them. She has never known the love of a heavenly father. Show God's love from His word and your actions. Just don't have any expectation that she will believe like you do. That will hurt her in the long run." When Danny slowly nodded, he continued, "If she doesn't believe you, that doesn't mean you take your love from her. You can't hurt her for what she doesn't do. Marriage doesn't work that way." His eyes showed he knew what he was talking about. "Care for her and, if or when love comes, take it slow. Show her in small ways you care for her. And you will find her voice. It might take a while. But it won't disappoint you. She will become a beautiful new creature before your eyes. One who can talk to you and share herself with you."

"Thank you for sharing that," Danny stood.

Stan pulled him into a hug. "God bless you, son."

As Danny left the office, he knew he was making the right decision. He hadn't felt that often in his life, but in becoming a cop and now doing this, he felt a peace.

It didn't mean he was without fear.

He still had to meet with the bishop who had raised him since he was ten.

Chapter Two

The dreaded meeting came sooner than Danny expected. On Tuesday, he and Priscilla met with the bishop. They sat across from the bishop. His adopted father. He wore the traditional, long Amish beard. He stared at the table, trying to ignore that James sat to his right a few chairs down. Priscilla seemed frozen beside him.

He had told Priscilla to say anything to get the bishop to agree to marry them. He was sure she wouldn't talk much, but he hoped to have her support. He, unlike her, knew his adopted father would not mind sharing all this gossip with his deacons or anyone else. Gossip spread like wildfire once the bishop got ahold of it.

The bishop rubbed his beard. "Why have you stepped in to marry her, Danny?"

Danny took a deep breath. "I want to marry her. I want to do the right thing."

"Are you the father of the child?" the bishop asked with thin lips as he glared at Priscilla.

Danny glanced at Priscilla, who stared down at the

table. His hands clenched and his chest burned. How could his dad treat her like this?

"I am doing the right thing."

The community knew James was courting Priscilla. He wouldn't shame her more and claim to be sleeping with her as well. Though he had come close when they'd dated. That guilt still sat with him. If he had done more on that day, would this child be his? Would she have been hurt? If he hadn't messed their courtship up, she may not be in this situation.

"The child is not yours," James spoke up. He had black hair cut into an Amish haircut. His brown eyes were dark, when he was charming people they would sparkle. But when the mask came down they showed only hate and indifferent. He had a leering smile that was as smug as he could get. His clothes were neat and smooth, as smooth as a snake. "Ask her."

Danny grabbed the edge of the table instead of grabbing James's neck. "I want to marry Priscilla."

The bishop frowned. "You have chances to marry anyone. James is right, the child is his child."

Priscilla took his arm.

"No," she nearly shouted. "The child is Danny's."

Danny stared at her and nodded. Her fingers dug into his arm. He knew then if he couldn't get the bishop to marry them, he would go to the courthouse and leave the Amish faith. He didn't want his children to be raised in it anyhow. No way would he let James near her again.

"You are a Jezebel," James muttered.

The bishop frowned. His face turned beet red.

"Fine," he shook his head. "You will make this right and marry her this Sunday."

Danny almost sighed with his relief. "Good. I will."

James stood up, knocking his chair over. "Now wait here. I have been courting her for a long time. I should marry her."

Priscilla held Danny's arm tighter. He was relieved because it kept him still. Danny rose with Priscilla, her arm still on his. "We will see you on Sunday."

He moved to the door.

James stormed out before them, slamming the door in their faces.

Danny tried not to glare after him. He didn't want to upset Priscilla anymore.

The bishop walked over to them. "You will make this right and marry her, covering the mistake she caused."

Danny nearly swore. Walking up to his dad, he pointed at his chest.

"Don't ever talk to Priscilla like that again. And never call our..." he bit his lip, "never call our child a mistake."

With that, he took her arm, gently, guiding her out of the room and out of the house.

Priscilla looked up at him. She saw a man who was angry over the injustice of what was happening to her. Her eyes glowed with gratitude. What he had just done was better than anything other men had done for her.

∽

"Will you take a walk with me?" Danny asked Priscilla a few days later. He had come over for supper and stayed to clean up. Even though it wasn't a man's job.

She looked up from the dishes. Did she want to go? She looked outside. It wasn't even close to dark, but what if Danny tried something? She mentally shook her head at herself for thinking he might hurt her. He never had in the past. But things were different now. She was damaged.

How could she even think that? She knew Danny. He was always a gentleman and that hadn't changed. Or had it? Because she could make him fall? She would make sure she never let or made anyone do that to her again. She had to stop thinking of him treating her like that. She had to start trusting him.

Again.

She timidly nodded a yes to him.

Her sister, Annie, wouldn't mind finishing the dishes. She had two brothers as well. They were a small family for the Amish.

Once outside, Danny led the way to the pond in her backyard. They had gone fishing many times here. It was where they had their first kiss as young teens. The water shone in the sunset. Priscilla took a minute to study the man she would marry. He didn't look a bit Amish. His eyes were dark, almost black, when he got mad. Which wasn't often, from what she could tell. His skin was tan from many hours outside. He had long brown hair with slight curls; it was wavy and pulled back in a ponytail. No Amish boy would wear hair like that. Why had he never been shunned over it? Maybe it had to do with the bishop.

"I thought I would share some things about myself, since when we were courting you said I was hiding myself from you," Danny told her. "You were right. And I will try to be honest with you from now on. Can we both be?"

She nodded without looking at him. But deep down she had no plan to do that. Wasn't that what a good Amish wife should do? She knew many wives just told their husbands what they wanted but did another. Others actually did what the husband wanted. She couldn't do what he asked. So she chose to do the first. She had to be a perfect wife who wouldn't make him fail again. She was a Jezebel after all. Even if the words still stung, it was her fault she that was in this mess. She could do it.

He knew she wouldn't share her opinions with him, as much as he wanted her too. Would he be able to share everything with this woman he loved? He didn't know how. Only his English parents had gotten a close look at his heart, and then there were still times he held back. But he would try to make this marriage work. He loved her too much to let her go again.

Priscilla studied Danny. He didn't speak like the Amish. That he had learned not to have an accent was beyond her.

"You know we moved here three years ago to upstate New York. I was happy to get out. Our order had too many laws." His eyes were dark. "Though I wouldn't want to give that time in my life up. It made me who I am. As you know, my papa became a bishop last year. He was a bishop back home, too."

He frowned, but then changed the subject. "I enjoy living here. It is peaceful, but close enough to the city to work."

He motioned for her to sit on the bench. And she did but made sure they weren't touching.

"Where do you work?" she asked to relax. She felt shy for asking. He may not like it.

"I don't mind if you ask me anything. I will try not to hide anything from you." He couldn't tell her the full truth about his future job, though. It was too dangerous for their relationship right now, and she wouldn't understand. "I work as a rancher. My boss cares for people in need, and I help him out. It's good pay for us to live on. You won't have to worry about money. He is a generous boss."

He hadn't lied. His boss *was* a rancher... along with other things.

"I would like to see his ranch. I have never been to one."

"I will take you one day."

She nodded. Being near him was exhausting. She felt so many things. She didn't want to ask him the next thing, yet she needed to know. "Why did you stand up to marry me? Why not let.... him... marry me?"

The words shuddered out of her. She looked at her hands.

Danny touched her cheek and lifted her face.

"I am glad you asked me, dear," he looked deeply into her eyes, trying to show her how worthy she was of love. "I know what that man doesn't know. You deserve the best, honey. So does this baby. He does not deserve a hair on your head. While I might not either, I will try to be worthy of you."

Again, he wanted to tell her he loved her, but it was harder than he thought. Was he afraid she would reject him? She probably didn't love him any more. Not with the way she acted after their break-up.

Priscilla looked down again. She didn't understand what he meant. She wasn't worthy of anything. She didn't understand him. This was all confusing to her.

"How did you know he..." she paused, "how do you know he was..."

Danny touched her arm. "I heard the bishop and deacons talking. One of the deacons was furious at James."

She looked up. "Was it my dad?"

He shook his head. "No. It was Paul. You know he preaches against the bedroom courting. He walked out furious. He knew you didn't consent. Even if you had consented, it would still be wrong to do that. It's called spiritual abuse."

Her brows came together, and she eyed him. "How did he know?"

He frowned. "I don't want to say, but I will say he was wise enough to see you. The goodness in your heart."

She didn't have a good heart. She had let James take from her, and everyone said she wanted him to. "I like Paul."

"If I had a choice, Paul would marry us."

She nodded. Then suddenly her stomach turned. Nauseated, she ran to the closest tree and emptied her stomach. Feeling ashamed, she touched her head, which throbbed.

Danny came over and wished he could make this better for her. "Priscilla, I am sorry. Was it the talk of the wedding that upset you?"

She shook her head. Leaning against the tree, she started to shake. Her face was pale. "You deserve someone who is not sick all the time. You want someone who understands what you are talking about. You deserve someone who is pure. I ain't. You deserve your own child. This child ain't."

The look of shock and hurt on his face surprised her. He seemed to really care for her, even after all these months apart.

He opened his mouth, then closed it. He was silent for a long time before he spoke next.

"Priscilla, maybe I will have to move slower, at your

pace. I can see you never had real love. I hadn't either for a long time. I promise I want you and only you. But I won't force you into this marriage. If you don't want me. I will step back. But I won't let you marry James. Ever." He rubbed his temple. "I will help you find assistance if you want to give this baby up for adoption. Or raise it." He met her eyes. "But I think you are crying out at me in fear. Don't let fear take the baby from you. You need this baby. This baby needs you."

Priscilla inhaled deeply. He was right; she had cried out at him in fear. She wanted him to walk away and leave, but he hadn't. She could see him one day loving this child. She knew what his love felt like, and it was safe.

She touched her flat stomach. "I am so sorry for saying those things. I don't know what is wrong with me…"

He put a finger to her lips. "Never apologize about being honest, even if it does hurt me. I want to know what you are thinking. And always will."

He smiled lightly.

She closed her eyes, her lips still tingling from his soft touch. A part of her wanted his lips on hers but another was afraid he would go too far. This would be a long journey with him. But for now, she had to trust him, or at least try. She might fully trust him one day, but as long as she didn't love him again, she would be fine.

No man would have that control over her again.

∽

A few days later, Priscilla found herself back in the barn. Just to get time alone and to check on Missy, the family dog. Though she wished the dog belonged to her so she could take Missy with her when she married. Her mother was packing stuff away in her chest and her sister was baking. She was to be married in a couple days. To a man she didn't love anymore or trust. Not what she wanted, or even how she'd ever thought her life would turn out. She had dreamed of marrying him once but that was before she knew she was a tramp and made men touch her. She would make him fail, even if they were married; she was a jezebel, a bad woman. And she would be the one hurt in the process. Would her baby be hurt too?

No.

Only she would be or could be hurt that way. It was her wifely duty. She shuddered. She didn't want to be married to him. She kicked the barn wall, wanting to cry when she thought of her future. But as long as she stayed in the community, she would be all right. They would help her through this. She knew it. The women would help get her dawdy house ready and then give her the stuff for it. The men would see that Danny had everything he needed. What if they told him he had a right to her as a husband? She shook her head to clear the thought. He had promised he wouldn't do that, and she had to keep that in mind. She would think of how she would be an Amish wife and, of course, a mother. She would fit in with friends her age.

Though her best friend, Annamay, wasn't married. In all honesty she probably wouldn't ever be. Not to an Amish. She was too busy running around and...

She heard footsteps and flinched. Turning, she saw her monster. James. A smirk on his face. His eyes were dark and evil. She hated them. She was alone in the barn. What if he hurt her? Her baby? She couldn't breathe. She started to shake.

James's smirk became leering; he saw the control he

had over her. He walked closer, and with every step, he showed so much control and cockiness.

Priscilla's stomach cramped. He was going to hurt her.

"You know the child is mine. And so are you," he smirked. "I know you didn't sleep with him." Now he stood in front of her. He stunk and his eyes were so dark. She shivered. "He will see soon enough that the child is mine, and so will the community, and the truth will be out."

He touched her kapp in a rough way. Not gentle at all.

She closed her eyes and tried to wish him away. Her whole body froze. She didn't know what to do. When she opened her eyes, he was gone. She fell to the ground, tears running down her face, and she cried.

She heard someone come in again. Too afraid it was James, she didn't look up, but stood and began hitting him with her fist. "Don't come near me."

"Priscilla, Priscilla, easy. It's me." Danny frowned. He caught her arms. "Easy, Priscilla. It's me, Danny."

She stopped fighting him and fell in a heap, sobbing.

Danny had never been so worried. "Now honey, what is wrong? Is it the baby? Are you having issues with the baby?"

He knew some ladies had challenges in the early months of pregnancy. He sat next to her.

Priscilla's face flamed. She didn't know what he meant, but the mention of the baby brought her more shame. No man should ask about her baby. It wasn't an Amish man's place. Danny was strange.

Danny's voice was like a growl. "Now Priscilla, if you don't answer me, I am taking you to the clinic. Please tell me, honey."

Priscilla didn't want to go to a clinic. That would be

more shameful. She wasn't married yet. She tried to calm down, but her panic brought on hiccups.

Danny could see she was just upset, and she didn't look sick. He got a rag from the office of the barn and wet it with a water bottle he had brought and wiped her hot face as she tried to be calm. His heart felt like it would break..

Danny remained silent, though he wanted to talk. But Stan had taught him to be quiet.

Her brother came out to the barn, and he frowned at them in the stall. "What are you doing, sis?"

She flinched, and so Danny spoke for her. "We are talking. We need time alone. Go back to the house, Ben."

He expected Ben to listen, though he was a year older. Danny was used to people listening to him.

Ben frowned at him. "Dadae will be mad about this after what Priscilla has done to shame the family."

Danny grunted. "Go back to the house and never say that again."

Ben just shrugged and left.

Priscilla moaned, leaning against the wall.

"You don't have to marry me," she whispered.

Danny had expected this.

"Well, I am marrying you," he said simply. "Can you tell me what happened earlier?"

She looked at her hands. "James... was here... just came in the barn."

Danny teeth ground. "I will ask my boss to be off until Sunday. I will be here the rest of the days."

She shook her head. Her blonde curls were coming out of her kapp, and he wanted to calm those curls down and make everything better. She was a wildflower, wilted now, but with love and care she could bloom again.

"It's fine. I will be all right. You don't need to do that."

Danny didn't respond. He just sat there, hay slippery under his boots, and the smell of the horses filling the air. He enjoyed the smell; it brought back good memories of her in this barn. When he first got to know her, and then when he courted her.

Surprisingly, Priscilla found that Danny sitting next to her was comforting. Not safe, but nice. He was quiet and kind. Usually, he liked to talk and be funny, but he could be quiet when he wanted to. He was helpful.

Unfortunately, she needed to use the bathroom. As she stood her head began to spin, he took her arm and helped her. After steadying her, he let her go. She walked to the pen where the dog and puppies were kept. Missy lay in a box with six nursing yellow puppies.

She knelt down by them and she sighed. "I hate to leave Missy. She got me through…"

Danny stayed silent, listening.

"My dadae found her at a flea market." She leaned against the stall door and looked longingly at the pups. "I begged him to get her. Since she was so thin and big with puppies; he did it to get the puppies. Now that this is her last litter, I worry about where she will end up."

Danny moved to where he leaned on the other side of the stall door and met her eyes. "The puppies are little, but if we are still in the dawdy house, we could take her. I just don't know where she will go when we leave. And to put a dog like that in an apartment doesn't seem right."

"We could stay in the house out back," her eyes got bright.

He hid a groan. Stay on her parents' land when they had allowed her to get raped? No way.

Then she looked down. "Never mind. I know all of this is not what you wanted."

She was what he wanted.

He touched her chin and met her pretty blue eyes. "Everything is worth it. I will do my best to keep Missy with you. You are worth everything."

She didn't believe him, but it was nice to hear.

Chapter Three

Danny walked into Walmart, needing to pick up some items for the new house. His new home. He had lived in an apartment for so long that it would be nice to live back in the country. Even it meant living among the Amish and their church rules.

After a long day of work and then training, he wondered how long he could keep from Priscilla. He was training so much but it would be some weeks before he was done and officially a cop. He was looking in the appliance aisle when he heard someone behind him. He glanced over his shoulder and saw his best friend and partner, Zack Johnson, standing there.

"Hey, buddy," he could tell something was on Zack's mind. He was normally outgoing and loud.

"Well..." Zack paused. "Well, is it true?"

Danny eyed him. "I don't enjoy playing mind games."

"Are you getting married?" he finally asked. "To an Amish babe?"

"Yep," Danny nodded calmly and added, "that is what I hear."

"Why?" Zack crossed his arms. "Talk to me, Danny."

He sighed. "It's her only way to safety, and I need to do that. She is pregnant with James Miller's child," he paused, "I have prayed about it and feel called to do it."

Zack's jaw hardened.

"That is what I heard. Man, I wish I could get my hands on that man," he said bitterly.

Danny frowned. He hated that man so much for what he had done to Priscilla. Anger hit him hard in the stomach every time he thought of that monster.

"I would be there first," then he saw her beautiful smile in his mind and her soft voice. "She is special."

"It helps that you love her, but do you still think she loves you?" Zack asked.

"I do care for her. She is sweet," he told his friend honestly. "She has something special about her. I think in time she will care for me again."

"But you understand marriage is going to be hard," Zack had always been honest with him. Danny expected nothing less.

"Yes. I do," Danny assured him. "I know what I am walking into."

"Well, can I come to the wedding?" Zack knew he might not be able to come. Some English were allowed but with Danny's English parents coming he didn't want to impose.

"I want my parents there for it, at least. I don't want to draw attention, and this wedding is already such a rush and filled with drama," Danny paused. "I don't think the community would like me bringing too many English people since it's not planned."

Zack understood and took no offense. Danny was

thinking about Priscilla and how it would go for her. Danny didn't care what the Amish thought of him.

"So, when do I get to meet this girl?"

Danny finished shopping and headed to the front, Zack following. He grinned at his friend. "Hopefully soon, but I don't want to scare her, you know."

Zack laughed. "I promise I will put on all my charm."

Danny chuckled. "That is what I am afraid of. Though Ash has never let that charm rub off on her."

Zack burst out laughing.

"That's 'cause your sister knows me too well and has the same problem," he winked. "She has too much charm."

Danny laughed. "That is true."

As they turned to head to the front, Danny nearly ran into an Amish woman. Her kapp was on tight on her head, hiding her face, and she was looking down. Her shoulders slumped like she had a heavy weight on them. He thought he recognized her clothes. She was of his order of Amish. When she looked up, he was delighted to see Priscilla. She looked shocked and took a step back.

He beamed. "Well, Priscilla, it is a sweet surprise to see you today."

She nodded. "Hi, how are you?"

"Good." He wished she looked a bit happier to see him, but he could tell she was trying. Maybe he was too excited. But he was glad that at least one of his close friends could actually meet her. He looked at Zack, who was watching with great interest, but acting like this was the most normal thing in the world.

"Priscilla, I am so glad I ran into you. I would like you to meet my friend, Zack." He looked at Zack. "Zack, meet my fiancée, Priscilla."

Priscilla looked at his cop uniform with some suspicion while she gave him a shy, small smile.

Zack held out his hand. "It is a delight to meet you."

She shook it but pulled away as soon as she could. "It is nice to meet you as well."

She eyed his uniform again.

Zack noticed her distrust and looked at Danny with surprise, but said nothing.

"What are you doing here, honey?" Danny asked.

Priscilla smiled lightly.

"I was getting some stuff for supper and then items for the..." she stuttered. "That is, Mamm said I could get some items for..." she stopped again, "for something."

Danny knew it was for the wedding or the house. "Well, that is good. I will let you get to it."

She nodded. "Have a good day."

Danny said softly, "Have a delightful day, darling."

Her eyes widened, and her lips parted. A bit embarrassed, she muttered, "*Danke*."

He dipped his head and then moved with Zack to the front. He knew Zack was thinking this marriage was going to be a mess. After they checked out, Zack walked him to his jeep.

Zack finally said what he had been thinking. "She is not comfortable with cops. You can spot it a mile away."

Danny shrugged. "We will cross that bridge when we come to it."

Zack jabbed his arm. "Well, she is hot."

He winked at his friend.

Danny chuckled. "Be careful, my friend. She won't marry you. You're a cop."

Zack laughed.

"And your partner in a couple of months." He turned serious. "You are very blessed."

Danny nodded. "I am. Very much so."

He just wished Priscilla would see what a blessing she was to him.

⁓

Danny drove his horse into the Yoder's driveway. He was working on getting to know Priscilla more. His only motivation to be nice to her parents. It wasn't easy when he saw the pain in her eyes. Pain James had caused and her parents had allowed. But with his soon-to-be line of work, and being raised Amish, he had gotten used to hiding what he thought and felt. If there was one thing the Amish had going for them, it was how to act and put on a good show. It was pretty much how the Amish worked. He didn't like it. That was not sure how Priscilla felt.

He dismounted and then tied his horse, Spirit, to the post. As he walked to the house, he met Priscilla when she came over from the side yard, carrying a basket of laundry. He moved quickly to get the basket from her. "Here, let me get that."

Priscilla stared wide-eyed at him, but nodded. "*Danke.*"

He was glad she let him take it. Many Amish women would say it wasn't a man's job. "You're welcome. How are you doing?"

"Fine," she spoke simply.

They started the short walk to the front door.

"Would you like to stay for supper?" Priscilla asked as they entered the house.

"I would. Thank you for the offer." He paused. "Only if there is enough."

She nodded. "Of course. Dadae likes us to make extra in case someone visits."

A shadow passed over her face.

He wanted to ask what was wrong, but knew she probably wouldn't tell him. Not yet.

She took the basket from him. "I will be back."

Danny nodded. He was left in the living room. There were no curtains on the window and there were just a plain couch and a couple chairs in the room. Though it was strange to have a traditional Amish house and have electricity. There was a bookshelf next to the couch. He walked over and looked through the books. He enjoyed reading. He saw a few Christian fiction books and smiled. Whoever read the books had good taste. He would have to tell his sister, Ashley, about Priscilla's love for reading. They would have something in common.

Priscilla walked back into the room. She looked so pale.

His heart broke at the sight of her. He tried to smile at her.

"If you aren't busy, would you mind sitting with me?" he asked, motioning for her to sit in the chair across from him.

"Of course." She sat in the chair, her back straight as a board, though the chair was comfortable.

He frowned. He was getting tired of that line.

He sat across from her. "Are the books yours?"

Priscilla glanced at the bookshelves. Then nodded. "Some of them are."

"What books do you like to read?"

"Christian fiction and some clean fiction." She smiled a little. "I like historical fiction too, and the ones about medicine are really interesting." Then her eyes got wide. "Is that all right?"

He frowned deeper. He wanted her to say something against him. To argue with him. Most Amish women could only read what their husbands' approved. Before marriage, reading was regulated by fathers.

A thought came to him as he thought of his English mother asking her husband what she could read and he smiled and relaxed a bit. His English mother would never ask him about that. She was a bit of spit fire, and he knew his English dad loved her for it.

"You can read anything you like. I don't care. Which is your favorite?"

"That is like picking a favorite star in the heavens." She smiled brightly. It was so beautiful, it took Danny by surprise. Man, she was a true beauty, inside and out. He had always loved that about her.

She stood and then walked over to the bookshelf. She touched them tenderly, like a favorite child, to a Christian historical fiction series. "These ones are probably my favorite. She is an amazing author."

Danny nearly laughed.

"Yes, she is." He could see she wanted to ask him how he knew, but he wasn't ready to go there yet. He wasn't ready to tell her. "I enjoy those books as well. I have read a couple of them."

Her eyes softened. He liked to read like her. "Oh, she is wonderful."

"Do you plan to bring your books with you?"

She looked at the books, then at him. "If you have room, I would like to."

"We do, believe me." He smiled. "My sister has many more books than this. She has a whole library."

Her eyes widened with excitement. "Really? I didn't know the bishop's daughter liked to read that much."

"Oh," he paused. "Well, it's a long story."

She looked confused, but nodded.

He felt guilty for not explaining. Maybe he should...

Just then, Annie called them for supper. He stood with Priscilla, and they walked to the dining room where the family was sitting. Her father, John, sat on one end and her mamm, sat at the other end. Her sister, Annie, sat next to her.

Danny sat next to John, though he didn't want to. He made himself. He couldn't stand the man who hurt his bride.

John bowed his head and spoke in Pennsylvania Dutch: *Lord, bless this food. May you forgive Priscilla's sin and make her see what she did to this family. Show her how her jezebel spirit made men lust after her. Make her see mistakes. Amen!*

By the end of the prayer, Danny wanted to hit the man. He made himself not look over at Priscilla. He didn't want to see either her tears or her hiding what she felt. It took him a few moments to gain control of himself.

Priscilla handed him a plate of food. He hardly tasted it because of how he felt. He wanted to make the man who sat beside him see what he did to his own daughter to be abused.

The family was quiet as they ate. Then, after a bit of time, John said, "Where do you work?"

"I work on the other side of town. On a ranch."

John nodded. "Where do you live?"

"I live next to the Bilour farm. I rent their dawdy house now. I have lived there for a while now."

"Why? Did you plan to marry Priscilla after you got her pregnant, and so you rented that place?"

Danny put down his fork. "I care for Priscilla and am doing the right thing for her. And I have a place to live and can provide for her."

John grunted. "She made you lust after her. She has a rebellious heart."

Danny stood up. He could see the shock on John's face. "Sir, thank you for the supper. I am taking Priscilla for a drive."

He walked over to where she sat. She stood up and took his arm. And they walked out.

On the porch, Priscilla muttered, "It is not Saturday night."

Danny nodded. "You're right. Will you be in trouble for going out tonight?"

Priscilla looked back. "No. You are the head of our family now. Dadae will see that."

He hated hearing her call him a leader. "Good."

He took her arm and helped her into the buggy. They drove for some time in silence. But this silence was relaxed and easy. He stopped by the covered bridge. He helped her out, then tied the horse. Walking to the side of the bridge, they looked over the river.

He knew to make this marriage work, he had to be open. Though he wasn't sure if he could be completely open with her. His stomach churned as he thought of being this exposed. This vulnerable. He softly started to talk.

"I was adopted by the bishop when my Amish mother passed away," he could feel her eyes on him. "My parents died when I was ten and the bishop took me in. I was an angry kid going to him. I hated him. His family would have been nicer to me had the bishop let them, but they got attacked for being kind to me. By the time I was fifteen, I was out of control. I had spent time with an English family since I was ten. I would stay there over the summers and holidays. They really loved me and I went to live with them at fifteen. I was still angry, but the dad, Stan, really invested in me. And my English mom, Pam, is a true angel. She taught me what it was like to be loved. My sister taught me to be kind and to love to read. I went back to the bishop's house because he made me and I was a minor but when I talk about my family, it is the Taylors. Not the bishop's family."

She looked up at him. This meant so much he would share it with her.

"*Danke* for sharing with me." She smiled lightly. "I would love to meet them."

"They already love you." He looked down at her. She hadn't rejected him. For some reason, that meant so much to him. His heart began to soften and even trust her. A little piece at a time. "Priscilla, honey, I am not your leader. I am your partner."

She looked at the river, gently nodded and then placed her hand on his. He sure wasn't going to move. It felt like she had just given him the world. His sweet wildflower.

~

As Danny drove his buggy to Priscilla's house the next day, he passed Amish barns, houses, fields and beautiful green landscape. He passed by the creek where Priscilla and he had really been emotionally intimate for the first time. He let the horse take him where he had been many times before, and let his mind go back to a summer day almost one year ago.

The sun had been bright as they sat next to the covered bridge. The bridge was big and black with pillars. The grass had been lush and always stayed green due to the shade trees that covered the river bank. He loved taking her there. He had to rent a car and driver. Though by that time he could drive.

She wore a light pink dress that made her blonde hair so beautiful. A white apron. She didn't wear any shoes and let her feet in the water. She was so wild and fun. She laughed at life and was carefree. They could always talk of anything. He had shared more with her than any other Amish person but that wasn't enough for him. He was leaning against a tree and she was sitting in front of him, sideways, looking half at the creek and half at him.

"Annamay's party is in a few days. Do you wanna go?" Priscilla had asked.

"Are you asking me out on a date?"

She rolled her eyes and chuckled. "What if I am? What's your answer, mister?"

He leaned forward and kissed her. Then an idea came to him. A bit of a naughty one, and he knew the bishop would kill him for. But he never cared what he thought, so why worry now?

He gave her a bit of a smirk. "I get to do something first."

Her eyes narrowed but held a side of mischief. "What?"

He leaned a bit closer. "I get to see your hair."

She looked at him with those soft blue eyes and seemed to take in his question. "Fine, but you are going to the social."

Then she shyly smiled and took off her kapp, and then she tugged at her pins but one got caught. She frowned when it got more stuck.

He reached up. "Let me."

He got it unstuck and then ran his hands through her hair. It was so soft and smelled like roses. His breath caught as he memorized the feel of her hair. She shifted a bit closer. He moved closer and kissed her. He let her know he loved this side of her and thanked her with his kiss.

He rested his head against hers. One hand on her cheek, the other tangled in her hair. "Thank you for showing me."

She melted under his touch. Became like putty in his hands.

He pulled back, knowing he had to get control of himself or he might lead her astray, and he wouldn't do that. He enjoyed the soft wind brushing through her hair. "Why did you let me see this side of you? Especially with what you believe the bishop says."

She shrugged.

"I guess I wanted to show you a deeper side of me because I want you to know all of me," she looked over the creek. "I want to know all of you, but you hold yourself from me."

She met his gaze with sad eyes.

She was right, and as she looked at him that way, he felt she could see all that was in his heart. All the anger. The hurt. The betrayal. He leaned close again and kissed her. "You know all I can give."

She shook her head. "I want all of it…"

As he pulled onto their street, he sighed. He wanted all of Priscilla too. He wanted that wild girl back. But he had lost her the autumn day she got in James's buggy. Not at once, but he had seen the slow change in her. Even while dating James, he would still touch her hand in church or at a social, and she would react to it by touching him back lightly or with a shy look or a blush. She would try to hide it but he could still get a reaction from her. Then he missed many Sundays in a row, and when he came back finally, the change in her had been shocking. She had become reserved and quiet. Her eyes had stopped brightening when they looked his way. It seemed like she tried all her hardest not to look at him and wouldn't let him close anymore. The changes worsened until that day he found her in the barn. If he hadn't gone out to see her that day...

He wouldn't think about it.

All that he knew was that he had to get his fiery, funny girl back. He would do anything to do that.

Chapter Four

The day smelled like spring as the sun rose in the sky. Priscilla used to love Saturdays, the time spent with family and friends. A restful day, and fun as a child. But when the abuse started, she began to hate them. She pushed out of her mind why she hated Saturdays. They brought the disgusting feeling.

This Saturday, she and her family were going to the Johnsons' for supper. Danny would go too. She was glad for it because he was calming to be around, and he handled nasty comments well, while she just wanted to hide. She didn't know how he did it.

She got up and decided she wanted to look nice for Danny, though she didn't know why she should try ,and got out one of her best dresses. A light pink one. Looking at her complexion, she felt almost pretty. Then she looked at her middle.

Though she wasn't showing yet, she was afraid of how she would soon look. She didn't want her body to change. She wanted to be pure again. Be a normal bride on her wedding day. She had skipped that part and was to be a mother. She sighed. Having a baby made women feel fat. Going downstairs, she made breakfast for her family. She ignored how the smells made her feel. She hoped her morning sickness wasn't too bad.

By midmorning, Priscilla was hot and grumpy. She didn't feel well and wasn't sure why. What she wouldn't give for a hot bath and to be left alone. To not have little cousins running around her, or siblings asking her for help.

Danny would be here soon to come with to visit the Johnsons. She went to wash her face in the washroom. Afterward, she looked in the mirror. She saw her face was old and tired. She fixed her hair, thinking it would have to do.

Walking out, and into the kitchen, she nearly ran into Danny. She screamed lightly. She looked up at his tall frame. He stared down at her with concern.

"Are you alright, Priscilla?" he asked so softly.

She loved the way he said her name. Soft and almost caring.

She nodded.

He slightly frowned, seemed to not like her answer, but then stepped back so she could go back to the summer kitchen which led outside and get the food for today's lunch. He followed her, asking if he could get anything for her.

She frowned at him and nearly told him to get out, but knew she couldn't do that. He was just too nice and all. What was he wanting to do with her? With all this niceness... she sighed and hid her discomfort. She didn't want to upset him. She finally told him he could take out two pies, but there was an added bite to her words.

Danny just nodded and did it, pretending she wasn't

acting like a brat. She didn't like herself for treating him that way.

He helped her into his buggy and told her mamm they were going ahead. He was gentle with the reins as he guided the horse to the small, country road. A soft touch did just as much as rough hands at times.

When Priscilla drove the buggy, she made sure she was in control, but also gentle. She liked looking at Danny's strong hands holding the reins loose. Something warm stirred in her. But she wasn't sure what. She pushed the feeling away.

He began talking. She kinda loved how he didn't have an Amish accent. He didn't pester her with questions about herself, but he did ask about her family and the farm. She didn't mind that topic as much.

After some silence, she got the nerve to ask. He didn't want to talk about the past. She hoped he would know. Would he trust her this time with the answer? "How do you not sound like an Amish man?"

He grinned, winking at her. He was so cute. "When living with the Taylors, I learned to get rid of the accent. I can bring it back if I want to, but I rarely do anymore. I like to be upfront and honest with people, so I just talk the way I want to. And keep it the same. Do you like my voice with no accent?"

"Yes," she said it without thinking. As he eyed her, she blushed to her roots.

"Well, it is a... fine voice," she stuttered. Her heart softened. He had trusted her with this. It meant a lot to her.

He smiled broader.

"Well, thank you, my dear." He winked at her again. "I enjoy listening to your sweet voice."

She looked away and blushed deeper. She couldn't get

used to this man. He was so forward. "I don't have much to say."

"Well, maybe that will change, my dear."

When they got to the Johnson farm, she was feeling better. Though still a bit grumpy, like she didn't want to have to talk to people and be friendly. As they walked in the house, she saw her best friend Annamay was there. Running up and giving her a big hug. Annamay took her into the kitchen before she could see if Danny minded.

The kitchen was empty, as the other women were in the summer kitchen. They would often cook outside when it was hot or muggy in the house kitchen. It was a bit early in the year to do it now.

"Well, what is the wild man like?" Her red hair was bright under her kapp. It almost shown in the sun. Her green eyes were always mischief and trying something new. She was a bit wild in the community and she ran around with too many of the boys. Some Amish and some English. Priscilla worried about her.

Priscilla almost laughed at hearing Annamy call him that. If anything, Danny was not wild. He was… she wasn't sure yet. Not this new Danny. Was he even the same man she had once been in love with?

"Well?"

Priscilla shrugged. "He is kind."

"And hot."

Priscilla's mouth dropped open. She didn't know what the word meant but surely it wasn't appropriate to say. "Annamay, that is a bad thing to say. What if the bishop hears yaw?"

Annamay had been in the world too long and knew strange words like that. She was enjoying rumspringa, where she could explore the world without being punished. Priscilla had never wanted to do that. She had to be a good Amish girl.

"Who cares? It's the truth," Annamay giggled.

Priscilla didn't know how to handle her friend, who was enjoying running around a little too much. She wondered if Annamay would ever stop and join the church. Just then, someone outside screamed. They ran out of the house towards the ear-piercing cries. They were coming from the barn. As Priscilla ran in, she saw one of the Johnson's little girls holding her leg as she screamed. She sat near a farm tool with blood on it. The other siblings came around her and stared, as children do. Priscilla knelt down by the girl. Meg was her name, if Priscilla remembered right.

"Now, why don't we look at this leg for a minute? Can you show me where it hurts?" she spoke gently.

Danny dropped down beside her. "We should take her to the house."

Priscilla shook her head. "No. Let her answer first."

Meg's screams turned into sobs. "It hurts here."

She held up her dress a bit and touched her leg below the knee.

Priscilla used her apron to wipe some of the blood away, making sure she didn't touch the wound. It wasn't deep, but it wasn't good. It was bleeding a lot, which could be good. She heard Danny gasp. Her lips went tight.

Danny looked worried. "Do you know what you are doing, Priscilla?"

"I do." She looked at him. "Can you carry her to the kitchen now?"

He gently picked Meg up and carried her to the house. Priscilla followed, thinking of what needed to be done.

Meg's parents met them in the kitchen. Their eyes widened in surprise.

"What happened?" Meg's mamm asked.

One of the children started to tell the story as Priscilla instructed Danny to place the girl on the counter by the sink. Thankfully this family had running water. Many Amish homes didn't have electricity, even though this community allowed it. Some liked to be stricter.

She then moved everyone out of the way Mrs. Johnson stood close by but didn't do anything to help. Mr. Johnson said he would be outside.

Priscilla wasn't surprised by this, many men didn't think helping with scrapes and bruises were women's work. For Danny to stay was strange. But she had expected it. He was different, and she always loved that about him. As she started to clean Meg's leg, she realized what she needed.

She looked at Danny. "Can you go to the buggy and get my clutch?"

Mrs. Johnson looked shocked. Men did not get clutches for women, or were demanded to do something in that way. But Danny did not seem to mind and left.

"Well, you are being awful bossy to your man," Mrs. Johnson muttered.

She should be more concerned about her daughter than Priscilla. So she ignored the comment. There was worse going on about her right now. And that could be why Mrs. Johnson was acting this way. Priscilla was a fallen woman, after all.

Danny came back and asked her what she needed. She rinsed her hands and then looked through the clutch he had brought. The cut needed stitches, but she would do her best for now. Many Amish families didn't like to go to the English doctors. And they had their own healer who often did not have the knowledge or skills for injuries.

"Meg, I am going to put a bandage on it," she said lightly to help the little girl calm down.

Just then Mrs. Johnson pushed Priscilla out of the way, roughly. "No. I don't want you to do that."

Priscilla furrowed her brow, eyes narrowing, "But why?"

Mrs. Johnson looked down at the bandages. "I have never seen one before."

"Well, they are perfectly safe. It's just their name. They help wounds heal without scarring," she paused. "If you don't let me do this, we will have to take her to an urgent care."

"Ah, no," Mrs. Johnson said. "I don't want to. That will cost money."

"Well, then, let me bandage her," Priscilla told her. "I have to stop the bleeding."

Danny wanted to speak up, but he had never seen this side of Priscilla before. Even when he knew her in the past, she had never acted like this. Even while courting her, he had never seen her this open. She was bossy and actually talking. People didn't talk back to authority, especially unmarried women, But here Priscilla did, and he couldn't be prouder of her.

He watched Mrs. Johnson and Priscilla do a stare down and then Mrs. Johnson finally nodded. "Fine. Do what you want."

Priscilla nodded and went back to work, talking to Meg gently as she bandaged the cut. Again, he was amazed at what he saw. She was a wonder, this woman.

When Priscilla was done, Meg gave her a big hug.

"*Danke*, Priscilla," she whispered.

"You're welcome." She looked at Danny again and he felt so much emotion for this petite woman. "Can you move her to the coach?"

He would take the child anywhere for Priscilla. After settling her in, he took Priscilla aside. "How are you feeling, my dear?"

She shrugged. "I am fine."

He touched her cheek. "What you just did was amazing."

She pulled away. "No. It needed to be done."

She was like most Amish women. They were taught to not accept compliments. Compliments were prideful.

"Well, you did very well."

He wanted to shout to everyone that she was the most wonderful woman in the world. One day he could. Maybe after they married tomorrow he would be able to.

∽

The winter air was cold, and Priscilla wrapped tighter in her blankets. Maybe because it was so cold, he wouldn't come. She could only hope. But after staying awake for an hour, she heard footsteps. She found it was easier to stay awake than to pretend to be asleep. Neither mattered if she would be hurt. After he was done with her, she would lay there and stare into space. Crying didn't help. Nothing helped...

Priscilla screamed. She wiped her sweaty face with her quilt and sat up. The air had a chill to it that said spring had arrived. She didn't get nightmares often, but she hated it when she did. She looked around, loving her light pink room. It was the color her parents had allowed. She had wanted it cherry.

But then she thought about how she was getting

married to do that. This was her wedding day. She had never been so nervous and scared as she was today.

That wasn't true. She got out of bed. She had been more scared when James had...

She wouldn't think about that. Especially not this morning. This was her day, even if she didn't quite feel like it was. She put on her best dress, wishing she could wear white. With small open-toed white shoes with slight heels. They would make her look delicate and feminine. She had seen them in a store window while shopping with Annamay.

She slid on her big black shoes, knowing she shouldn't wish for stuff that would never happen. She combed and then tied her hair back but of course it didn't listen. She used mineral oil on it, especially after washing it last night.

But her datt hated seeing her blonde curls. Maybe she'd been born sinful. Maybe it's why the abuse had happened to her. It was what she deserved, after all, for having wild blonde curls.

She hated her curls even though Danny loved them. She could still feel his fingers running through her hair. She poured oil on her hands and put way too much on her hair but the curls stayed back. She set her kapp on her finally tamed hair. After washing her hands, she grabbed the tote that held the few dresses she owned. She would have to sew more to fit her figure. She wouldn't be staying the night in the house like most Amish couples did the first night of marriage. Her datt hadn't wanted it. She wasn't sure if she felt more rejection or just indifferent at this point. She was a terrible daughter. Touching her stomach, it tossed and turned; she felt nauseous.

She walked past the kitchen where her sisters readied breakfast. She left the tote by the door. She walked to the barn and milked her cow. She went through the motions without thinking and feeling. She had milked a dozen times every other morning. She moved to where Missy fed her puppies, praying Danny and she could buy her one day. Before her father sold Missy and she ended up in bad hands.

Kissing Missy's soft head, Priscilla let her fur catch her tears. She was scared to marry Danny, but she didn't have a better choice. What if he lied to her and hurt her though? Hurt her baby? Touching her flat stomach, she knew she would never let anyone hurt her child. She was sorry for thinking of ending their lives.

"I do love you, baby." She had just felt so hopeless until Danny grabbed her and literally threw her on the hay.

"Priscilla, time for church," her sister called.

Giving Missy one last kiss, she got her bag and then walked with leaden feet to the buggy. Sitting in the seat next to her siblings, she felt dizzy. Was she going to pass out? Knowing it would make her dadae angry, she took deep breaths. Thankfully, the house they were getting married in was close by. Though it seemed to take forever to get to the farm that housed the church service and wedding.

When she got out of the buggy, her knees nearly gave out. She walked to the side of the house and threw up. While she was dry heaving, she felt a hand on her shoulder. She moved away and knelt by a tree. The person followed and just stood there, not moving or talking.

It had to be Danny. He was the only one who would stand there without talking. Others would try to help her or tell she made her own bed and now she had to lay in it.

"Is it the baby or wedding worries?" he finally asked.

"Both," she cried out. She had thrown up often since

finding out she was pregnant. But she wasn't as bad as her mother, who was always throwing up when with child. She looked at him. "I am sorry. We should go inside."

"There is nothing to be sorry about. Are you all right?"

She nodded and stood. He was so caring and kind. She had loved it before but now she felt he was going to try something. He wore a very sharp pressed white amish shirt and black vest. Along with amish pants. But he still wore his black cowboy boots, which were forbidden. The light breeze blew his hair in his eyes, and she almost wanted to push it away. But she couldn't. He was so cute though. In the bright sunlight his face was so tan.

"We should get in or they will gossip."

Danny crossed his arms. "They will gossip anyway. It's what they do best. Well, you won't have to put up with it long."

Her eyes got wide with a bit of fear. As Danny looked down at her, he thought of how pretty she looked in her black dress and white apron. Her hair pressed. It was a contrast to the fear he saw in her eyes.

"So will we leave the church?" her voice sounded afraid.

He sighed.

"Never mind," she straightened, her chin lifting. "You are the head of the house. We will leave when you want."

Though her body didn't want to follow. She wanted to fight him.

Danny took her hand. "We are equal partners, which means when we leave the church, it will be both our choice. You will have a say in this marriage, honey."

She didn't even blink. Just nodded like an obedient new bride.

What did he expect? This was the way she had been

raised. It was all she knew. He took her hand and led her to where they were supposed to be.

When they walked in the church, Priscilla felt like all eyes were on her. Did they see her stomach? She wasn't showing yet. Would she soon? She clutched her Bible, knuckles white.

Finally, the long service was over, and now she and Danny would marry. Everyone went outside while the women got the building ready.

Danny came to her side as they were ready for the wedding and smiled wide. One arm was behind his back.

"Hey, beautiful. Ready?" He gave her a wink.

All she could was nod. He was so cute looking at her like that. Like a schoolboy. He deserved someone pure. Someone good. Not her.

"I got you something," he said.

He was silent for so long, she asked, "What?"

He pulled his hand out to show her a bouquet of flowers. Wild flowers, with lots of sunflowers.

"I know you can't hold them at the ceremony, but I wanted you to have them. They remind me of you," He cleared his throat. "Not that you remind me of weeds but... these flowers are pretty like you."

He faltered and looked at the flowers like they had been a bad idea.

Priscilla took them as she met his eyes. "*Danke*. They are pretty."

"Not as beautiful as you," he said in a low voice.

She blushed to her roots as she took them. He thought she was beautiful. Was it because he wanted more? Wanted to use her? Still...he had brought her flowers.

Her dadae never brought her mamm flowers.

Minutes later, she sat with her sister. They would have

a three-hour service and then they would do a short ceremony. After the long service, which, like most Sundays since the abuse started, Priscilla didn't hear a word. She had always struggled with how judging this bishop was, but after the abuse. It was too hard, so she didn't try. She just sat like a stone and tried to forget what she was going through. She knew that was a sin, but what was she to do? She just had to survive, just like now, as she walked to stand by the bishop. She met Danny's gaze. She couldn't bring to make herself smile, even though Danny gave her a small one. His eyes shown with love for her. She always loved that look, but now it made her feel ashamed. He deserved someone better than her.

She was so glad James was not here. He hadn't come to a service since she got engaged. Though this was the first one.

As the bishop spoke the words that they were married, she was glad she didn't have to kiss him like English weddings. Though she had many times. She didn't want the pressure to perform. He touched her hand, just touched the back of her hand. It made her tangle and even now it still touched her. She used to feel safe when he did that.

As she looked at him now, she almost felt that way again.

The service ended, and she was a married woman. But to a man who wasn't the father of her child. She felt sick and not because of the baby. This was her future. Because her people made it this way.

There were rows of tables in the large living room of the home. There was baked chicken, mashed potatoes, and many different kinds of bread. There was cake and different kinds of desserts. People visited and greeted Danny and Priscilla at the head table but there was also a bit of tension in the air. It was like no one to mention why this couple was getting married in the first place. Everyone saw it wasn't for love.

The dinner seemed to never end. Priscilla felt exhausted by the end of the day. She had never been so tired. She stayed by Danny's side and did what he did. She never moved from him except when Annamay pulled her aside.

Priscilla hugged her.

Annamay giggled. "You are married."

Priscilla smiled. "I am. Who thought I would get married before you?"

She laughed. "Oh, I knew you would, but never to that man. No one thought an Amish girl could get him. He is so rebellious. Though he is cute."

Priscilla actually laughed at her friend's words. "Do you think so?"

She nodded. "Everyone thinks so. He is kind but has a mind of his own, unlike so many Amish boys."

Priscilla knew that was true. Danny was set in his mind. She gave Annamay one last hug and went to her new husband.

Danny took Priscilla's hand when she came back to him and smiled down at her. He could see circles under her eyes and the sleep she needed. He bet she was exhausted. He was tired too. It had been an emotional day.

He leaned down and whispered, "Do you want to go, lovely?"

She nodded shyly, almost smiling at his name for her. He never seemed to run out of nicknames. She kinda enjoyed it. Then she tensed at the thought of going home with him.

"If you want to? If you want to stay, then I am fine."

Danny wanted her to tell him what she felt, but he knew that would never happen. When would she be open with him? Maybe even vulnerable.

He would get her to trust him one day. Soon he would show her and she wouldn't know what hit her.

He tied the horse to the post and led her through their new house, dawdy house. He wanted to carry her over the threshold but that would scare her, and the Amish didn't practice that tradition.

He showed her all the light switches. She smiled brightly at them. She loved them. It was a small house, smaller than he remembered, but it was pretty. Pam and her girls had decorated very well but also in a way the bishop would approve. It looked homey and clean. The whole place shined. He flipped on the lights, then he went out to get her bag, came back in, and put it on the large bed. A beautiful, colorful quilt covered the mattress, just like he had asked for.

Priscilla hadn't moved from standing in the bedroom. She seemed in a daze.

Standing in front of her, he put his hands on her shoulders. "Honey, are you hungry? I asked my English mom to buy some food for us until you go shopping."

She shook her head.

He hated how she must feel. He wanted to pull her into his arms and tell her she was safe, but knew he couldn't.

And that hurt him, too. She looked so lost. Her gaze at nothing, the way she held her around herself.

"Then why don't you go to bed, honey?" he said softly.

Her eyes got wide.

He took a deep breath. "I am sleeping out here, Priscilla. You will have the bedroom alone. I will not come in at all."

She nodded and gave a big sigh. Then covered her mouth.

He smiled. "G'night, Priscilla."

She nodded and headed slowly to the bedroom.

Danny went to the sitting area and sat on the small couch. He knew the room couldn't hold a bigger one. Though he was tired, he needed to pray. He wanted his life and this marriage to start off right.

He knelt down by the couch and prayed for his new wife to feel safe, and for their relationship to strengthen.

Chapter Five

Priscilla couldn't remember when she had ever felt so alone. She lay on the bed in her clothes, after taking off her shoes. She pulled the pretty quilt close to her. Normally a couple spent the night at the bride's family's house, but she didn't want to share a bed with him. Especially not the bed she was abused in. Her parents had agreed she didn't have to and would not even have her come over to clean up after the wedding. She was happy she didn't have to face them so soon after being married.

She started shaking then. She almost cried, but was too exhausted to even do that. She didn't know what to do, so she just lay there awake for hours till she finally closed her eyes and fell into a peaceful, restful sleep.

∼

When Priscilla woke up, the shine was shining bright despite a coolness to the air. Kentucky was showing off its beautiful spring. Priscilla sat up quickly, afraid she'd overslept. She looked around to see her new room. Then it hit her. She was married to Danny. She had dreamed of this day when they courted. Especially once she'd fallen in love with him. But now she wasn't sure who he was anymore, or who she was.

She wasn't the same woman she had been before. She didn't deserve him. But now there was no backing out. Her people didn't believe in divorce.

She looked around the room. White ruffle curtains hung neatly over a big window, a pink rug graced the floor, and the plain walls made the quilt even more beautiful. It had every color in it. She pulled it around her shoulders, not wanting to get up, but she had to relieve herself. Since getting pregnant, she always had to. As she got up, she touched her stomach. Was it the baby that made her feel like this, or her new marriage?

She pulled her hair back out of habit. Her dadae hated it when she let it loose, even around the house. Wrapping her robe around herself, she walked down the short hall to the kitchen and then found the bathroom. When she went outside, she took the time to look around. The house was a pretty little place on a farm surrounded by corn fields. A little barn to the left must be where Danny kept his horse. She didn't mind Danny's horse, but he was so dead broke, with no will. Probably from past treatment because she knew Danny was gentle with him. It was one of the first things she noticed about Danny. He was always so gentle.

Walking around, she found a place for a small garden, then what looked like a woodshed. She went back to the house and imagined the garden she would grow. She wondered if Danny wanted to farm, or if he farmed at the ranch he worked at? She would plant corn here. She was sure she could get him to stay Amish.

"Good morning," he said from behind her.

She jumped and turned around, her hand over her chest.

"I am sorry to scare you," Danny looked down at her and wanted to smile. She had pulled her hair back and wore a robe, though it didn't hide her shapely form. She looked so adorable that way. Still mussed from the night before.

She shook her head. "It's fine. Do you want me inside to cook you breakfast? I should have been up earlier. I am sorry about that. I won't sleep this late again and I will..."

He put a hand on her arm, and gently smiled at her. Amused.

"So, how I get you to talk is...in the morning." He winked.

She blushed.

"Honey, you can sleep as late as you want. I don't mind. And I can cook, so I made my own breakfast already. Come in and I can make you some."

She nodded. Her eyes didn't meet his and looked all around her, like she had done something wrong. She rushed back to the house. She couldn't believe she had let her new husband make his own breakfast. It just wasn't right. She should have been up but the wedding and baby took a lot from her. No matter, she would make him breakfast every morning from now on.

Inside the small kitchen, she looked around. It was plain white, of course, but still cute. Off the kitchen was a table with four chairs around it. She walked into the room to find a small sofa and two fluffy chairs. The room was teal but with the same ruffled curtains that hung in her bedroom. There was a soft peach rug on the wood floor. It was small but cozy. She wouldn't mind living here for a while. She knew they would move to a big farmhouse before the baby was born so they could fill it with lots of children. She paled at the thought. Her hands shook a little. She didn't want to think of more babies.

Turning, she saw Danny watching her. "It's a nice house."

"I am glad you like it. I will start your breakfast."

Her mouth fell open. Then she shook her head and nearly gasped. "You can't. That is my job."

She took off her robe and put it on a chair while going into the kitchen.

He disagreed but didn't tell her that. It would take time for her to see they were doing things differently, and he didn't mind cooking. Though he didn't think he could cook as well as her. So, he wouldn't mind her cooking for him. He just didn't want her to feel like she had to.

Priscilla couldn't believe she had stayed outside so long, daydreaming, while her new husband was starving. She got to making herself breakfast, feeling like a terrible person. Her dadae would be yelling already. Danny must be hiding his anger from her. She made herself something quick, with extra for Danny. Then sat down at the kitchen table across from Danny. He just poured himself some coffee. Then she prayed the Amish prayer, which was to be silent and formal, and dug into her food.

Danny also bowed his head but seemed to take longer to pray than she did. She stopped eating and stared at his bent head. "God, thank you for this food that my wonderful wife made. Bless this marriage and be with us always. Help us grow in you. Grow together. In Jesus' name, Amen."

Frowning, she decided she didn't like him praying that long. Was he judging her for making him wait for his meal? Her dadae used to pray for so long, and then tell her and sometimes her siblings and even mamm what they did wrong and what God expected from her. As Danny looked up, she looked away before being caught staring. Her datt hated her staring at him but then yelled louder when she looked away. It was confusing.

"This is really good, Priscilla," Danny said after a few bites.

She looked up to find his eyes soft. Not hard at her, like he was judging. She looked away and nodded, unsure what to say. No one ever told her she did something well. She ate in awkward silence and soon enough she felt better and not so in knots. How was she going to stay married to this man?

She felt exhausted all over again.

"Well, I am going to get some chores done." He stood up. "If you need me, I will be in the barn."

He put his dish in the sink. Then stopped at the door. Looking at her again, he said softly, "*Danke* for breakfast, Priscilla."

Then he left.

She sat there, staring after him. What a strange man? She had never been thanked for doing anything before. And not for something as simple as breakfast. She stood there far too long in thought. Getting up, she started to clean. At least cleaning made sense, unlike her new husband.

∼

A few days later, Priscilla woke up in the living room from a nap, still feeling tired. She looked around her and thought how quickly this had become to feel like her home. It had been a long time since she felt safe. She had gotten used to being at the dawdy house. It was cute and small. She wished she could decorate it the way she wanted, but she wasn't sure how, and most Amish didn't waste their time on doing that.

Danny walked into the small living room. He had gotten off early that day. Sometimes she wished for a bigger house so they could have their own space.

He sat on the chair across the room. "How are you feeling, honey?"

Though she wasn't comfortable being around him, she was coming to love his nicknames for her. They just ran off his tongue in such a sweet way. "Fine. I should get supper on."

Danny shook his head. "Would you like to go out? We could get supplies in town if you want."

She nodded.

"Sure. I would enjoy that," she stood up. "I will go get ready. When do you want to leave?"

"Does four work?" he asked.

She nodded. Why did he always ask her what she wanted? Her family never had, and she hadn't met many men in the community who did. He was a strange one, for sure. She walked into her room and got out a light pink dress, and then fixed her hair. She was ready before he told her to be. She didn't want to make him late. Grabbing her shawl and her purse, she walked outside but she didn't see him. He must be hooking up the buggy or doing the horse. Though it was a drive into town, he enjoyed the ride. She enjoyed the smell of the spring in the air. Fresh grass that held a bit of dampness from the rain earlier. The trees were starting to show their leaves.

Just then Danny came up from the side of the house.

He seemed to be more careful in the way he walked, in order not to startle her. She was thankful for that.

Before Danny could say anything, a car drove into the driveway. She recognized Danny's police friend Zack from their meeting at Walmart.

Danny explained, "I thought a car ride would be more comfortable."

She nodded. "That sounds nice."

Danny walked up to her and took her arm. As they slid into the back seat together, Priscilla was glad he had decided to do this. She had only been in a car a few times, and not for some time. She loved car rides. How comfortable they were, how air and heat could be used whenever she liked and how the wind blew in her face when the window was down. Looking out the window, she was thankful Danny stayed quiet this time, though usually she enjoyed hearing him talk. She looked around as they drove down the road, studying the rolling green hills dotted with Amish farms. That world, though she hadn't left it, seemed so far away when she rode in an English car. She couldn't imagine driving every day to go to work.

They pulled into a parking lot for a place called Hobby Lobby.

"Do you want me to go in with you, my dear?" Danny asked. "I do need to run into Tractor Supply for something. It's right next door."

Priscilla shook her head. "That is fine. I haven't been to this new store."

Getting out, she smiled and almost did a happy little jump. Some women in the church had talked about Hobby Lobby, but Priscilla hadn't gone yet. Her datt thought shopping useless. Pushing the guilty feeling away, she entered it. Feeling so much joy, her heart skipped a beat as she took in all the pretty decor, the spring stuff that was in so many aisles, and how the wall art hung all around. She didn't know how one store could do that.

The colors and items were overwhelming. She walked down the aisles and just stared and looked. She spotted a tall, beautiful woman in one of the aisles. She wore jeans with flowers down the side of them and fancy black boots. Her bright pink top was paired with a colorful scarf. Her long, blonde hair was done in a sassy bun that gave her a flirty look. Her bright blue eyes didn't seem to miss much. Priscilla met them, then looked away. And kept looking around. This place was just wonderful.

Seconds later, a crashing sound came from where the pretty lady stood. Priscilla rushed over to find the woman on the floor, holding her ankle and boxes all around her.

"Let me see if I can help you," Priscilla said. Her heart beat a mile a minute. She paled, her hands shook a bit.

She knelt and put her hand on the lady's ankle. "You should keep your boot on if it is sprained."

The lady nodded, her face pinched in pain. She pushed her long blonde hair back. "Okay."

An employee came by. "I can call 911."

The woman shook her head.

"No, the ankle doesn't hurt that badly." She sighed and Priscilla's heart went out to this beautiful woman who had been enjoying the fun of Hobby Lobby until this unfortunate accident. "Could you get me some ice, if you have it?"

The employee nodded and headed away.

Priscilla dug through her purse, remembering she had put a wrap in there when her little cousin's ankle twisted.

Pulling it out, she said, "Here, I will wrap it."

The lady shook her head. "No, it's fine. I don't want to bother you."

Priscilla shot a glance at her. "I can help you."

She finally nodded.

"Please, let me know if I am hurting you," she said softly but firmly. "Is there someone you can call?"

Then the lady nodded.

"I am not sure what to do. My parents are away and I can't drive with this ankle. I could call my brother, but he just got married, and I don't want to bother him," she frowned.

"I am sorry," she said. "I am Priscilla."

The lady smiled a little and, again, Priscilla was surprised by the beauty of this lady. "My name is Ashley Taylor."

They shared the same last name. Strange. Though Taylor was a common name. She decided to make conversation as they waited for the employee to come back and Ashley decided what to do.

"That is exciting about your brother getting married. Tell me about it."

Ashley smiled brightly. "He is funny, sweet, and will make a great husband and father."

Priscilla assumed Ashley's brother had lived with the girl before, which was common enough in this day. What would people think of her when she got married? She finished wrapping her foot.

The employee came back with a pack of ice.

Ashley thanked the employee then met Priscilla's gaze.

"Well, I could call my friend..." she looked deep in thought.

A pair of boots smacked against the floor and Priscilla recognized Danny's stride. What if he was upset she had helped someone? She stood up and straightened her dress just as Danny and Zack came around the corner.

Danny took in the scene and then ran to Ashley's side like she was a long-lost friend. He knelt down beside her. He sure loved to hug people. Those hugs at the beginning of their courtship were wonderful.

"What happened, Ash?" he asked.

Priscilla kept looking between them. Wondering what was going on?

Ashley sighed from where she still sat on the ground. "Oh, you know me."

Danny looked at her ankle. "Can you walk?"

Ashley nodded.

"Just give me a second." She bit her lip. "This lady here is helping me."

Danny stood and moved closer to Priscilla. "Thanks for helping, Priscilla."

Ashley's mouth dropped open. "You are *that* Priscilla? Danny's Priscilla?"

Before Priscilla could say anything, Zack spoke up, "Man, nothing gets by you, Ashley Taylor."

Ashley stuck out her tongue at him. "Well, if I hadn't just fallen, I would have figured it out."

"Really? And when have you ever figured something out that quick? You would have sat here all day and not known."

"Oh, what do you know," she bit back playfully.

Zack crossed his arms. "What have I told you about shopping? This store is dangerous, both for your wallet and now for your body. You should listen to me more."

Ashley rolled her eyes.

"That will be the day." She held out her hands. "Now do something useful and help me up."

Zack shrugged, but took care as he helped her stand.

Ashley leaned heavily on him as she turned to face Priscilla. Reaching forward, she suddenly hugged her.

"Oh, my. I have wanted to meet you." She let go and gave Priscilla a side grin. "Though I thought it would be more graceful than this."

"Well, there would have to be a graceful person in the meeting," Zack teased.

Danny laughed, and Ashley chuckled. "Just ignore him. That's what I've tried to do my whole life."

Danny laughed loudly. "And she is still trying and somehow fails."

Ashley crossed her arms. "Here I am, hurt, and everyone picks on me."

Danny gave her a side hug.

"Sorry." He winked at her. "It is good to see you. What are you doing in town, besides hurting yourself, that is?"

"I'm in town for Paulla's baby shower, and I've been dying to meet your new bride."

"Why don't we go out to eat, or do you want to get off your feet?" Danny said.

Ashely looked down at her ankle like she had forgotten it hurt.

"Sure, why not. I can hurt at a restaurant as much as I can at home," she smiled at Priscilla. "And I wouldn't give up this time to spend with my new sister."

Priscilla smiled back feeling happy to meet and spend time with Ashley. Ashley's natural personality made it easy to be around. But for some reason she felt some regret. The way Danny interacted with his sister and even how Ashley and Zack flirted with each other. She didn't have that with Danny anymore. It was taken from her. She felt a huge loss at the thought and wondered if she would ever get it back.

Chapter Six

A few days later, Priscilla stared outside, feeling a little ill. Danny had told her he wanted her to meet his parents. They were going to eat supper in their home. She was so nervous. She was just tired of new things. She wanted to be left alone and have time to relax. But she had meals to make every day for him. And now she was making him clothes. It was just all so much. She hadn't planned on this a month ago. Or even two weeks ago. She was so tired of worrying all the time. Of performing for him.

But as a wife, she owed him.

Why should she try to be a good wife when he wasn't even growing a beard? He remained clean shaven as if he were still single. And that bothered her. Didn't he care how that looked? She had no idea how he'd been approved to join the church, based on his actions. He didn't follow their rules well at all.

And it annoyed her.

He didn't seem to care about their new marriage.

Well, she didn't either. She was just surviving. She wondered if she would lose control over her emotions and just say she was done.

She was done performing and being perfect. Even though she had lived through six months of abuse, this survival was different.

She set her chin and straightened her spine. She would make it. She had to. For herself and her baby.

Just then, she heard Danny's boots on the porch. She turned to see him walk through the door.

"Hi, my dear." He smiled lightly.

She tried to smile back. "Are we still meeting your English parents?"

He nodded. "I would like you to."

"I will go get ready." Then she walked to the bedroom and locked the door, as she always did. She didn't want to go, but she would for him.

Closing her eyes, she took a deep breath and sighed. She could do this. She picked out a nice, pressed purple dress, put it on and wrapped an apron over it. When she started doing her hair, she felt all thumbs. Nothing looked good or worked. So she just finished without thinking more about it, and donned her kapp.

It wasn't like her hair ever looked good enough anyway. Sighing again, she walked out to where Danny waited in the living room.

He looked good, wearing newly pressed fabric Amish pants with suspenders, an olive-green shirt, and his hair pulled back into a small ponytail. Despite the clothing, he didn't look Amish at all. But he was handsome. Or as Annamay said, he was hot. She wet her lips, cheeks burning. Her stomach fluttered, and she told herself it might be the baby. Her mouth felt dry as the word 'hot' bounced around in her mind, though it sounded too worldly.

"You look nice. Ready to go?" Danny asked gently as he held out his hand.

She looked at it, trying to understand why he always reached out to touch her. At times, it confused her. Few Amish couples touched in public, and if they did, sometimes it was gossiped about. She just nodded and finally took his hand, it was strong and gentle. She let go of it as she followed him outside to the car. Again, she saw Zack sitting in the driver's seat. Danny held the back door open for her and she slid in and buckled. Oh, her pulse thrummed, how she was becoming to love traveling this way. It was so much faster.

It wasn't long before they pulled into town and then onto a private street. Nervously, she held her hands together. When they stopped in front of a cute little fenced yard, she looked around, trying to imagine him growing up there. Running and playing in the yard.

Then it hit her again: she didn't fit into his English world.

Danny got out and came to her door. Opening it, he waited. Closing her eyes and trying to calm down, she took deep breaths. She couldn't do this. Her stomach churned.

"Honey, if you don't want to meet them, we can wait," he sighed. "This is a bad idea. We will just leave. My parents will understand."

She looked up at him. She had expected him to force her to get out. He ran a hand over his hair. Concern showed on his face about her. It felt strange. He dropped his hands, and she impulsively took one of them. She could see she surprised him by this. She had surprised herself with it. But he didn't wait to clasp her hand in hers, and his look turned tender.

She glanced at the house. Would they hate her? They knew this child she carried was not his. Would they think badly of her? She didn't deserve to be married to Danny. She wasn't good enough, and they would see that.

Allowing him to help her out, she fixed her dress and let go of his hand. Touching was too much. Too soon. He let her pick the pace to the house. He didn't push her like she thought he might. Then they were in front of the door. He knocked, though she figured he normally didn't. Much faster than she wanted, the door opened, and his parents greeted her.

His mother smiled brightly. She had a look about her that showed so much kindness. She now remembered seeing her at the wedding in a brief encounter but it was so busy and overwhelming, she didn't meet her. Being the only English couple there, they had been easy to spot.

"Well, my dear, come on in."

They walked in, and Danny's mom pulled him into a side hug. He introduced Priscilla and she shook their hands.

Danny led her to the couch and as she sat, she put her hands in her lap.

Danny talked with his parents comfortably. They didn't ask her a bunch of questions, possibly seeing her fear. Pam, his mother, was pretty with graying, blonde hair, and sharp, kind, blue eyes. She seemed to have energy coming off her. She wore a long maxi-style dress and a shawl over her shoulders.

Stan, the father, seemed so relaxed as he talked, and that reminded her of Danny. He was a sharp-dressed man, with salt-and-pepper hair and brown eyes. She could almost feel the calmness he emanated. It was soothing and very different from his energized wife. She still held herself from him; so many men in her life had rejected her. And this one wouldn't be much different.

By the time Pam got supper on the table, Priscilla felt a little better. She enjoyed listening to them talk. Sitting at the table, she looked around and tried to imagine Danny eating many meals here. She could see he was comfortable. His eyes almost shone, and he looked content. Then she realized he didn't look like that at church, and especially not at the bishop's house. When they had previously courted, she had spent time with him there. And it had been tense. Yet this place totally relaxed him.

Stan bowed his head. "Dear God, bless this food. Be with us always. Thank you for having our new daughter Priscilla here. Bless her, Father. Thank you for blessing Danny with such a wonderful wife. In Jesus's name, Amen."

She stared at him. How could he say all those things about her? She had heard no one say nice things like that before. Not about her. The Amish didn't praise each other or anyone. That was prideful. He must not know about the baby if he said such nice things. She was sure of that. She started in on the food and tried to relax again.

As Danny sat next to Priscilla, he could tell she was shocked and probably uncomfortable by his dad's prayer. But he knew his parents wanted to make her feel at home. He felt so proud to have her sit next to him. Like a real man. And she looked so beautiful. Her hair was looser around her face and the soft curls escaping her kapp framed her face. He wanted to reach out and touch one, but knew it wouldn't be a good idea. It was too soon.

"Have you always lived in the area, Priscilla?" Pam asked.

Priscilla nearly jumped, startled by hearing her name, and her eyes widened a bit. She nodded. "My parents came from Ohio, though. Across the river. Most of my relatives still live there."

"That is nice. Do you visit them often?"

Priscilla shrugged.

"Some," she looked at Pam, trying to ease out of her comfort zone. "Have you always lived here?"

Pam glanced at Danny, and he shook his head. He hadn't told Priscilla about his past. Not the whole story. His mom seemed to understand, though he knew she wouldn't agree. He wasn't willing to go there yet. It wasn't a simple story.

Pam answered softly, "Well we have moved around a bit in Ohio and northern Kentucky. My kids were homeschooled, so it was easy to do."

"Was it for the jobs you moved so much?" Priscilla's eyes lightened curiously.

Again, Pam looked at Danny, but this time Priscilla noticed and put down her fork. "I am sorry. I am being rude."

"No, my dear. You are just fine." Pam patted her hand. "My husband changed his job a lot, so that was why it was so easy to move."

Priscilla nodded, still looking a bit bewildered. She darted her eyes from each of them.

Danny could kick himself for that. He didn't want Priscilla to feel like he was hiding something. But he didn't know how to tell her about that part of his life. She wasn't ready... or maybe he wasn't.

"We did a lot of traveling together. They took me to

Washington DC and other places like that," he touched her hand. "I would love to take you one day."

She pulled her hand away. "That would be nice."

He was taken aback by her quick reply. He wished she liked him more. This was so hard. He felt like he was giving all of himself, and she gave nothing of her true self —the woman he loved before. Cooking, cleaning, sewing. Nothing personal. But, he told himself, this marriage was worth it. He would make it worth it.

When they finished the meal, Pam brought coffee and a bundt cake to the living room. Priscilla felt more comfortable. Though she sat tightly next to Danny, he didn't seem to mind. This time she joined in the light conversion.

As they got up to leave, Pam stood next to her. "Do you mind if I give you a hug?"

Priscilla looked at Danny and then back to Pam. "Sure."

His mother wrapped her in a big hug. She felt so comforted by it. Pam smelled of cinnamon and felt warm and soft to the touch. Despite that, she remained stiff. Only had Danny in the past given her hugs where she felt something.

Then Pam said, "Oh!"

She stepped back to hold her shoulder where Priscilla could see a tiny spot of blood. What had happened? Then she realized it was her pin from her dress that had picked Pam. it must have come loose.

"Oh, my. I am so sorry."

Pam chuckled loudly.

"Oh, it's fine. I find myself in these situations often," she waved her hand like it was nothing. "It happens sometimes, my dear."

Priscilla's mouth dropped open. "I am so sorry."

"Honey, it's fine," Pam hugged her again. Then put a hand on her arm. "Now don't give it another thought."

Priscilla was sure she could die of embarrassment. But at least Pam made the embarrassment so much easier to bear. After one last hug to both of them, Danny led her outside. As he greeted Zack and then opened the car door, he winked at her.

She actually hit his arm.

"Don't," but smiled despite herself. "It's not funny. Your poor mamm."

He chuckled. "I think she found it funny. That's what my mom is like."

Priscilla slid in the car as she softly blushed, embarrassed. The day hadn't been as bad as she thought. Maybe her marriage would look like his parents', but she wasn't so sure.

It might end up looking like her parents', and that wasn't good.

~

Kentucky was giving them a wonderful spring. It wasn't too hot or wet, like usual. As Priscilla did chores, she learned to become used to doing things by herself instead of in a group, since she was used to working in a big family. She always had sisters or close cousins helping. She had just finished the laundry when her mamm came up the drive, riding in a rented car. She walked out to the driveway and greeted her mamm who looked pleased to see her. She thought of how often Danny would hug her when they courted and how she had learned to accept them. Now sometimes he would kiss her forehead. She would still stiffen at his touch. She was sad at how much she missed this marriage.

She realized how much she had missed her mamm. Her family. "What brings you here, Mamm?"

"I thought you would want to go to town with me?"

She could go with Danny anytime she wanted. He loved going to town, and especially liked taking her out to eat and just a walk down by the River. But it was always emotional being with her husband.

It would be fun to go with her mamm again.

"Sure. Let me get my purse."

Going back in the house, she put on her bonnet and kept on her apron. She hoped it hid her growing belly. She didn't want people to know when she was due. Maybe she was pregnant with twins, and that was why she was so big. Frowning, she made those thoughts disappear as she got in the van, the driver greeted her.

Shopping with Mamm was such fun. Her favorite place to go, of course, was the town library. It was an older building in the middle of downtown. It was pretty large and had some great Christian fiction books. Her mamm had to go to a different store so she told Priscillia she'd pick her up after she ran her errand.

Priscilla found a couple of books to borrow and then sat down in a booth by the window to read one by A.S. Harrison. She loved this author and had read all of her previous books.

As she dug into the first few pages, she felt someone standing beside her. Glancing up, she saw Danny's sister.

Ashley smiled brightly and sat down across from her.

"Hi, Priscilla. It's great to see you here. Now I can get off to a better start than the other day," she laughed at her own joke.

Priscilla chuckled.

"Well, you are looking better. It's nice to see you again." She paused. "What do you like to read?"

Ashley laughed like Priscilla had just told a joke.

"That book," grinning, she added, "I also work here part-time. Well, when I am in town, I do."

"That's like a dream job," Priscilla beamed at her. She cocked her head. "Danny never told me where you work."

Ashley's smile died a bit. Then she said, "I live and work in Fort Wayne, Indiana, and I come back as often as I can."

Priscilla nodded. The response didn't answer her question, but she was fine by that. Why did she need to know what Ashley did for a living? But for some reason, she felt left out. She liked Ashley and felt a connection with her.

"That's great."

Ashley nodded. "Yeah. It is great. I have a wonderful church family there."

"What do you mean by church family?"

Ashley looked confused. "Didn't Danny tell you?"

Priscilla blushed. Maybe this was something her husband was supposed to tell her. Not her sister-in-law. "No. Sorry. You don't have to tell me."

Ashley shook her head.

"No, I will tell you," she paused and made a face that Priscilla couldn't read. "Well, a church family is like the friends you have at the church you go to. You have fellowship and connections with them over the faith you share."

Priscilla felt a little confused. "Faith, like traditions?"

She shook her head and touched Priscilla's hand on the table. "No, it's a faith and relationship with Jesus Christ. A one-on-one relationship with Him. Like He is like our Father."

Priscilla flinched at the word *father*. If He was like her dad, she would get anger and indifference.

Ashley looked at her with such soft eyes. "He is a perfect heavenly Father with no faults. He only has your best in what He wants for you."

Priscilla looked at the table, and a tear unexpectedly ran down her face. She didn't know what overcame her but she whispered, "Then why did He give me a babe?"

"Oh, my dear, a man did that," Ashley wiped her own tears away. "God did not want you hurt, and He brought you Danny."

Priscilla rolled her eyes, brushing at her eyes angrily.

"Great, a man I don't love." She wiped at another tear. "A man I am afraid of sometimes."

"I know this might not help now, but there is nothing to fear about Danny," Ashley reassured her.

Priscilla sighed. "It doesn't help much."

"Just know it is true for both Danny and God."

She nodded. For some reason, she felt better. Letting things out with Ashley helped lift the weight from her, but she didn't want her mamm seeing her upset when she got back. Her mamm would want to know why, and she didn't want to go there. Trusting her mamm was very hard right now. Her mamm didn't support her.

So she pushed her hair back with her hands and lifted her chin. "What kind of books do you like to read?"

Ashley looked down at the book on the table. "The books I write, probably."

Priscilla's eyes widened. "You are an author?"

Ashley nodded.

"I am. And I am having a hard time getting into a new story." Her eyes shone. "Do you think you could help me with it?"

Priscilla shrugged. "I don't know. I am not that good at writing."

"Well, it's the plot I am having a hard time with," Ashley pulled out her tablet and showed her the outline. "Would you like to help, Priscilla?"

Priscilla smiled. Then they started talking about the story. It seemed as if no time went by and they talked for over an hour.

When Mamm walked in, she looked exhausted. Priscilla stood nervously.

Mamm looked at Ashley, then at Priscilla. "Well, it's been a day, the van tire broke, and we had to take it to Walmart, and it took forever to fix."

"Sorry about that, Mamm," Priscilla said. "I wondered why you were gone so long."

"Well, let's go, it's late and Danny will be upset you wasted the whole day," Mamm snapped and walked out.

Priscilla looked at the clock on the wall and realized it was around supper time. Danny would be home and might see how lazy she was and might regret marrying her. She had to do better.

She had to be a better wife.

Ashley stood and hugged her.

"Don't worry. I know my brother. He won't be upset," she smiled. "Thank you for your help today." She pulled out a card and put it in Priscilla's book. "I know Danny has my number, but call me anytime you need to. And can I ask you something?"

Priscilla looked at the door and back. "Of course."

"Would you be up to helping with plotting more, if you don't mind?" Ashley smiled.

Priscilla was shocked. "Really? I would love to. But Danny said you go back to Indiana soon."

"I will find a way to stay connected, sis," Ashley hugged her. "Now you need to go."

Priscilla was a bit stiff; she wasn't used to all this touching and nodded. Holding the books to her chest, she got in the van. She was so glad she went to town today. Not even her mamm complaining about the day could upset her.

She had found a friend and sister all in one day.

Chapter Seven

Priscilla needed the outhouse the next morning, and she didn't have time to dress, so she put on her robe and hurried outside. When she came back in, she nearly ran into Danny. He was again in the kitchen, baking. He looked over at her from the rolls he was making, then he looked back. Then his eyes came back to her, wide and with surprise shining in them.

It was hard to get over him always doing her duties. Even though she was starting to get used to it.

Then she realized her hair wasn't in a bun. Oh, she must look a mess, her hair all this way and that. She put a hand on her hair.

He wiped his hands on his apron and reached out slowly to touch her hair, and she stayed so still. She let him touch her, and for some reason, his closeness didn't bring her any fear. His touch was gentle, though his hand was callused.

"Your hair is so beautiful."

His words warmed her heart. She wanted to argue with him but didn't know what to say.

He moved his hand away, slowly, like he didn't want to. His hand then fisted as he turned back to the rolls. Was he mad?

She went into the room and readied for the day, still feeling petite and delicate near him. She never thought she would feel this way again.

Then she remembered that feeling this way before had ended badly. What if that happened again?

Shoving her feelings down, she finished her hair.

Danny banged the pot as he made breakfast. Seeing Priscilla with her hair messy, this way and that, she looked so adorable. Her hair had grown so long and beautiful. She looked so stinkin' cute. He wanted to pull her into a hug and run his hands through her hair. When he had taken a chance to touch her curls, the experience was better than he expected. Her hair was soft and silky. He wanted more, but at the same time, felt like he had been given the world. It was kinda fun romancing his wife like this. He couldn't think of anything he would rather do.

After breakfast, Danny left for work and Priscilla worked on chores. Memories of kissing Danny invaded her day. She kept feeling his fingers in his hair, seeing that look in his eyes. By the time supper arrived, she was a mess. Priscilla didn't know what was wrong with her, but by supper time, she was a mess. She had burnt the pie and the meat wasn't cooked all the way through. At least the vegetables looked good. She quickly pulled out leftovers from the night before and put those on the table. She hoped Danny wasn't too upset.

She heard Danny being dropped off, but she wasn't ready to face him. She set the table with the food and stood next to the table as he walked in.

He gave her a broad smile. "Good afternoon, my dear."

She gave him a small smile but it didn't match her eyes. "Hi, I got supper for you."

He looked at it and his face seemed to dim but then he nodded. "*Danke*. It looks great." As they sat, he took her hands and prayed for the meal. She had come to be more comfortable with him praying. He prayed almost like God was a friend. Someone he knew personally.

As they ate, Danny made small talk. She was used to that. It was easier than deep conversations, and she got to know things about her new husband as she listened to him. And she even laughed with him because he was funny and could always make her laugh.

After dinner, she served him a dessert of leftover brownies. She put fresh whip cream on them and then covered them in chocolate syrup. He seemed to enjoy it, and she had a little too.

When they finished, she put the dishes by the sink. He walked up beside her and took her hand. She flinched but didn't pull away.

"I have something for you. Do you mind sitting in the living room with me?"

She let him lead her to the couch. He left space between them and let go of her hand. Then he reached behind himself and held out a box.

As she took it, her hands shook a bit. He was giving her a nice gift of plates, but that meant he wanted something in return. She knew without asking what he wanted. And her fear grew. She knew of some husbands who would do that with their wives. She opened the box and saw plates because she didn't care.

What if he wanted her tonight? Would he hurt the baby? She stood up. "*Danke*."

Then she ran from the room to spend the rest of the

evening in the kitchen, and then her bedroom. Danny stayed in the living room.

Later that night, Danny rolled off the small sofa, startled. As he lay on the floor, he thought of what had woken him. Then he heard it. An ear-piercing scream. He came fully awake and ran into the bedroom. Priscilla tossed and turned in her bed, screaming. Oh, no, not again. She'd had a nightmare last night too, but had fallen back to sleep before he reached her.

He knelt by her and tried to wake her up, taking her arms so she didn't hurt herself. She finally settled down and turned over like she was going to sleep. Danny wasn't sure what to do. He laid down on the big bed. It was the only big thing in the small house. It was so much more comfortable than the sofa he slept on that he put his arm behind his head and fell sound asleep.

Priscilla woke up with a jerk. Her eyes landed on Danny surprisingly sleeping at the far end of the bed. She didn't feel fear. Just care for this gentle man. He looked so peaceful and relaxed, like he belonged there.

She had to get up. She walked into the kitchen and found herself in a mess. This time she wasn't sure if she could ever get out. It was a crippling part of the past she wanted to forget. But here it was, and she couldn't escape.

For the second time that night, Danny startled awake. This time his training took over. He ran into the kitchen to find Priscilla crouched on the counter and a couple broken plates shattered all over the floor. He saw his slippers by the table. Slowly putting them on, he met Priscilla's wide gaze. She wasn't looking at him. His foot bumped a chair and she screamed. She threw a plate, and he ducked, but it had nearly hit him in the head. It hit the wall instead and shattered.

"Priscilla, honey, it's me, Danny," he spoke softly.

She screamed again when she heard his voice. "Stop. You can't talk me into doing anything. You are just a man!"

Those words hurt Danny more than he could say. Did she say them out of fear or was that how she felt? How was he supposed to care about her when she feared him? Even hated him. Was he wrong? Had he moved too fast? Were his emotions getting away from him? He was a man, after all, but he had been gentle when he wanted to move much faster. He prayed he would stay calm and be able to handle this.

She threw another plate and it hit the sink. "I hated him. I let him court me. I let him come by and talk to my parents. I accepted gifts from him. He told me I was pretty. I was special to him. I couldn't stop him after he hurt me. Nothing worked."

Danny stayed very still. He tried to remember his training. This was different though. He loved this girl more than life itself. How was he supposed to get her to calm down? Was she even awake? This was so unlike her.

The tears on her face, the pain in her eyes, and her damp hair hung in her face. Danny's heart broke at the sight of her.

"I wanted to be a good Amish girl. Danny wasn't that. I accepted any care James gave. It was my fault, even though I didn't want it." She looked at the ground in shame, and her face crumbled in so much pain.

Danny took the chance to walk closer, and that's when another plate hit his shoulder. He stopped, but closer to her. When she talked again, it was fast, and he caught every other sentence.

"Don't touch me again," she sobbed. Her chin quivered. "He bought me with gifts, and you gave me these plates."

She threw another, and it was ear-piercing loud as it smashed against the wall. "He expected me to give him my body for gifts. Now you are expecting the same."

She shook her head. "No one will take that from me again. Ever!"

She put her hands on the edge of the counter as she sat there.

"When I even pushed Danny away, he stopped. I thought James would too. I never thought he wouldn't listen," she sobbed. "I felt so used when he left that morning."

She covered her face with her hands.

Danny took a minute to calm his beating heart. If he could get his hands on James right now, he would be dead. He didn't get angry often but people who hurt weaker ones made his blood boil. Moving slowly, he wrapped Priscilla in his arms and carried her to the sofa. Hearing the glass crush under his slippers felt like his heart cracking open. And maybe the sound of their relationship shattering.

Laying her down, he pulled a blanket up over her as she continued to sob. He sat on the floor by her and prayed. He also dealt with his own demons. Anger at James. At himself. Maybe he had taken it too far with her while they were courting. If he had been a better Amish, she wouldn't have courted James. When she finally slept, he gazed at her while the sun started to rise, feeling such a love for her. He would always love her. Touching her stomach and kissing her head, he got out his cell phone. He went outside, feeling exhausted but knowing he couldn't sleep for a long time.

He hit Stan's name on the phone, sure his friend was just pouring his coffee as he prayed for his officers. Wiping an angry tear away, he knew he could use those prayers.

"What's up this fine morning, Danny?" Stan answered.

He groaned as he walked over the grass. "It's not good."

"What happened?" Stan waited for an answer, like the wise man he was.

Danny was quiet for a long while, then he spilled out what happened, ending with, "She doesn't trust me. Now I see that. I brought her home a gift last night. Just to show her my love and care, and she took it this way. She didn't even act like this last night. But then she always hides what she feels. You think I am a master of hiding feelings, you should get to know this lady. What's the point of this marriage if we are both unhappy? If you can even call this a marriage."

"Are you afraid she will leave?" Stan asked.

"Oh, no. She would never do that. We will just live in misery for the rest of our lives," he snorted. "I can't seem to make any headway with her. She hates me. At least in her nightmares she does because I am a man." He sat on the porch and held his forehead, glad Stan was quiet enough for him to admit it. "Maybe she is right. Maybe I can't be her man. I ain't strong."

A rustle in his ear sounded like someone else had gotten on the phone, and he knew it must be Pam on the line. His parents always did this, and that was the reason he called the house and not Stan's cell.

"Oh, my boy," Pam said compassionately. "It's not you. It's not her."

"Then is it God pulling us apart now?" he asked, a bite to his words. "'Cause I am tired. She has had nightmares for the last two nights and I am tired. I have comforted her and held her long into the night."

He sighed. He made sure they knew he had done right by her. Not that they didn't expect it. They had taught him well. But had he moved too fast? So maybe it had been his fault. His face felt beet-red with anger at himself.

"It is God doing it." Pam paused, knowing Danny would wait to hear her wise words. "She is having nightmares and flashbacks because her body and mind are finally letting her heal. It takes time. She is working it through and her doubts are coming in. This is the process she has to go through to heal. God is letting you be the one to see her heal. This is the valley of the shadow of death. Light will come, my boy. It will come and be more beautiful than you've ever seen."

Pam's words made Danny bow his head as tears ran down his face. He sobbed for all his wife had lost, for his own loss in what had been lost with her, and for his anger at James again. His chest heaved as he sobbed.

This hurt more than words could say. Was God going to hear his own heart? 'Cause it was breaking.

~

That morning, Danny glanced back at Priscilla. He had cleaned up the mess from the kitchen the night before like nothing happened. He had put a bandage on his face and told her it happened over the night with something falling. It was true. She didn't need to know she had thrown it. He wondered if she even remembered it. For now, he wanted to just let it go and hope they could move on from this.

He got the peanut butter out, and Priscilla leaned past him. Reaching for something in the cupboard, she touched his waist with her hand, the other balanced on the counter. He moved away quickly because it tickled him.

To his delight, she noticed and smiled shyly at him. Forgetting what she was reaching for, she asked softly, "You wouldn't be ticklish, are you?"

He grinned at her. "Not at all. Are you, miss?"

Her eyes widened and she blushed.

"No," she squealed.

He put his hands on her waist. "Really, Priscilla?"

She backed away, and he let her.

Shaking her head, she giggled.

"Not at all," she mimicked his words.

He laughed. "We are both bad liars."

She giggled. "That we are."

She moved as if she wanted him to catch her. He loved the playful look on her face.

He took to the chase and she ran in the small house. He caught her, tickled her and she laughed. He loved hearing it. He chased her and they both tumbled onto the small couch, continuing to tickle her and laugh with her. She laid on her back, and he hovered over her gently without thinking about it.

Then, all of sudden, she slapped him across the face. He sat down, shocked and hurt. What had just happened?

She backed away from him, pulling up her knees up to her chest.

"Don't touch me again," she whimpered.

"Honey, what did I do?" he asked softly. He backed up to give her space.

She started shaking. "You hurt me, James."

She closed her eyes as tears escaped.

"Stop touching me..." she whimpered.

Danny felt his heart break. He had never been in so much pain over someone. It physically hurt. She sounded so defeated, like she had given up. He wasn't sure what to do. He sat there and did the only thing he could think of: pray. He didn't take his eyes off her as he prayed. She sat there shaking and in a daze. Not seeing him.

Finally, her eyes closed and she leaned into the corner of the sofa, falling asleep in a fetal position. He kissed her head and walked outside to the porch. His face was still stinging from her slap, but his heart was in worse condition. Oh, how he wanted to make this right.

He picked up his phone and hit his father's name. He didn't need to talk to his family. He needed to see them. He needed his mother's hug to see his father face to face tonight.

Tonight was different from the other nightmares, and he knew it.

His wife had thought he had attacked her. Was he wrong to play with her? Was it too soon? He walked out in the dark and didn't bother turning on the light. He sat on the swing and waited until he heard their car drive up in the dark.

His strong mother was out by the time the car stopped, and she calmly walked up the stairs to him. He didn't move. He was now numb. It was easier than feeling this much pain. She sat next to him on the porch swing and pulled his big frame into her arms.

"Oh, my boy." She rubbed his head.

Her touch did him in, and he let out a sob while she held him. She whispered sweet things in his ear but never tried to stop his cries. He loved that about his parents.

They never kept him from showing emotion, no matter how much he hurt.

He sat up as mother handed him a hankie. He wiped his face. He looked at his dad leaning against the railing, boots crossed. His face was emotionless, like it became when he was concerned. He silently waited to hear Danny's story.

Shaking his head, Danny ground his teeth in frustration. "She thought I did or would hit her, and it came way too close to home tonight. I was not ready for it. Why would she think that? She thought I was her abuser! Why?"

Mama rubbed his shoulder. "It sounds like she went into a flashback. So, she couldn't have known it was you. It was her mind blocking anything in order to survive."

He crossed his arms. "I have never seen a flashback like that before."

Dad shrugged. "They come in different ways. Just know it is not you she is mad at or scared of. It's him. You can't change how you are with her because of this. If you do that, she will know you are holding back, and she won't be able to trust you."

He rolled his eyes.

"Oh, she doesn't trust me. I can see that for myself." He looked down. "How am I supposed to act like me if I am scared she will do this again?"

"Time," his mother said. "It will take time on your part and hers. Look at me, honey."

When he looked at her, she took his face in her hands. "Her having flashbacks and letting out what she feels means she is feeling safe here. And that can be scary sometimes. She has never been allowed to be herself, and you let her. So those old memories are coming, and not just with James, but probably some of her parents. Since her parents must've known, but even if they didn't know, they let her get hurt while living there. She was taught her father is her protector, but he wasn't. Know she is trusting you and it scares her a bit. You are a good man and can help her through this."

He closed his eyes and thought of what she said. Letting it sink in. "You're right. I will do anything for her."

Chapter Eight

Priscilla woke up, feeling bruised all over. Why was she in a ball? Had she had another nightmare? She sat up and remembered some of what happened. Danny tickled her and she had loved hearing his laughter. It touched her heart and felt like a breath of fresh air.

Then she remembered slapping him.

How could she have slapped her sweet husband? Holding her arms around herself, hugging herself, she couldn't believe she had done that. Would he get mad and punish her with words? Or even hit her back? She deserved it. What if he did more than hurt her? She gave him a reason to.

She held her throbbing head. She was panicking now.

She got up to get a glass of water and heard voices by the porch, so she walked over to the open window and saw Danny sitting next to his mamm. Her attention moved to his dadae. Though Danny and he shared no blood, they were so much alike. He leaned against the porch just like Danny always did, his black boots crossed. She loved the gentleness of the older man and how he looked at her with such kindness. He seemed to see the real her. She hadn't expected that from men before. It was like God made those two men different from the others.

She heard Stan say softly, "You know she may do that again for a while yet. Do you think you can handle it?"

She glanced at Danny through the small window. He touched the cheek she had slapped. A tear ran down his face.

"It's hurt more than I ever thought," he shook his head.

She backed up, stinging at his words. She had made her tough, kind husband cry. She went to lay back on the sofa. He wasn't going to punish her. Worse, he was giving up on her. Curling her arms around her stomach, she held her baby and thought, *I am sorry, baby. I thought I found someone to take care of us. I messed it up, baby.*

Again.

She closed her eyes and let her mind go to the time in the barn where everything had been perfect until it all ended for her.

Priscilla met those beautiful brown eyes. Danny always looked at her with such delight and made her feel so special. But as much as she cared for him, she wasn't sure how this courtship would work. She wanted to be a good Amish girl.

And she knew Danny didn't want to be Amish.

She looked outside the hay loft window, crossing her arms.

Danny walked closer to her. "What's wrong, love?"

"Everything," she sighed and looked at him. "I don't know if we should keep courting. You are going to leave, and I don't want to. I want to be a good Amish wife. I want to go to heaven."

Danny's eyes widened. "So going out with me will make you go to hell? I love you, Prissy."

She knew that, and she loved him too. Though she had a hard time saying it.

"Staying Amish won't get you to heaven." Danny had told her this a dozen times but she didn't understand. It was like he spoke a different language.

She shook her head. "I don't know. I just feel torn."

Danny touched her hand, like he always did in church or in town. They weren't allowed to openly touch. No couple, married or not, did that without being gossiped about. So he often just touched her fingers with his. It was soft and gentle and made her feel so cherished. Safe.

She always felt safe with him.

"I know you. I know everything about you. What you love, what you think, what makes you laugh and cry." He tickled her a bit.

She giggled but stepped back, looking up at him. "That is true, and I know nothing of you sometimes. I feel like I don't know all of you and never will. If we marry, will I know you?"

He kissed her.

"Let me show you who I am," he whispered and kissed her again.

She melted in his kisses. She kissed him back. His lips moved passionately over hers. He took off her bonnet and dug his fingers through her curls.

She had always loved him more than anyone else in the community. She hadn't planned on courting him but he became her friend first, and then when he asked, she had a hard time saying no to that cute face and those pouty lips. He was fun and wild. He came up with the greatest ideas of things to do. He had shown her touch could be good. She had come to love his hugs. She had never been hugged by anyone else, not even her parents. But he loved hugs and then kisses. And he was always careful that she wanted them too, and if she ever said no or backed away, he would respect her.

She loved the feel of his mouth, and wanting more. How could she want a man so much? Want his touch, his kisses, his love. The emotions overwhelmed her. She loved him so much.

"Danny boy," she said.

As he pulled her closer, she knew this wasn't right. What if the bishop saw her? When she asked that, Danny always asked her what God thought. What would He say? She knew He wouldn't want them to fall like this. She wasn't Danny's and she may never be. She knew what she had to do and if she didn't do it soon, her body would take over.

His lips came back to her, and he kissed her. She kissed him back with all the emotions she felt, running her hands through his forbidden hair. In the kiss she also told him goodbye. She knew what was coming, and she needed a good Amish man. Though she couldn't imagine loving another man as much as him. So she would settle for a good Amish man and give up this love. Putting her hands on his chest, she almost pulled him closer. How could her body and mind fight each other so much? It was almost more than she could bear but she pulled away with tears in her eyes.

He looked at her worried. Kissing the tears from her eyes. "What is wrong, my love?"

"This is not good," she cried. She wanted him to just kiss her and ignore her words.

But he frowned, sat up and shook his head. His face crumbled in guilt. "You're right. I am sorry. I let myself get carried away."

She sat there quietly, her hair all over her face. She pushed it back, unused to it being out, and definitely not used to a man seeing it. Her husband was the only one supposed to see it. And Danny was not her husband. Now, and probably ever.

She stood up. "I don't think I can do this."

He followed her movement. "What do you mean?"

"We can't court anymore," her eyes stung as she said the words.

"What? Why? Is it because I went too far? I am sorry. That won't happen again." He took her hand.

She pulled away. They were just too different. "We want different things. It's not good."

With that, she went down the ladder and half-ran to the house.

Now she knew she had gotten what she deserved from James because of making Danny fall in the barn. She had wanted him. Had desired him. Had wanted his love forever. She was a sinful girl. It was all her fault.

She only had one option now, and she hated that one. She had to leave.

A while later she heard a car drive away, and then Danny's boots against the floor. He came over to her and picked her up. She didn't show she was awake. When she felt the bed on her back and his arms move away, she almost called after him not to leave her. But she knew she couldn't because he didn't want her after what she had done. When he left the room, she grabbed his pillow. It smelled like him.

She cried into it, dreading what she had to do.

∽

Danny woke up late the next morning. It had taken forever to get to sleep, but he sat up, feeling rested and refreshed. Walking into the kitchen, he made coffee, feeling like he could take on the world. Or at least his cute little wife.

They would get through this, and he felt confident in that. He had assured his parents of that last night, and he wasn't alone in this. They would be there for him and Priscilla.

As he sat down at the table, drinking his coffee and reading his devotion, he looked at the clock. Man, Priscilla was sleeping late. Was something wrong? She had seemed fine when he carried her to the room last night. He had wanted to stay and hold her.

But he knew she wasn't ready for that. How he wished he could love her the way he wanted to. He would have to love her at her own pace, and he could do it. Love was patient, as his dad reminded him last night.

Time and patience would be the best step for her.

Glancing at the clock again, he decided to check on her. She must be very tired, or maybe she remembered yesterday and was embarrassed. Knocking on the door, he heard nothing. He called her name softly. Finally, he opened the door and found the room empty. Walking in, he saw the bed neatly made and a note on the bed.

He didn't want to pick it up, afraid of what he would read. What if she had done something worse than he expected?

He opened it and read:

Danny, I am sorry for letting you know like this, but I didn't know how else to do it. You are a good man and deserve someone better. Me and the babe will be fine. I have to leave. Please don't come after me. In kind regards, Priscilla.

Sighing, he rolled the paper into a ball. Had he not written the same letter to Pam and Stan at one point, he might have been more worried. Where would she go? At least he said the baby would be safe.

Knowing she probably went to someone in the Amish community, he forced himself to hook up his horse. He wasn't willing to let them get shunned yet, and driving his jeep around looking for his wife would do that in a heartbeat. He could borrow a buggy to go home.

He rode to the Yoders and was shocked not to find her there. Would she really go back to her parents' house? He shook his head and turned his horse towards their home.

Tying the horse to the post, he walked inside without knocking.

"Priscilla," he called out. When he got no answer, he walked to the kitchen and saw her sister, Annie. She didn't look surprised to see him.

He crossed his arms. "Where is she?"

Annie looked hopeful and something like awe was in her eyes as she met his gaze.

"In the bedroom, getting the washing," she walked closer to him. "Don't let her..."

She started to say, then stopped as she looked around. Her eyes dropped to the ground.

Danny felt her pain and walked closer. Taking her chin in his hand, he made her look at him. "I understand what you are saying. I love her."

She looked at him with such longing. "I know, but you show it differently than other men."

Inwardly, he kicked himself. He should have been a better brother to his wife's siblings. He just hadn't wanted them to hurt her. He knew most of them blamed her for the baby.

"That's because I love her differently. The way God wants me to." He heard someone at the door, and Annie backed up, getting back to work. He understood that. "Annie, know that if you need anything, you can always come to me or Priscilla. No matter where we are. You are my family too."

Again, she looked at him with longing and nodded. Glancing at the door, she went back to being emotionless. He held her gaze until she turned away.

"What are you doing here, Daniel?" Ben asked with a grunt.

Danny grit his teeth.

Annie spoke up, "Priscilla came today to help with some chores, and Danny is here to pick her up. That is nice, Dadae."

He sat at the table, turning his back to Danny.

Danny met Annie's gaze before he left, and she gave him a shy smile much like Priscilla's. Taking the stairs two at a time, he went to where he thought her bedroom might be.

He knocked and heard her say, "Come in."

He walked in and shut the door. She spun around, and when she spotted him, her eyes widened. He tried to stay relaxed, but his legs spread apart. Boots planted on the floor. How could she go back to the home where she'd been hurt?

"Well, Priscilla, aren't you going to say something?" he asked.

She held a blanket to her chest and didn't meet his gaze.

"I told you in the letter," she muttered. "How did you find me?"

He crossed his arms. "I thought you would go to the Yoders. Why come here?"

She dropped the blankets on the floor and fisted her hands. "Because the Yoders like you. My family doesn't!"

He hurt at her words. He was handling this wrong.

Getting mad at her was not going to help. When her eyes flashed regret, he knew she didn't mean to say that.

She backed up and turned around.

He didn't come closer. "Love, why did you leave?"

She hung her head. "Because I hurt you. You deserve better."

He walked to her. "Honey, I want you. I don't want anyone else. Ever."

She turned around, glaring at him. "Really? Even now, I hurt you with my words. I make you sin. You deserve someone who doesn't make you hurt. Make you sin."

"What are you talking about? You have never made me sin." He ran a hand through his hair. Was she talking of the time they made out in the hayloft? "Ever."

She lay on the bed then, facedown.

"I made you cry. I slapped you," she cried out, "I made you sin by crying."

Confused, he knelt down beside her. "Honey, what are you talking about?"

She closed her eyes, biting her fists as a baby would. "I made you sin by crying. It's a sin for a man to cry."

Danny had no idea where she got that idea. "Honey, who told you that?"

"Dadae. He yelled at my brother for crying over his broken foot. It's a sin."

He was glad Priscilla couldn't see his face. He hardened his jaw. "That is not true at all. It's not a sin for a man to cry. Did you know David cried often in the Bible? And Jesus wept."

She sat up and opened her wet eyes in surprise. "Really?"

"Yes," he paused, knowing he would come back to this

topic. But first he had to handle something bigger. "Now there is something else wrong."

She closed her eyes. "How did you know?"

"I know you, honey. Can you tell me?"

What he saw surprised him and hurt him to the core: A hopelessness in her eyes that went deep.

She didn't look as at him as she said, "I make you fall. I am bad because of what I did with James and, because of that, my baby is a sin. I am a sinner and so is my baby. You deserve to be with someone pure, who is not a sinner."

Her chin shook. "I will never be pure again. You should have taken me that time in the barn. At least you would have been the first. I wanted you then, and that is why James hurt me later."His mouth dropped open. He could not believe what she had just said.

"Who told you this?" he asked when he finally found his voice.

"My dadae and the bishop when he found out." She met his gaze. "So your datt thinks I made you fall, and this baby is my fault for that."

He couldn't breathe. He had never felt this much anger before. He knew the church had its problems, but this was crazy. He stood up and walked to the other side of the room. He needed to calm down or he was going to say something wrong. Mother had tried to warn him that the Amish could treat women like this, but he hadn't been ready for it to be *his* woman. She knew things he had missed before because he wasn't really a part of the community.

His girl had been treated like this. Why hadn't he found out she was pregnant before anyone else and protected her from those words? Those actions. If her father was right here, he would have put him into next week. His hands were in a fist, his face hot. His chest physically ached. He had never felt this kind of rage before.

At James.

At her father and at the bishop.

Finally, he started to pray, knowing he had to talk to her. She must feel like he agreed with her. How did he convince her otherwise? She had believed the lies for so long. It was like a cut that stuck around until someone tried to heal it, and that meant it hurt to be healed.

He walked over to her and knelt down beside the bed. She was shaking again.

"You can leave," she said, dejected. "I will divorce you so you can have someone else in English."

He took her hand.

"Honey, I had to calm down over there for a minute. I didn't want to respond to the anger I was feeling," he squeezed her hand. "Not at you, but toward the men that hurt you. You and our child did nothing wrong. I have to ask you some tough questions. Can you answer me?"

Fear entered her eyes but she nodded like the obedient wife she was.

He had to get her to see she was a victim. Not a sinner. He spoke in a steady voice. "Did you want what happened to you?"

She flinched and shook her head.

He hated her reaction but kept at it. "You didn't want him to touch you?"

"I didn't," she whispered.

Her hands trembled in his. "He hurt you, didn't he?"

Her chin shook again. "Yes. He did."

He placed his hand on her cheek.

"By what you said, you are a victim and survivor of what he did to you. You didn't want what happened to you. You didn't want him to touch you. He hurt you against your will. That makes him an abuser. An evil man. It makes him the sinner. It's his fault," he paused. "You are the victim. Our baby is a gift. You are not a sinner, and it was not your fault. You are innocent of what he did. And this baby is a gift. All babies are a gift from God. He blessed us with this baby. God blessed me with you. Do you understand?"

She blinked. "No, but I am trying."

He gave her a small smile. "That is all I can ask for, honey."

He just knelt there by her, still holding her soft, pale face, her hair escaping out of her kapp in the adorable way he loved.

Her face softened and she closed her eyes.

"What did I do to get a man like you?" she whispered.

"I wonder every day how God brought you to me. You are my whole world," he rubbed her cheek. "Come home to me."

She nodded, and his heart sang.

He leaned his head against her forehead. "You are so brave, my girl."

He stood and then helped her to her feet. His legs tingled, having fallen asleep, but he wasn't about to complain.

"Will your datt be outside in the field by now?" he asked, trying to keep his voice light.

He must have failed because she looked at him, concerned. "Why?"

"I don't think I can face him at the moment." He knew he couldn't. Not without punching the man to within an inch of his life. What kind of father could tell his daughter those lies?

She didn't seem to understand his words and glanced at the clock. "He is outside."

He nodded. "Good. Are you ready to go home?"

She looked surprised again. As if trying to figure him out.

She picked the blankets up off the floor. "I will take these down to Annie. I should help with laundry, since I agreed too."

He shook his head. "She will understand. Let's go."

He didn't want her here. And he was afraid of what he would do if he stayed much longer.

She frowned, sighing, but nodded. Her eyes darkened a bit. She would make this work. This marriage.

He was glad to see some fire back in her eyes, that look he remembered. That he missed. Even if it was at him. He didn't want to push her so he didn't carry the blankets for her. Love was patient, he reminded himself.

After giving the blankets to Annie, they kept the conversation short. Annie looked pleased they were leaving together.

On the drive to their house, he was glad he didn't ride by her datt in the field, but he did drive by his own father.

Like a good Amish girl, Priscilla waved at the bishop. He waved back.

Danny knew it might be childish, but he was too angry at the man who had raised him for years to wave at him. That man had hurt his girl. Badly. He ground his teeth.

Priscilla glanced at him in surprise when he didn't wave. But she stayed silent. As usual.

At home, he helped her down from the buggy that he borrowed from her datt, but then he didn't let go and kept her in his arms. He needed her close for a moment. To know she was safe and where she belonged.

She looked up at him, her hands on his chest. Her eyes were at peace for the first time since the flashback. "I am sorry for leaving."

He leaned closer to her. "I will always come for you. No matter what."

She leaned against his chest, finally feeling at peace, and as if she had come home to him.

Chapter Nine

Priscilla woke up that afternoon, still sleepy. After Danny brought her home, she had gone into her room to get away from him and had fallen asleep. Glancing at the clock, she was shocked to see it was late in the day. Her stomach grumbled. She was famished. Annie had fed her this morning, but she hadn't been hungry and didn't eat much. She was too afraid with her datt around.

She heard a knock on the door. She pulled the blanket up and called for him to come in.

Danny walked in carrying a tray of food.

She sat up, glad she was still dressed. She felt so exposed. Danny seemed to be in a good mood, not bothered by what happened earlier. But that was Danny; he was always so relaxed. It bugged her sometimes. She didn't know how he managed it.

He sat the tray down by her.

"Mom brought some food over last night." He smiled. "It is what she does when she comes over. She thinks she needs to care for everyone."

She looked at the food, not sure what to do. She had

never seen a man serve a woman. It was a woman's job. Not a man's.

"I should have made something, especially on your day off. I am sorry I was a bad wife," she tried to stand but Danny took her hand and she sat back down on the bed.

"Please, eat." His eyes were gentle. "You are a wonderful wife, the way you care for me, how strong you are, and this is what I like to do for you. I want to take care of you, and this is one way I can do it." He squeezed her hand. "Now please eat, babe."

She didn't want to, but her stomach growled and he heard because his eyes turned amused. She moved to get comfortable and took a bite of the food. It was delicious, and her stomach welcomed it like a lost friend. Being married to Danny, she sure ate a lot of takeout and other people's food. She knew some Amish ate that way, but her family never had. She liked it. Especially the time she spent with Danny over meals.

As she finished the food, she took a bite of the garlic bread. "This is delicious."

She took a long sip of the sweet tea she had come to love because of this man. "So, your parents came over last night?"

She didn't want him to know she had watched him with his parents.

He nodded, turning serious. "They helped me through some things. Before parting ways last night, I told them I wasn't giving up on us. On what we have. That I will do what it takes to make this work."

For the first time, she really heard what he said. It hit her heart it had never done before. Her eyes watered, and she looked away. She tried to stop what she was feeling.

He came closer and put his hands on her knees. "Love, what did I do?"

She shook her head. "Why do you care? I have never had someone care like you."

Tears fell for the first time since being married to this wonderful man. She wiped at them, afraid to let them out. They might never stop.

He took her hand. "Let your tears come, it means you are feeling. Feelings are always good, even if they hurt."

She shook her head again. "You make me feel things I never felt in my life. It's overwhelming."

"That's because you never had this before, love. I care for you."

She put her head in her hands. "Why? What did I do to deserve you? Why do you care so much?"

He kissed her head. "Because I love you."

She abruptly stood and walked over to the window. He made her feel so vulnerable.

Gazing out, she whispered, "No one has ever loved me."

She heard him stand up and come over to her. But he didn't touch her.

He spoke softly, "Well, that is not true. I know Annie and your brothers love you, and I know your mamm loves you. You have just never heard the words. I hadn't heard them till Pam told me. I believed Pam loved me first. It took a while to trust a man and to believe Stan loved me."

He leaned close. "But I now know unconditional love. And that is what I have for you. My love will never leave."

She turned around and put her hands on his chest. It didn't take him but a minute before he decided to hold her tight against him.

Priscilla felt his heartbeat against her ear. To know she held his heart in her hand was scary. She had no idea what it was to give her heart away.

Danny took her chin in his hand and met her gaze. He looked over her face with such longing and desire. It made her tingle and feel beautiful and precious.

"I trust you," he said.

She melted under his gaze and then hid her face in his wide chest. He was trusting her. He was giving her a chance, knowing he might get hurt. That meant more than words could say. She finally slid her arms around him and hugged him tightly. It felt scary and just right. Like she was at peace.

"Oh, my brave girl." He hugged her tighter and kissed her head. "You are so strong, love."

He seemed to know how hard it was for her to hug him or accept his hugs.

~

Priscilla got up the next morning and started baking bread. Then she decided to make Danny a green shirt and, for herself, a matching dress. She'd learned that he loved when couples dressed alike. This would be her way of telling she was working on their marriage, and wanting it.

Maybe.

She wanted to please him. She heard a knock on the door as she was pulling the bread out of the oven. When she went to the door, she found her mamm on the other end. She was surprised to see her so early. But then again, she had slept later than usual due to all she had been through.

"Hi, Mamm, do you wanna come in? I was about to make myself some breakfast."

"It's near noon and you haven't eaten yet?" Mamm walked inside. She poured herself some coffee and then sat at the table. Her mom was dressed neatly and seemed like she had come with a mission.

Priscilla looked at the clock and shook her head. It wasn't even ten yet. But she couldn't remember the last time she'd slept that late. She hadn't seen her mamm since shopping. She didn't want her mamm to bring up her running away. That she would be a terrible wife and she knew it. Guilt pained her heart. She started some toast. Eggs might be too much on her stomach this early. She asked her mom if she wanted some, but she didn't.

Finally, she sat down with the toast and coffee. She was glad Mamm let her eat in silence; she just needed food and to not think. When she finished, Mamm was done with her coffee, so she refilled it.

"You can't hide from the topic all day," her mamm said.

Priscilla shrugged. "I wanted to try. I am tired."

"Being pregnant does that," her mamm said, matter-of-fact.

"Well, I don't wanna be." Then her hand went to her stomach. That wasn't right to say. What if her baby heard her? She was a terrible mother.

"Well, this baby is a gift from God. All children are."

She sat down in her chair. "Really? I thought children are here to do chores."

Her mamm looked a little hurt. "Do you really feel that is how it was growing up?"

She shrugged. "More by Datt. But that is one of the

reasons I ran. I don't deserve Danny. And he deserves someone better than me."

"That is not true. But you need to make a decision. Do you want this marriage to last?"

Priscilla looked at the wood table. Did she? She really didn't know. She didn't love him anymore. He could have anyone but he chose her. She didn't deserve him.

"Yes," she heard the weakness in her own voice.

"Well, with emotion like that, you will go far," Mamm told her dryly.

Priscilla might have almost chuckled, if she didn't feel so tired. So defeated.

"How do I decide to want this marriage?"

"Do you believe in divorce? In leaving?"

"No. I don't. And I knew that going into this. I knew we might both be miserable our whole marriage."

"Or you can make it work and be happy. You can have both." Her lips were in a thin line. But her eyes showed so much love to her daughter. She wanted her to have hope.

"Can I ask if you are happy with Datt?"

Mamm shrugged. "I am happy with my children. My community. Not everyone has it great, but you can have it better. I see the way Danny looks at you. He adores you. He loves you."

"He told me yesterday that he loved me." But then he had loved her for a long time. She knew that.

"That is wonderful, and everyone can see it. Can you?" Mamm asked.

"Do I know what love is?"

"Probably not. I know you didn't see it in my marriage or in the home enough. But Danny is different." Mamm took a sip of coffee. "You need to decide if you want the marriage to just last, or if you want to make it happy and loving. There is a big difference. And take it from someone who knows that making it happy and loving is the difference."

Priscilla nodded. Her mamm was right. She needed to do more to make this marriage good. Danny *did* love her.

And that made her definitely feel something, but she wasn't sure what.

Chapter Ten

Priscilla had gotten used to Danny having more time off than most Amish men. Since they didn't have a farm to work, she had more time with him too. In the future, having a farm would be nice. But right now, this marriage was too new. And like she had told her Mamm yesterday, she wanted to make it work.

After running back to her home, she kind of felt ashamed. She shouldn't have done that.

She took out some items for supper, and then started making cinnamon rolls.

Danny came into the kitchen a few minutes later. He had been reading on the sofa. He enjoyed reading almost as much as she did. It was nice to have something in common with him. She enjoyed talking to him about books.

She looked at him, surprised to see him wearing jeans and a white t-shirt. Combined with his hair, he looked English. She wasn't sure what to say.

He looked reserved, even a bit nervous. He ran a hand

over his jaw. "I hope you don't mind that I wear this. When I lived alone, I wore it all the time."

She rolled it out into rolls as she blinked.

"I want to be able to show this side of me in our marriage. But only if you are comfortable with it."

She looked at the dough. He was right. She wanted this marriage to be honest too and that meant accepting his new clothes. And it wasn't like anyone else would see them.

"I don't mind but please don't let the community see it."

He nodded.

"Of course." He smiled softly at her. "Do you mind if I help you? I want to show you something."

She nodded. She was curious about what he wanted to show her.

He took out fresh produce. She had never cooked with this kind of food before, but she had seen them in the store. He cut one in half and took out a big seed.

She finally got curious enough to ask, "What are you making?"

"Avocado dip. I bought other stuff to go along with it. Avocado is good and healthy for you."

"I've never had it before."

Danny didn't look surprised. "I didn't either until I lived with my English parents."

She worked beside him, and they moved well together. He was careful when he touched her and she was thankful for that.

"What was it like, living English after living Amish your whole life?"

Danny tapped his boots, showing how proud he was of her. He thought of the answer as he looked down at her.

She looked cute, her blonde hair tucked inside her kapp. Flour dotted her nose, and he wanted to kiss it away. Instead, he thought about how adorable she looked. Having her in his house still took some getting used, even though they'd been married. It didn't feel like it had been a couple of weeks.

"The first time I saw a TV, they must have thought I was crazy because of how I acted," he said, tossing the avocado skins in the trash. "It was wild. I started watching old shows like Andy Griffith. I loved their shower and took one almost every day. That was before the bishop installed indoor plumbing. I loved learning the most." He paused. "Most don't know this, but I have my GED."

Her eyes widened as she looked up at him. She cut it into a roll and then put it on the cookie sheet. There was a flour mark on her face.

"Really?"

He nodded, not feeling any judgment from her like he usually received from the Amish community. "I wanted an education past the eighth grade level."

Priscilla's head dipped.

"I want to learn more, too," she said the words barely above a whisper.

He reached for an onion, and his hand faltered to it. He was so touched she would tell him that. It was forbidden to learn more than the Amish teach a person. It was prideful. He wanted to wipe that cute flour from her face. But he just enjoyed watching her instead.

"You know, if you want to learn more, I can help you and get you the books too."

She shook her head hard. She stood across from him. "No, the bishop wouldn't like that."

He didn't like her answer, but he understood it very

well. "If you change your mind, let me know, my book queen."

She looked up at the sound of the nickname. "What did you call me?"

"My book queen. Do you mind if I call you that?" He leaned a bit closer, meeting her eyes.

Her eyes were soft, and she shuttled a bit from his touch. "I don't mind."

He touched her face with his hand, wiping the flour off. His touch was so soft and gentle on her skin.

"My book queen," he said softly, his breath smelling of spices and masculinity. Some may say it wasn't a romantic smell, but it fit for how she felt: light headed on her feet.

She stood still for a moment, looking like she enjoyed his touch. Then she pulled away and moved to the other side of the kitchen.

Priscilla didn't know how she felt about Danny's touch. She liked it, but then she felt like she was bad for wanting the touch. He had wanted to touch her before, but then another man had raped her.

She touched her stomach, almost feeling the baby grow inside of her. Would she love the child one day? Would the child know his or her father was a rapist? So many thoughts overwhelmed her. Fear ran through her thoughts.

Even though she wasn't sure about Danny's physical closeness, he could still call her his book queen. Those words touched her heart like nothing else. She always loved when he talked to her. His voice comforted her. She had known he wouldn't judge her for wanting to learn more.

Danny had finished stirring all of the ingredients into a bowl. He grabbed the chips from the cupboard and scooped a big, green chunk of dip onto a single chip. Grinning at her, he popped the loaded chip into his mouth. She felt awkward staring, but his enjoyment of this strange concoction was too cute. She loved this new side of him, something she got to know before. It made her feelings deeper for him. More than just the physical like before. She enjoyed being with him and seeing him in this light.

After he swallowed, he said, "You should try this, book queen."

If he kept calling her that, she would eat anything he gave her. She took a chip and dipped it. The creamy avocado, mixed with onions and spices, tasted rich and good. It smelled heavenly.

"I like it." Her eyes brightened. She gave him a shy grin.

"Well, you don't have to act so surprised," he joked.

She smiled.

"I wasn't sure what it would taste like. It's really good," she held her stomach when it felt nauseous. Like she may need to go to the backroom "Maybe it's too spicy for the baby."

"What is wrong? Are you all right?" he asked, concerned.

She went to get some water, and the spasm passed. "Ache. I am good."

"You don't seem as sick as most mothers," he commented.

She blushed. Her face burned so hot. Women didn't talk to men about pregnancy or birth. Ever. It was bad to talk about. She sat the cup down and looked back at the dip and where Danny stood.

"It was good. Maybe I should try it after I have eaten something else."

He nodded. "Why don't we do that? I want to make sure you're eating good food, and enough of it."

She softly smiled. "You are different."

He grinned. "You will have to find out more about me."

She wanted to know more about him, but she was afraid to know more as well. What if she found out something terrible about him and their life would be ruined? She pushed the thought away. That wouldn't happen. Could it?

∼

Priscilla looked out the window when she heard something. She smiled thinking about how close she felt to Danny after cooking with him yesterday. In the distance she saw a bunch of buggies pulling into her yard. White bonnets and black hats. Had she done something wrong? Her husband, for sure, was always doing something.

Ashley joked that even when sleeping, Danny was probably breaking a rule. They had all chuckled. But Priscilla felt like it might be true.

Danny came up behind her and she felt him tense. Without thinking about it, she took his hand.

Turning to face him, she met his gaze. "It will be all right, Danny boy."

His eyes widened at her nickname for him.

She hadn't realized how much she liked using that name for him. They heard a knock on the door.

He kissed her head. Still holding her hand, they went to the door. They greeted five couples who Priscilla had known most of her life. She hugged Miriam and even Paul, though it wasn't common for the community to do so. The couple did it to everyone. Priscilla felt better with them there. They may be able to stop the others from attacking them.

The bishop was with them. Priscilla knew when Danny spotted him, his hand tightened in hers. She squeezed his hand. She knew if the bishop was there it wouldn't end well. Her heart started beating faster.

They invited them to sit under the tree in the front yard since it was a nice evening. They all sat on the ground.

Danny helped Priscilla sit down, though she wasn't that big yet. She was hardly even showing. She sat crossed legged. He was always a gentleman.

Danny sat next to her but didn't take her hand again. Their friends wouldn't like that. They all started talking about different daily things, and it was a nice visit, but Priscilla knew something was on their mind. Normally visitors brought their children.

Finally, the bishop cleared his throat and everyone went quiet. "We came because we are concerned about your family, Danny."

Priscilla wanted to run. The last time they had a meeting, it had ended badly. She had felt so ashamed. That old shame was coming back.

Danny remained silent.

"You wear cowboy boots, and you haven't grown a beard. That is not allowed by the church. You are married now, and your face is still clean shaven," Eli, one of the deacons, told him. He had been there when they were to be married and had pushed Priscilla to marry. Though he didn't seem to push James into marrying her.

"I do it for work. It's hard for me to grow facial hair." That was kinda true. He just really didn't like facial hair.

He had liked kissing Priscilla without it. Though if he did grow a beard, he would still enjoy kissing her.

"Well, then, that job is taking away from our ways and you need to quit," the bishop said.

Danny's eyes narrowed. He took a deep breath. "I am the supporter of my family, and I can't do that."

"Money is not worth more than morals," Eli said firmly, his face stern.

"No, of course not. But tell me what is the moral behind having a beard?" Danny asked respectfully.

"It's the way we have always done it. And if you don't follow the rules, you may be put in the band and shunned," the bishop's face started to turn red.

Priscilla flinched. She didn't want to be shunned. That is what the band was. It would be terrible to be cut off from her family and friends. She looked at the faces of the women she loved. She saw the worried looks on their faces. The concern. They didn't want to shun her anymore than she wanted it. They loved her too. And she knew that. She didn't want anything to change. Ever. She had to try better at making Danny want to stay.

Danny glanced at her. His love shone as he met her gaze as she sat there looking so forsaken. He knew he couldn't let her down but that meant standing up for what he believed in. Although he loved her more than life, he had to stay by the Lord first.

He looked at the group. "I will try to follow the rules better. I do want to serve God. That is my biggest desire above all else."

"Well, that is good," Paul Yoder agreed with him. "That is what we should all want to do with our lives."

The bishop nodded. "Yes, but remember the rules are

important. We have ways to do things, and we don't want to change them."

"God is more important than rules," Paul said.

The bishop grunted. And the talk went back to everyday stuff like farming.

Priscilla sat back, resting on her hands; she was pulled into a talk with Miriam Yoder and Ida Yoder. Priscilla bought milk from Ida and other milk products she'd carried over in her buggy. In the last few weeks she had grown close to her.

"You need to get your husband under control more," Ida said suddenly.

Priscila just stared at her. She was trying to make this marriage strong, and this lady wanted more from her. Well, she didn't have it in her.

"Ida, that is harsh. What is Danny that is doing so wrong?" Miriam asked.

"He doesn't follow our ways," Ida said. She frowned. "I'm not sure I should sell to you."

Priscilla's mouth dropped open. How could she be so mean to her?

"What have I done to you?"

"Nothing, but your husband has been breaking rules," Ida said.

Priscilla shook her head. Tears came to her eyes but didn't fall. "My husband has shown me more love than I have ever felt in my life. He is a good man and loves the Lord with all his heart."

While she might struggle to trust him, she still knew he was a good man And that he loved the Lord with all his heart.

Ida threw up her hands. "Well, who is to argue with that?"

Priscilla gave a sarcastic laugh. That sounded like something Danny would say, and it sounded funny. Maybe she was becoming like her husband.

"So, my husband could abuse me and be a good Amish man that follows all the rules, and he wouldn't be talked to?"

Ida nodded. "Well, if he was abusive, it means you are not submitting enough."

Priscilla flinched at her words. She got up and walked away. She couldn't handle this any longer. She knew Danny noticed, but he couldn't leave their guests and not be rude. She was probably being rude enough for both of them. She wiped her eyes as she marched toward the house. Her breaths came short.

She ran the rest of the way to the house, dodged into the bathroom, and threw up. Wiping her mouth with a rag, she stood at the sink shaking, feeling so ashamed.

Then she heard Miriam come to the doorway.

"Oh, my dear," she said compassionately.

Priscilla wasn't one for hugs but she wrapped her arms around Miriam. Tears ran down her face as she cried against her friend's shoulder.

"I wasn't good enough. I didn't submit enough to him. That is why he did it," she cried. "If I don't submit to Danny, will he do the same?"

She couldn't imagine the shame and despair if he hurt her.

Miriam held her. "You did nothing wrong, my dear. Nothing."

She pulled away and wiped her eyes. "I shouldn't have said anything."

Miriam took her face in her hands. "You didn't do

anything wrong now or then. He *was* and *is* evil. It was his sin. Not yours."

Priscilla didn't believe her, though it was a nice thought to have. Everyone else thought she was the one who had made him do it. And she hadn't submitted to him, and it had hurt her. She had fought him.

"I can't deal with all this. They hate us."

"That is not true, dear," Miriam shook her head.

"Well, they hate Danny."

"If that were true, he would have been shunned already, and the bishop wouldn't have allowed you two to be married," Miriam told her gently.

Priscilla reluctantly agreed.

"Again, remember our home is open to you if you need a break, honey."

Priscilla knew that. But leaving Danny wasn't the answer. She wasn't going to run again. "Thank you but I want to try to make my marriage work."

Before Miriam could reply, she heard boots on the wood floor. Danny and Paul appeared in the doorway.

"Are you all right, love?" Danny asked.

She nodded. "Nothing I haven't dealt with before."

Paul frowned. "Sadly, that is probably true."

Danny went hard, his back straight. His eyes narrowed, seeming to be angry at Paul but Priscilla wasn't sure if he was angry at her.

"Do you want to stay for supper?" Priscilla remembered her manners.

"We would love to, but we have to get back to the kids." Miriam gave her another hug and whispered, "come to me anytime, dear."

Priscilla hugged her back, eyes watering. She wasn't

sure why, but to have someone love her like this felt strange.

Like Danny's unconditional love.

Danny must have seen the rest of the couples off. Danny and Priscilla walked them out. And Danny said little. Priscilla wanted to ask him what was wrong, but held back. She didn't want to be too outspoken. She needed to be more submissive.

And besides, there was hardness to Danny's expression, and it didn't seem like he wanted to talk about what upset him so much. He had never been like this before. Had the bishop hit a sore spot? She felt confused and that closeness went away. Was she losing him due to the conflict of the community?

∼

As Danny took a sip of his coffee, he found himself enjoying breakfast with his wife. He ran a hand over his smooth face as he thought of what the community thought of him. Oh, what would they think of the car he hid behind the bushes. Oh, he wouldn't care. He only cared about what he was hiding from his wife.

Pushing the thought away, he said, "So I was thinking we could go to Augusta for a festival and eat supper there. Have you been?"

She nodded. "Yeah, but never for a festival. It's the Art in the Garden, right?"

"Would you like to do it? I think Zack might meet us there later."

She wasn't sure she wanted to be around crowds of people, but spending the day with Danny meant more to her than facing the people.

She asked softly, "When do you want to leave?"

"How about noon? I can help you around here till then."

"Clean?" Her mouth opened a bit.

"Nah, I thought I would trash the place for you!" He winked at her.

She smiled at his joke. "Well, thank you, but you work hard all week. It's my job to work here."

Danny took her hand that lay on the table. "Well, today I am going to help. It's a beautiful day, and I would love to help you."

Priscilla looked down at his hand and nodded. If they were back home, he would work outside. There was always work to be done there. But they weren't home.

"*Danke*. Sounds nice." But she wasn't sure how she felt about her husband doing so much.

Chapter Eleven

Later that day, they walked down an Augusta sidewalk lined by vendors on both sides. The festival overlooked the shining river. Priscilla smelled a mix of different vendor foods and the scent of the river and summer air. It was wonderful. Though there were a bit too many people for her liking.

When someone passed too close, she moved near Danny, who took her hand.

He smiled down at her. "You better hang with me, honey."

She smiled lightly and nodded, this time wanting him close. He was her protector. She turned back to the vendors, awed by them. They sold so many unique items, like the Amish often did. Goat soap, scented candles, candy, essential oils, and many other things. Then she saw a vendor that sold books, and she pulled on Danny's hand.

"Can we go look at the book one?"

He grinned.

"Of course." He looked at the booth. "I love that author very much."

He chuckled.

She looked at him, confused, but pulled him over. She didn't know what overcame her, but she had to meet this author. A blonde had her back to them, but Priscilla saw Zack behind the table.

Zack sat there like he belonged.

Letting go of Danny's hand, she picked up the Christian fiction book. Then the author turned around and Priscilla's mouth fell open.

Ashley?

Her husband's sister smiled brightly. "I didn't realize you two would be here today until Zack showed up."

Priscilla was still shocked. "You are A.S. Harrison?"

Ashley stepped around the table to stand in front of her so she could give her a hug. "Yeah. I should have told you. But people get weird when they find out, and I just wanted to get to know you as a sister and friend."

Priscilla put the book on the table.

"I understand." She crossed her arms. "But next time tell me, got it?"

Then she laughed and gave Ashley a big hug.

Ashley hugged her. "I will promise."

Then Ashley reached over to hug Danny, who stood there in shock.

Who was this Priscilla? She wasn't acting like the woman he knew at all. Apparently he had a sassy, bossy wife... to his sister at least. He wanted her to be like that with him. He found a place to sit behind the table with Zack while the girls chattered like best friends.

After some time, he offered to get lunch for them all. He and Zack walked to the food area, leaving the girls to giggle over books and writing.

"What's wrong, man?" Zack asked finally.

"Who is that woman back there? She doesn't act like that with me."

Zack shrugged. "She is still in her shell with you. You need to bring her out of it."

Danny crossed his arms. "I have tried, and it only gets me more hurt over this woman. She is like ice sometimes."

The sun shone in his eyes so he put his sunglasses back on. "No, she is broken. It's harder when you love them."

Danny looked at him in surprise. "How could you tell?"

"How long have I known you?" Zack laughed. "It's all over your face. It's in the way you look at her, and how you treat her."

Danny gave him a small grin. "I do. I just wish she loved me back."

They got to the line of Augusta's local world-famous rotary burgers. Getting four, they brought them back to their women, who didn't seem as if they missed the guys much. But Danny was okay with that. He loved seeing Priscilla happy, and if his sister could do that, he was thankful.

In time, Danny prayed Priscilla would love him, and they could have a real marriage.

∽

As Danny drove home a couple of days later, he listened to the radio. A song by Mercy Me played loud. He loved this band. He'd grown up without it until Stan had shown him the pleasure of music. He sang along as he parked at the neighbors, who kept his jeep for him and then walked home from there. Though many mornings a friend picked up since he drove by. He still wasn't sure about telling Priscilla about the vehicle.

It was hard keeping it from her, but he wasn't sure she was ready. Their marriage was still tenuous. Even though they'd had fun at the fair, and made avocado dip together, and even had shared that one special night when he told he loved her, he knew she wasn't ready to find out that her Amish husband drove an automobile.

She hadn't even told him she loved him back. And he hadn't expected her to. But it still hurt.

He pushed the memory away and strode up the short. He walked up the short lane to the small house. He couldn't wait till they moved. He just didn't want the move to be too hard on her. She had experienced enough changes, and her parents and friends visited often, though he hated seeing her parents and knowing that they had allowed hell for their daughter for six long months.

But he had learned self-control at an early age and was friendly to her parents.

As he neared the house, he heard music. Walking in, he heard music coming from the kitchen. Quietly, he moved toward that room.

What he found made his eyes go wide.

Priscilla was dancing. She had her own moves and, though not perfect, she was graceful. The look on her face said it all; she was so peaceful, like she was serving a kind, loving God. Danny had been praying she would find God for herself. The loud Christian music came from his cordless radio. The song was the same one he had been singing in the car.

Priscilla closed her eyes as she danced to the music. Having never seen anyone else dance before, she made her own moves. She felt beautiful and graceful, something she knew she wasn't. The music changed to the next song. Still feeling a bit sinful since she knew the bishop would never allow this especially the dancing but it was healing. She loved how the lyrics made her feel like God really might care. She let the music take her away to another place where she was safe with just Danny. Of a time when she was safe with just him before the abuse happened. She turned and her eyes landed on Danny.

He leaned against the door, boots crossed, grinning like a fool, his arms folded. "Hey hottie, having fun?"

Her jaw dropped open, and she quickly turned the radio off. "I am so sorry. I didn't mean to. I just found the radio in the back room one day and thought I would listen. I am sorry. I know the bishop says it's bad."

That guilt she felt early filled her. She was sinful for doing this.

Danny walked up to her and put a hand on her lips.

"Shh," his face was full of concern and care. He didn't look angry at all. "Why do you listen to it?"

Priscilla didn't want to tell him but felt like she had to. Not because he was her husband but because he was her friend and honestly cared for her. Loved her.

"Well, I like it. It helps me feel..."

Danny took her hand and leaned against the counter as he waited.

She looked at their entwined hands, how big his hands were over hers.

"It makes me feel better..." she finally admitted. "When listening, I forget what happened."

Her face crumbled. She hated being so weak.

Then Danny's arms came around her, and she went willingly. Leaning her head against his chest, she closed her eyes. This was better than listening to music.

"Do you want to dance?" he whispered in her ear.

She looked up at him, confused. "I don't know how."

He kissed her forehead. "Well, let me teach you."

She gave him a shy smile and nodded.

"Take off your shoes."

She blushed, but did as he said. She left her stockings on, too embarrassed to take off more.

He didn't seem to notice. "Now put your feet on my boots."

She looked up at him. "I will hurt you."

He grinned. "I wear steel-toed boots, honey. You won't hurt me."

She did as he asked, and he turned on the radio quieter. He changed the channel to another song. Something soft and beautiful. He took her arms and placed them around his neck. He wrapped his arms around her waist. Holding her close, he swayed gently and slowly.

Priscilla loved his touch. His words. Her heart warmed, and she leaned against him, tightening her hold. She wanted to run her fingers through his long hair, but she didn't think that would be proper. She had to keep her walls up; she couldn't let herself be close to him because she didn't want him to think she was ready to be close again. She was not ready at all, but he might take advantage of her weakness.

She didn't know how much time passed, but when she heard his stomach growl, she realized she was hungry, too.

Stepping off his shoes, she covered her mouth with a hand. "I should serve our supper. I should have realized what time it is."

He kissed her forehead. "I would rather live off of love than your good cooking."

She chuckled, not wanting to move. She touched the

edge of his hair. Looking into his dark eyes, she felt like she could get lost in his gaze. He parted his lips and leaned towards her. She felt lightheaded, and it had nothing to do with hunger. He was going to kiss her. She was waiting for it but a bit uncertain. Then his stomach growled again, and he blinked and pulled back.

Feeling cold, she moved out of his arms.

Before she could walk away, he took her hand. "Come here, my love."

She followed him, and he told her to sit at the small table. She was so surprised by his action that she did. He then went to the small kitchen and got the supper she had pretty much finished. He brought a bowl to the table and then sat down. She looked at the casserole and felt terrible.

She was the wife. She was supposed to do this. If she didn't, he wouldn't care for her and see her as lazy. She didn't want to be lazy. She might lose him and her reputation in the community. She had to keep up appearances.

"Love, look at me." Danny used a gentle tone.

She obeyed, but didn't feel like it.

Danny wished she'd tell him to stop being bossy but, of course, she obeyed. "Honey, this is a small thing for me to do, and I wanted to do it for you tonight."

"Men don't serve." She lowered her eyes again. "I am sorry for saying that."

Taking her chin in his hand, he made her look at him.

"Love, you never apologize for being honest with me. Ever." He paused when she blinked. "Now, I know Amish men don't serve their women, but I like to. I enjoy it and doing things like this for you makes me happy. I feel like I am closer to God when I do. Jesus served a lot on this earth. Will you be all right if I keep doing it?"

"No." She gave him a small grin. "But I will try."

He smiled widely. "Good, my love."

After he prayed, they were both silent for a while, then Priscilla asked, "God served while on earth."

She hadn't read the Bible much. It was in German, and she didn't read German very well. It was confusing. She loved to read English and read some gospel in her Christian fiction books, but to actually know who Jesus was new to her.

Danny nodded. "Yes, He did. I will show you in the Bible how He served others."

She looked thoughtful. "I often wonder about the God you talk about and the God the Amish serves."

His eyes brightened. "It took me a long time to realize that God is both just and kind. The Amish see God as only just. You can't have one without the other."

She nodded, still thoughtful. For now, the subject was dropped. But Danny was seeing the tables turn for Priscilla. She was finding the true God.

Chapter Twelve

Priscilla loved Sundays. They were so relaxing, and she could read more. Tucked in a blanket on the sofa, she was reading while sipping sweet tea Danny had brought her.

Though she tried to not cook or bake on Sundays, Danny told her he enjoyed baking since he didn't get to cook as often as he liked during the week. She enjoyed the smells that came from the kitchen, and she had learned the taste that followed was even better.

As she was thinking of her husband, he walked in. He gave her that boyish grin she had come to love.

"Want to come on a buggy ride this afternoon? We can eat? I have picnic food." He paused. "We don't have to if you don't want to."

She sighed. She had told herself she'd try to make a happy marriage. And that meant doing things like this. It could be fun.

"I would like to, Danny."

He held out his hand, and she took it as he helped her up. When she stood, he let go. After using the bathroom, she walked outside to see him standing by the buggy. As he helped her in, she was glad she had never taken a buggy ride with a man before. Danny hadn't liked to do buggy rides. They had always taken car rides.

As Danny got in the buggy, she folded her hands in her lap. She tried to push back memories.

Danny looked down at her and gave her an adorable wink before snapping the reins. When he looked at her like that, forgetting the past was easy. It brought memories of before the abuse. Leaning back, she enjoyed the soft breeze and the sweet spring sounds. Oh, how she loved this area. Though, like most Amish, she hadn't been to many other places. That was fine with her. Even if she hadn't traveled much, she still wanted to learn more than she had in school. But she knew it was prideful to learn more than what the bishop wanted.

"Priscilla, can I ask you something?" Danny spoke softly.

She nodded. "Sure."

He didn't ask much of her. Well, so far.

"What would you like to do in the future? If nothing was holding you back?" he leaned a bit closer, and his eyes stayed on her. He knew the horse knew where to go.

She wanted so badly to tell him she dreamed of being a nurse. But she couldn't do that. It wouldn't be submissive, and she didn't want to offend him.

She looked down and muttered, "A homemaker," then she added, "Like most Amish women."

"But what about you?" He looked deeply at her. "You aren't like most Amish women."

She shrugged. "Well, I am."

He looked disappointed but returned his gaze to the road.

She had to get to know her husband. "What about you? What would you like to do?"

Danny's heart jumped. He could see she was trying at this marriage a little, but he still wanted her. The real her. The one he knew before. And he wished he could answer her question honestly, but he knew he couldn't. Not yet. But one day.

"I like the job I do now." He paused. "Maybe one day, I will find what I want to do."

"You mean when you leave the Amish?" She frowned.

He looked at her and nodded. "Probably. I told you before we married I would probably leave the Amish one day."

"But you won't go to heaven?"

He didn't want to have this talk right now. But he was glad she brought it up. Turning the horse, he looked ahead, where the horse took the turn. "Yes, I will. Do you know why?"

She shrugged.

He looked at her again. His horse knew where to go.

"Because I asked Jesus into my heart, and I serve Him. He has taken me into His family. Not because I stay in a religion or follow a man. Staying with the Amish does not mean I will go to heaven. Or even hell. That is up to the heavenly Father," He paused as the horse stopped. "Do you understand that?"

She looked at her hands resting in her lap. "I don't know. I have never heard anyone explain it that way. Well, except in books. But we were born Amish, and we are supposed to stay with our faith and traditions."

"But that is the thing, Priscilla. Traditions do not get you to heaven. A faith in God does that. A real relationship with Him does that." He touched her hand. "God made you to serve Him. Not a man. When we think staying in the Amish saves us, we are putting our trust in man and not God. The Lord made you in His own image. He created you beautiful and priceless. He created you for a purpose."

He paused. "The book of Ephesians says 'For by grace are ye saved through faith; and that not of yourselves: it is the gift of God: Not of works, lest any man should boast. For we are his workmanship, created in Christ Jesus unto good works, which God hath before ordained that we should walk in them.' I memorized those verses when I was young."

Her face showed she wanted to believe him but there was so much confusion. "I struggle with what you say and what the bishop says."

"Yes, it is. It took me years to understand what my English parents were saying," he frowned, looking at her from the buggy seat. "But I was also a very troubled boy."

He touched her cheek gently. "Just think of it this way, faith is a free gift, and if we had to stay in a religion to keep that gift, it wouldn't be free. But we are bought with a price."

He paused. Should he ask her this? "Aren't you tired of wondering if you are good enough for God? If He will love you enough to let you go to heaven?"

She frowned. He knew she struggled with that. She had told him so while they courted. She didn't feel invaded by the question, but felt his concern.

"Yes, I still wonder. Especially after it happened. I am trying…"

He stopped the buggy and touched her face. "But that is the thing; you don't have to try for me or Him."

She blinked. How did he know she was trying so hard

to please him? She wanted to believe she was good enough for both of them. The way he looked at her and touched her, she might believe it one day.

He pointed to the landscape.

When his hand moved away, her cheek felt his absence. She looked over the beautiful landscape, and he loved seeing the landscape through her eyes. Her face was priceless, how she loved everything she put her heart into. He wanted to kiss her so badly. The hilly landscape was uneven as their relationship at the moment.

"It's so pretty here. Can we eat by the lake?" she asked.

He would give her anything she wanted if she kept smiling like that. "Of course, my dear."

He got out of the buggy, and after helping her down, he grabbed the basket and then tied the horse to the tree. As he did so, she spread out the red and white checkered blanket. Just then a thought entered his head as he watched it blowing in the wind: wrapping Priscilla in that blanket and rolling around with her as she giggled. Oh, how he would love to hear that open free laugher come from her again. As he sat down, he told himself that in good time he would.

Priscilla seemed relaxed as they ate; she had her legs out in front of her, leaned against the tree, lifting her face to the sun. They talked of lighter topics, and Danny wondered if she was going to bring up what was on her mind. He could tell something was. Maybe it was because of how well he knew her or the way she pursed her lips once in a while.

Finally, after a long sip of sweet tea, she looked down at the blanket. She did that often when she talked about something serious.

"I have been thinking…" she paused. "You have been the one working at this marriage."

She crossed her arms. "For this marriage to be better… I want to make it real…"

Danny couldn't believe what he was hearing. Did she really want to make this marriage real? Give 100% of herself? Show who she was and not hold it back from him?

She glanced at him with fear but also determination in her eyes.

He took her chin in his hand. His eyes watered at the happiness he felt. "You don't know what you are saying does to my heart. I believe God put us together for a reason, and I believe He will bring blessings from us."

She smiled so shyly he wanted to kiss her.

"I want that too," she said.

On the ride home, Priscilla took another chance and laid her head against his shoulder. Her trust made Danny feel a million feet tall, like he'd been handed the world.

They might make it, after all. Would he get her to trust him? And if she did, how would she handle the truth? How could he keep that trust?

∽

Normally mamms were with their daughters for the first midwife visit, but Priscilla hadn't wanted her mamm there. There was too much shame. She was afraid Mamm would say the baby wasn't Danny's child. It would be so hard to bear. She touched her flat stomach and imagined being big soon, something she didn't want to be. Maybe she had wanted a baby one day but not now.

Not this way.

Right now, she couldn't do anything about it.

A knock sounded. She went to the front door and opened it to the midwife. She was a small woman with long blonde hair that hung freely down her back. Her blue eyes showed only compassion and acceptance of her.

Her mamm hadn't used this midwife, but Danny wanted an English one. Priscilla had decided to just go with what he wanted. If she didn't like the midwife, she would go with her mamm's midwife.

The woman held out her hand. "Hi Priscilla, I'm Christina Jones. You can call me Christy though."

Priscilla tried to smile and took her hand. She was suddenly nervous, and she didn't want to do this. She didn't want this child in the first place. She pulled her hand back and then crossed her arms.

Her manners took over. This was her house, and she knew what to do. She motioned for her to come in. "Do you want to sit?"

Christy occupied the living room chair.

Priscilla knew it would be rude to keep standing, so she sat on the sofa. She didn't know what to say.

Thankfully Christy took the lead. "During the first appointment I like to get to know each other. Do you have any questions for me?"

Priscilla lowered her eyes and shook her head.

"Well, I have been a midwife for twenty years. I have served this community for most of that time. I love getting to know each person here. I have been married to my wonderful husband for fifteen years and have three children," she continued to talk about herself and her work.

Priscilla kept looking at her hands. This wasn't going well. She couldn't relax. She knew this lady would judge her for being pregnant so soon after marrying Danny. She would know the dates. But maybe being English was different. She just didn't want to be judged.

Christy stopped talking and then said, "Priscilla, can you look at me?"

Priscilla's gaze shot up.

Christy pulled the chair closer and patted her knee. "You don't need to be scared of me. I won't judge you for anything. I am here to be your friend."

Priscilla nodded, not really believing her.

But it would be nice if it were true.

"Trust will take time." She patted her knee again. "But what won't take time is for that baby to grow. You need to start taking care of yourself and your baby. No matter when or how you got this baby, it is coming out."

Priscilla blinked. How did the midwife know she hadn't been taking care of herself? Did she look bad or ill? Or was it just a guess?

Her eyes filled. "I didn't want this baby, and I am so ashamed to say that. Can my baby hear me?"

Christy leaned closer. "Oh honey, you did nothing wrong. But because of what happened, God gave you a gift: a beautiful, precious baby. I can't say this will be an easy pregnancy, but you will get through it. You are not the first woman who has done this, especially in this community."

Priscilla felt sick. She held her stomach. "Really?"

She nodded. "I can't say who, but I know you are not alone in this."

Priscilla paled.

"I guess I will have to have this child at one point," she sighed. "It's going to be a long nine months."

Christy nodded. "Yes. It may be. But you also have a good husband to help you through."

Priscilla wanted to roll her eyes. Why did everyone love him so much? Even if she didn't feel good enough for him, she could still see his flaws. The other day he baked with her. What man did that? It was strange. But everyone loved him. Annemay would run away with him if she could. Given their personalities, they were probably a better fit.

Priscilla wasn't wild at all. Not anymore.

So she just nodded in response to Christy's words.

"Now, do you want to get started with me checking you?"

Priscilla stood and backed away. "You mean down there?"

Christy shook her head. "No, honey. I just mean your stomach. I will never touch you without you agreeing to it. All right? That is a promise. I will ask you first, all right?"

Priscilla held her stomach as she sighed. She sat back down.

"I am sorry about that," she sighed again.

"No. You are fine. Just let me know what you are totally comfortable with. All right?"

Priscilla didn't know if she could be that open, but she nodded anyway. "How did you know Danny's not the datt?"

"Rumors fly, and I heard of your situation."

Priscilla blushed. The Amish were like the world. They both liked to gossip a bit too much. And she was at the brunt of that gossip. She hated people knowing her shame. Her guilt. But that was how her Amish community saw her: she was bad and got pregnant without being married.

Christy's eyes were warm and comforting. The way she sat there, it seemed like a warmth to Priscilla. "It's why I wanted to be your midwife. I will show you how wonderful being a mother can be and give you some love along the way."

Priscilla bit her lip. "My parents love me."

Even as she said it, she didn't believe it. Letting their daughter get raped in their house? Was that love? She didn't really know.

Because if her parents really loved her and let that happen, she didn't want to know real love.

~

At the end of the appointment, Danny came inside. He smiled and greeted Christy.

"It's so good to see you again." He shook her hand and then sat next to Priscilla.

He looked at his wife and noticed that while she looked more relaxed than he expected, she was still stiff next to him and her face was whiter than normal. He wanted to reach out and hug her, but he didn't.

"Is there anything you can tell me that I can help with?" he asked Christy.

Priscilla's cheeks seemed to pale. She was embarrassed, probably, but he planned to help with this pregnancy and this child.

His child.

James would have no rights or say with the baby. He would make sure of that. Even if the law and blood was not on his side.

Christy smiled softly. "You can help Priscilla rest when she needs it and make her eat good food. Fresh vegetables and meat. Things like that. We already did what needed to be done."

Danny nodded.

"I can help with that." He made mental notes of what he could pick up. What should he add to the list? "I will go shopping soon."

Christy stood. "That is good, but I should go now."

They walked her to the door and said goodbye.

Priscilla just stood in the kitchen after she left. Frozen.

"Can you tell me what you are thinking?" he asked gently, closing the front door.

She met his worried gaze, her mouth dropped open a bit.

"You wouldn't like it." She leaned against the counter. "You want this baby more than me. And that is terrible for me to admit as a mother. I will be a terrible mother."

Danny shook his head. "That is not true. I may love this baby more right now, but you will learn to love the baby too. None of this is your fault. The feelings you feel ain't wrong. You will learn to love, but you have to learn the right way to love as well."

"What do you mean?"

"You have been shown conditional love growing up, but God loves you unconditionally. He doesn't have limits, and people can love that way as well. I love this baby unconditionally. It means he can do anything, and I will always love him no matter what." He stepped closer. "I also unconditionally love you, my dear."

Her lips parted, and she met his gaze. Those beautiful blue eyes looked at him with such wonder. It melted his heart.

"I really mean it, my love." He leaned closer and his gaze became intense.

Priscilla still couldn't believe he really loved her. Loving the baby was one thing, but her? She wasn't anything and, honestly, she still didn't want to be married.

But now as she looked at his deep brown eyes, her heart softened, and she felt her walls beginning to fall. She was afraid to let them down. But she couldn't help it. He was weakening them.

For now, she held onto them because the wall around her heart was all she knew now that the abuse had changed her. She couldn't experience that pain again.

Chapter Thirteen

Priscilla walked into the bishop's house on Sunday where service was being held. It was strange coming here after hearing some of the things Danny had told her about the bishop's family, especially the bishop himself. But, of course, like most Amish, she feared the bishop.

What he said was law.

She sat down next to her mamm. She couldn't sit with her sister anymore, since she was married now. She missed those days. During the service, she noted where Danny sat in the married men's pew, watching her. He was looking at her so adoringly.

She smiled shyly at him a few times. He still wasn't growing a beard. He shaved almost every day. And she knew the bishops or deacons would chastise him about it again and tell him he had to be a better Amish man now that he had a family. They didn't realize that he didn't care to be Amish. He looked so cute the way he was.

He said often he wanted to serve the Lord. But what did that mean?

The Amish did serve the Lord. They dressed the way

the Lord wanted them to, and they followed all the rules, even if they didn't understand why. She was sure she was doing the right thing in God's eyes. As the service ended, she had a hard time singing like she used to do. Singing was her love and joy, but since courting James, the music seemed to have been taken out of her. She missed it greatly.

When service was finally over, she started helping the ladies get the supper ready. Staying busy was better than talking with women who wanted to know how her marriage was going.

Not what she wanted to share. She still had so many fears.

She was getting the drinks ready when she felt a hand run all the way down her back. She knew it wasn't Danny. He would never touch her in public like that without asking. She jumped, pivoting to see James's back turned to her. She knew he had done it.

What was he doing here? He had been going to the other church district since she married.

The room was empty as she backed up until she hit the wall, trying to catch her breath. She knew it was him. She had forgotten how he used to do that when they courted, and how he did it often when he came to her room. Bile rose in her throat. She was going to be sick. How had she forgotten that? She was so stupid. She had to get out of here. She pushed into the dinning room where there were too many people and not enough air.

As she stepped outside, she nearly ran into Danny. Not knowing what overcame her, she wrapped her arms around him.

He reacted by holding her tight as he led her away from the door. But he didn't try to hide her from prying eyes. It didn't matter at this point. She knew they were the talk of the gossipers.

"What is wrong, love?"

She trembled and tried to calm her heart. Oh, that touch had scared her so bad. It was like she was back in that room. Scared, and she couldn't get away.

As Danny held her, she tried to calm down and then finally sighed. "I will tell you later. Let's go eat."

She looked around where they were standing outside by the back of the building and knew they were drawing attention with her meltdown. If she told him here, with James still around, it might end badly, and she didn't want him to cause a scene. It wouldn't be good for anyone.

He looked over at her face. "All right, but are you okay now?"

She nodded.

"I am," she sighed and stepped away from his arms. "Let's finish supper."

She walked back into the house. The men sat down to eat. That was tradition.

She saw Danny sit down next to some guys his age, but he hardly ate. She knew it was coming back home. He had been on edge all afternoon, and now this thing with James. It didn't help. She was mad at herself for letting it happen. She stood against the wall and watched for James. But she didn't see him anywhere. Maybe he had left with his new girlfriend. She had heard he had another one, but she thought the girl was from the other community.

Oh, that poor girl. Tears came to her eyes.

When it was the women's time to eat, she sat next to Annamay, who talked and giggled about her new boyfriend. She didn't seem to notice Priscilla was upset.

She didn't really care. That was just Annamay, and Priscilla was glad she treated her like normal.

Not like Danny, who treated her like a scared girl.

Maybe that was why she loved Annamay's friendship so much. She didn't act differently with her. After a few bites of food, she got up and cleared the table for the kids to eat next.

That is when Danny came next to her and leaned close. "Let's go, honey."

She looked into his blue eyes and saw a haunted look. He needed to leave. She told Annamay goodbye and then he helped her into the buggy.

His hands were tight on the reins all the way home, but he was gentle with the horse and didn't take his anger out on the animal. She knew he wouldn't. He never took anger out on others. He only took his anger out on himself, at times.

When they reached home, he helped her out and then hugged her. At first she froze at his touch, but then relaxed. His chin rested on the top of her head. He smelled of cologne and a bit of horse. Something she was familiar with, and it comforted her. He was so big on hugs. She knew the habit came from his English family. Almost every time she said goodbye to Pam or Ashley, they would give her a hug. She still wasn't totally comfortable with it, but she was definitely getting used to Danny's touch. It was gentle and always giving.

He kissed her head and then told her to go relax while he put the horse away.

She went to the porch and decided to sit outside and wait for him. It took him a while, or she was tired, because the next thing she knew, she was waking up to find him watching her. She blinked, feeling so tired.

"You are so beautiful. I love watching you sleep."

Her heart skipped a beat, and her face heated. Amish men didn't tell their wives that, or if they did, she had never heard it before. Those wives were missing out. She had the best husband, and she could finally admit that to herself. She sat up, suddenly famished. She hardly ate lunch and now her stomach growled loudly.

But she knew she needed to tell Danny what had happened. He still laid on the sofa like he had to plan to move. His face showed just the comfort and love he had for her. Though she knew he was still wondering. She sighed, feeling helpless and hopeless that she had let James do that to her.

"I forgot something from when James and I courted …" she stopped and didn't look at him as she spoke, but she knew he was listening closely. "He used to rub my back sometimes, in passing at church, and in the…"

She didn't say bedroom, but Danny got the idea.

And he had touched her back today.

He stood up, walked to the edge of the porch, and then came back.

Her eyes flew to his. Was he leaving her? For some reason, she didn't want him to. She had always been the one to leave, but now, for some reason, she didn't want him to do the same thing. She didn't want him to get tired of her. The swing felt suddenly hard and unforgiving against her stiffened shoulders.

Surprisingly, he knelt in front of her. "I am so sorry he did that. He won't again. I will not leave you alone at church or in public. He could be there."

She frowned. She didn't want to be followed by Danny. That felt suffocating, but with the worry on his face, she knew she couldn't argue with him. He was her husband, so he knew best.

Her shoulders hung. "I am sorry for panicking today. I am sure they will talk of it."

He shrugged.

"What's new?" he grinded his teeth. "I can't wait till we leave."

Her fingers curled into her skirts as she waited to see what he would say. She had thought she was convincing him to stay. She had been the perfect Amish wife for him so it hadn't worked. But this time, as he said it, she didn't feel the panic she did before. God would take care of them.

Where had that thought come from? God hadn't taken care of her so far. Why would He now? Maybe because she was being a better Amish? She wasn't sinning anymore. Her hands went to her growing belly. Maybe being a good mother was what God wanted? She would try that as well as being a good wife. Then God would be happy and take care of her.

She wanted to sigh again. Being a good Christian was hard sometimes. There were times she wanted to be like Annamay and just throw all the Amish rules away.

It might be easier than continuing to keep pushing through.

Chapter Fourteen

Priscilla enjoyed cleaning, even though the dawdy house was so small. She really missed cleaning and baking with her family. Maybe she would go soon and help out.

She was picking up Danny's socks on the floor by the couch when she noticed something under it. She pulled the object out. A phone?

Since her community allowed cell phones, she had seen them, and even knew how to use one, though she hadn't had the chance to often. She clicked it on and found a picture of herself on the screen. She was petting their driving horse. He must have wanted the horse in it. She hadn't known he had gotten the picture. It was tender and made her look beautiful.

Something she wasn't.

She opened the screen and saw another picture. This time, it was her profile. Still not fully on her, and she actually wasn't bothered by it. Had someone else had pictures of her, she wouldn't like it. But with Danny, she felt comfortable.

He loved her, he provided for her, and he had only shown her kindness. He made her feel safe. And even if she couldn't bring herself to love him back, he could take as many pictures of her as he wanted.

Well, she couldn't sit here all day and look through his phone. But it was private. She wasn't sure if she would bring it up to him. He had definitely hidden it, which bothered her.

Danny had said to be honest with him if they wanted this marriage to work, and she did. Going into the kitchen, she set the phone on the counter. She wanted to talk to him about it. She had a right to know why he kept it a secret. She had to be stronger and talk this out.

That meant picking hard topics.

As she cleaned and made supper, she kept looking at the phone, thinking of what they would talk about. What if he watched bad things on it? Was he looking at English women dressed badly? Was he talking to English women? Did he have a secret girlfriend? She had heard of Amish men doing that.

Though not often, because it was sinful.

She couldn't live with Danny acting that way.

Maybe it would be her fault if he fell into sin. Being pregnant and so newly married, she hadn't been meeting his needs. He might be tempted to look at other women. She wasn't totally sure what that meant, but it wasn't good. Though men looked at women. Some even in the community did, she knew.

But Danny had always been good and honest, so maybe he hadn't been looking at bad things.

By the time Danny was due home, she had given herself a headache with all the worrying. She decided to quickly put it back and snatched it off the counter, but then Danny walked.

"Hello, darling."

She stood there with the phone in her hand as she stared at Danny. He looked at her curiously.

"I am so sorry. I was just cleaning and found it. I had no right to look at it. I am sorry."

Her mouth went dry. She went into the living room and stood there, not sure what to do.

Danny shook his head regrettably. He closed his eyes for a second seemingly to try to know what to say.

"Honey, I should have told you about it. I know other Amish have it, but I was worried about how you would feel." He sat on the couch.

"Come here." He patted the seat next to him.

She sat stiffly and handed him the phone as if she had been burned.

"Honey, can you look at me?" he asked gently.

Looking at him, she was sure she had shamed him. She had done wrong, and he was going to tell her so.

"I am the one that is sorry. I should have told you about it sooner." He took her hand. His hand felt strong in hers. His hair fell right above his eyes in an adorable way. He gave her a sad puppy dog look. Her stomach flipped, her heart feeling a bit cold. "Will you forgive me?"

"Of course."

"Want me to show you how to use it?"

She shrugged, trying to hide what she really felt. She felt disconnected from him. What else was he hiding? Was it better not to feel than to be hurt? "If you want to."

He opened it fast, and that surprised her.

"All right," he grinned. "I have nothing to hide from

you, so you can use it anytime you want. You can even message Ashley on it."

"Really?" She smiled. A strange relief took hold of her, as well as a budding excitement. Maybe she was wrong and he wasn't doing anything bad. "I would like that, if Ashley wants too."

"She will. She adores you."

She chuckled. "I am not sure about that."

Danny then showed her how to use his phone and his apps.

When she smelled supper, she got up. "We better eat."

He smiled brightly.

"I reckon I can eat if it's your cookin'." He winked at her.

She nearly jumped. Her stomach did a flip. She held her belly. It must be the baby, though her cheeks felt pink.

Putting a bowl on the table of stir fry, she sat and took his hands while he prayed. As they ate, they kept the conversation light.

Then Danny said, "I know what some men do with phones, and I want you to know I won't hide anything from you. You can look at anything and go on any app."

"*Danke*, Danny boy." The feelings were at battle inside of her. She wanted to trust him and a part of her was afraid to get hurt. Now she had this to overcome. What else was he hiding from her? But she might like to talk with Ashley.

Danny leaned over the table. He looked at her so deeply, yet so gently. "You want to know something, Pris?"

She nodded. When he looked at her like that, she couldn't say no.

"I love you. Everything about you, I love."

She stared at him. Did he really mean it? Was he

showing her real love? Why would he hide the cell phone? Will his love be as destructive as James's, but in a different way?

∽

The air was stinky and hot. But that was normal for Kentucky, especially along the river. As Danny drove to the Yoder place on Sunday, he wished Priscilla would tell him what she was thinking. But she hid from him. Hid her true self. And that hurt. Though maybe he deserved it. He was also hiding things from her. How would this end up if they both hid things? He felt guilty over the other things he was hiding. They made the cell phone look so small. A car and being a cop would be much worse.

Maybe he was hoping all his cooking with her would help. Or that how he served her in so many ways would help. But it didn't.

The last thing he wanted to do was go to the Yoders' house. But it was a Sunday where they didn't have church so the Yoders invited them over. Priscilla wanted to go and since Paul Yoder was the only one who had defended her, he decided to go. Out of all the men in the community, Paul seemed the most decent. He had pushed for Danny and Priscilla to be married.

He drove the buggy up the driveway and came to a stop. He helped her get out since it was hard to do since she was getting bigger. Miriam and Paul came out to greet them. Miriam even pulled Priscilla into a tight hug.

Paul patted his shoulder. "How are you doing, son?"

"Fine. How are you?" Danny kept it to small talk.

The supper went well, and Danny hid his riotous emotions. The children and older girls kept the conversion going despite Danny's tight replies. He had never fit in with the Amish. He had rebelled all the time, and now he didn't want to be Amish anymore.

He wouldn't be here much longer anyway. He was still livid about what James had done. How could the bishop and deacons let abuse like this go on?

He was going to be a cop who wanted to turn in James.

"Why don't we go outside, Danny?" Paul offered. Though it was asked like a question, Paul's tone said it wasn't one.

"Sure," Danny nodded to Priscilla, and she just gave him a small smile. She went to help Miriam with the dishes.

Danny walked with Paul to the barn. Hayfields surrounded them and swayed lightly in the wind. The barn was typically Amish with a skylight to let in light. He liked how these barns were built, and when Priscilla and he finally had their own place, he wanted this kind of barn.

"So, what issue do you have with me?" Paul asked. Not in an unkind way, but direct. "Or is it just the Amish you don't like?"

"I don't have any issues with you," Danny said.

Paul laughed harshly. "Oh, really. You hide it so well."

Danny looked down at his boots.

"Look at me like a man and tell me you don't judge me just because I am Amish."

Danny glared at him. But then it hit him. Was he judging for that reason? He wanted to go to the law. But he knew nothing would come from it.

His dislike was more than just that, and he knew that.

It was his deep past.

Paul seemed to sense he was getting through to Danny,

so he changed the subject. "I know how you got married. Do you want to get your wife to love you and to have a real marriage?"

Danny felt like he was getting hit. It was a bit embarrassing to have the man acknowledge their marriage issues. Maybe advice would help. He would take a chance at trusting him, though, because of how the Yoders had handled their wedding and supported Priscilla.

"After we leave, it will get better."

"Oh, really?" Paul said. "Let me tell you, it won't. Especially if you don't enter her world."

Danny crossed his arms. "What do you mean?"

Paul ran a hand over his thin beard. "You want to know your wife. Enter her world by enjoying her friends and her family. Did you know that my wife has been there for Priscilla since we both knew she was being abused. Miriam visits her almost every week. We offered to move her in with us when the abuse started, but Miriam knew that Amish girls won't do that. And Priscilla wanted to stay with you after getting married. Miriam has helped her get the house ready. You need to learn more about your wife, and that means despite your wanting to leave, you need to love where she came from. Because once you leave the Amish, you know she will never contact her family or friends again. This is your chance to create a relationship with her before her heart hardens."

Danny thought about it and then asked, "How do you know so much?"

Paul sat on a barrel of grain. "I married Miriam after she had four children with a very abusive man. He died, and she married me because he left her with nothing. She had many walls around her heart. We both became believers, and even though that didn't fix everything, it helped a great deal."

"If you are believers, why do you stay Amish?" He sure wouldn't do that.

"We are what they call silent Christians, and we have led many people to the Lord. We may leave one day, but for now we are called to live here. I also help people leave the Amish if they want. I help many of the youth who run away from the Amish. Also, I help victims in the communities by getting them safe. I feel I can do more in the community than outside of it."

Danny's jaw nearly dropped open. If the bishop found out what Paul was doing, he would be shunned, and maybe even kicked out of their community.

He leaned against the stall door. Maybe he and Paul had more in common than he thought. But he had judged the man wrongly. He should be treated like a man and not just Amish.

"I had no idea you did all that, but I still don't think I can stay here. There are too many bad memories."

"You don't have to stay. And I know you won't. But loving your bride means acting in her world and, right now, that world is Amish." It was cooler in the barn especially since it was very warm outside. "By doing this, you will show you love and accept all of her. As you love her, you will show her your world. But take her out of her world before she is ready, and those walls will never come down."

Danny frowned. Paul was right. He was asking too much of his bride. She loved the Amish, unlike him. So, of course, she wasn't ready to leave yet. He had to do this the right way. He held out his hand to Paul, and the deacon shook it.

"I was wrong to judge you for being Amish. I just want to go to the cops. To the law, and I know I can't."

Paul shook his head sadly.

"Maybe that will change one day. It pains me more than you. Personally, I know how it works. If we went, nothing would come of it." He met Danny's eyes. "I wanted to go to the law for Priscilla too, but with her being an adult, I knew it would just hurt her more than help." His brow lowered. "I went after a man in another community and now he is serving ten to twenty years."

Danny's mouth dropped open. "Really? How were you not shunned or kicked out?"

Paul shrugged. "I left after we got so much hate for it. But we weren't totally shunned. I also helped a victim try to keep her kids from a rapist. He tried for custody."

"After raping her?" Danny was shocked.

Paul nodded. "Yup, and in the end, he got custody."

Danny crossed his arms, and his eyes darkened. "That will never happen to my baby."

"I hope so," Paul said.

It won't happen, Danny thought.

"So, to review, now you know the Amish are not just black and white," Paul's eyes lightened in humor. "There is a bit of gray in all of us, and we all have a bit of a rebel in us."

Danny smiled. Paul was right. He should have seen that before now.

Or maybe he hadn't been ready to see it before. Now if he only didn't have to leave. For some reason he didn't want to leave. Maybe he didn't want to take his bride from all of this.

Chapter Fifteen

Priscilla helped Miriam in the kitchen. She couldn't believe how Danny had acted tonight. He wasn't trying very hard to be polite. In fact, he had been almost rude. He didn't have to come if he didn't want to. It ticked her off. These were her people. This family was one of her closest ones. They loved her, no matter what she went through.

And her husband had treated them like dirt. Badly, giving them one word answers and not participating in conversation and not smiling. He looked grumpy. Maybe that is why Paul took a walk with him. Maybe he showed him how he was acting. For the first time she felt angry.

Miriam sent her older girls out after most of the dishes were done. They had kept the meal light and used paper plates. Miriam sat down at the table with a cup of tea.

Priscilla joined, though she hated tea. "You know Danny has started to pick up Dunkin Donuts coffee, and I love it. He makes it at home too."

Miriam smiled. "You seem fond of your husband."

Priscilla dipped her head. "When he is more pleasant

than today. I love the community, but I know he wants to leave."

"How will you handle that?" Miriam asked.

Priscilla blinked, unsure on how she felt about it. She would go to hell for leaving. "I have hardly any connection with my family right now. But then again, I think I can convince him to stay."

Miriam put a hand on Priscilla's arm. "That is not wise to do, child. You both need to want to do the same thing. Danny needs to respect you and what you want, but you also need to respect him and what he wants. Are you willing to do that?"

Priscilla bit her lip. "It's so hard to trust. I have come to care for him, and I know he won't hurt me. But to give him it all…"

"Do you want this marriage to last?"

Priscilla nodded. "I do."

"Then you have to commit to this marriage, and God will help you do it. Praying together helped me and Paul grow together."

Priscilla was always confused by the way Miriam talked about God. Not many Amish had that relationship with Him.

Well, Danny did.

"I have never prayed in front of someone. The bishop wouldn't like it," she said.

Miriam sighed. She knew what Priscilla was talking about. The bishop would make his people pray in front of him, and then tell them what they did wrong. Other times they had to pray out loud in front of the church and confess their sin. Miriam had been made to confess her sin when she became pregnant with her abuser's child and she had asked the church to forgive her.

She had never felt more dirty.

That is, until she had to marry that abuser and then have three more children with him. She was glad Priscilla hadn't been made to do that. She knew her husband wouldn't have allowed her to, either. Priscilla wasn't strong enough yet to voice what she wanted.

Miriam cupped her face and eyed the young bride in front of her with compassion. Priscilla's situation brought up old memories.

There had been a time when she wanted to forget her wounds, but as she sat across from Priscilla, she knew she had to bare her own past with her. The Bible commanded believers to bear one another's burdens.

"Growing together in marriage will take time, but as you grow in Christ you will be able to do it. He wants you to be free in Him, my dear. And He wants you to be free in this marriage He has blessed you with."

Priscilla just blinked at her and took a sip of tea. What did Miriam know about her marriage life? "I don't deserve him."

"Oh, child, you deserve the world." She patted her hand. "There is nothing you did wrong. Why do you feel like you don't deserve him?"

Priscilla couldn't answer that. It was too much to unpack.

"I don't know. There are so many reasons. I want to try to trust him but it's..." she didn't finish.

"It means opening those walls around your heart and trusting him."

Priscilla gasped. "That sounds painful."

"Oh, but Priscilla, it is so worth it. To be free with him. You will see you can be yourself with him and never have to hide. It's unconditional love he has for you."

"You make it sound so wonderful, but I have never seen a marriage like that before."

"You mean among the Amish?"

Priscilla shrugged. "Well, since that's all my life, sure I've never seen it."

"Well, I have seen it. You just don't know how to look for it. Have you seen Lydia and Samual? Or Jonathan and Sarah? Or any of my married children?" she smiled as she took a sip of her tea. "They all have fulfilling marriages, and you can tell they have love for each other. These are some of the happiest women in the community."

Priscilla thought about it. What Miriam said was true. Those couples were sweet together, and the women were filled with joy. Could that happen to her? Could she be that happy one day? She didn't know if it was possible with how much she had been through. But it didn't hurt to dream.

"It seems I gave the young bride a lot to think about," Miriam commented.

Priscilla cocked her head, smiled. "I never thought myself a bride. Not a pure one, anyway. But Danny calls me his bride. He loves to give me these little nicknames."

She chuckled.

"And what do you want to call him?" Miriam's eyes laughed with humor.

Priscilla nearly coughed. "Oh, I can't. It wouldn't be proper."

Miriam patted her shoulder. "I hear our men come in. Let's see how they are."

Priscilla was glad to find Danny laughing with Paul. He seemed in better spirits. Maybe it was Miriam he didn't like? As they sat down in the living room, Danny kept his arm around her like he normally did. And she was glad for it. She always enjoyed his touch. She even shared a special look with Miriam.

Knowing what her friend might be thinking made her blush. This had turned out to be an interesting day. She would ponder what Miriam said. Could she leave if Danny wanted? Eyes opening, she enjoyed this talk much better than the church services.

∼

Standing in the kitchen, Priscilla thought about how different she had been feeling since Sunday. She grinned, surprised by the lightness in her heart, and scooped her special strawberry pie off the counter. They were going to a barn building today. She'd been thinking a lot about what her mamm had told her, plus Pam and Miriam's advice, and she really did want a happy marriage. Her baby deserved two parents who loved each other.

Danny walked into the kitchen, and throwing him a saucy look, she said, "Take this pie out to the buggy, Danny boy."

He took the pie, winking at her. He loved when she called him that. Ever since Sunday, she'd been more relaxed. She showed her true self to him, and he loved it.

He wanted to do the same with her, but every time he thought about confessing that he was a policeman who drove a jeep, his gut twisted and his heart hurt. He knew he wasn't being honest with her, and the guilt of it kept him awake some nights.

He pushed those thoughts away.

This day was for them, and he would make it the best for her.

"I love when you call me Danny boy," he told her softly, almost afraid to share that with her.

She stopped saying it before. But that was his fault. With his free hand he touched her cheek.

She smiled and blushed. "Well, for you, I will do that."

He carried the pie out as she readied the other food. She was excited to bring some of the dishes she had made with Danny's help. She called them healthy food. She carried the special bread she had baked out. Danny took it from her and helped her into the buggy. She wore a light pink dress. It looked so good as he helped her into his buggy. It felt so special. He couldn't believe he had gotten her back, and he had resolved more than ever to get her to fall in love with him again. She was worth it.

"I am so excited for the barn building, and to see Annamay," she said. "I see her at church, but it's more fun at events like this."

He smiled down at her. He loved seeing her joy. "I am looking forward to going, and seeing the Yoders, too."

Since his talk with Paul, he had felt more determined to fit in Priscilla's world.

She grinned. "I am glad."

Danny wasn't sure what he had expected, but he was now seeing the woman he used to know. Was she becoming who she used to be? He didn't know; he only knew he loved the change. When they reached the barn-building party, he parked the buggy and then helped her down. He took the food over to the tables while she went to find Annamay. He saw her chatting and talking with her. Joy shone on her face.

He got busy helping with the building. He wasn't that good at carpentry, but he had done this before, so he caught on pretty fast.

Then he found himself working next to the bishop.

"I didn't expect to see you here," his adoptive father muttered.

"I wanted to help," Danny replied calmly. He wouldn't let the bishop get to him.

"Well, that's a first," his adopted Datt snorted with a scowl. "How is that bride of yours? Has she said anything about the real baby's father?"

He asked low so that no one could hear.

Danny straightened, fury blooming in his chest, and stepped closer to his datt, vision red, but Paul stepped between them.

His friend looked hard at the bishop. "That was out of line."

The bishop looked around and then just walked away.

Danny breathed hard. He stepped away from the barn, walking out to pasture. Despite how beautiful the view was, he couldn't seem to see it. Paul followed him.

"This is why I plan to leave the Amish," said Danny, his heart a cold rock in his chest.

Paul grimaced. "I understand. Just know not all the Amish are like that. Look around. Do they look like puppets, all following one man? Or people who care?"

Taking a deep breath, Danny did look around. And for the first time, he saw the men building the barn. He saw the community the way Priscilla did. He saw the closeness, the loyalty to each other, and how they all worked together.

"I know what you are saying. Sometimes I wish I could be a part of both worlds."

"Don't we all. But rarely do we get that," Paul said. "Just don't forget about us when you leave."

"How could I? There will always be an Amish boy in me somewhere."

Paul patted his shoulder. "That is true. Don't forget where you came from."

A shadow crossed Danny's face. "If only I could."

He caught sight of Priscilla, still talking with Annamay and some other friends who had joined them. She looked happy with them. He saw that this was her world.

He had a lot of things to feel guilty about, but taking her from this world might be the worst thing of them all. How would she do when she found out everything? His stomach churned as he thought of it.

Danny had shown Priscilla how to message Ashley when they got home last night after the barn raising. She wasn't sure if she should message Ashley. Feeling tired, she sat down on the rocker and picked up his phone. A message from Ashley lit up the screen. She tapped the notification, and the message popped up.

Hey, Priscilla, Danny told me you are using his phone. I thought I would message and see how you are doing. Writing in the mail is fine, but I like this way a bit better if you are all right with it. Hope this finds you well. Love, Ashley.

Priscilla wasn't sure what she would say, but she didn't want to give up this chance to get to know Ashley. Was Danny reading her messages, though? She wouldn't feel comfortable with that, but he had a right to. He was her husband, after all. It was taking time to trust him about that. Sighing, she decided to reply.

Hey, Ashley, I am doing great. I would love to talk with you over message, though I am not that good with it yet. I get lonely sometimes here by myself. And being with my family isn't always easy sometimes because of the baby and bad memories. I hope this finds you doing good. How is the book going?

Priscilla hit send after making sure everything was spelled right. Less than five minutes later, she got a reply.

It would be great to chat here! So glad you're doing well. I get lonely too, and you don't need more stress from anyone. How is my big brother doing? I haven't talked to the hunk in a while.

Priscilla chuckled and replied, though it took longer for her to type. *He is doing great. He has been working a lot lately.*

She wasn't sure what she was supposed to say about Danny. He would read it. She wanted to share how he made her feel. But maybe Ashley already understood what she was feeling.

Great. Wanna read a scene for me? I have been working on it since last night.

I would love to.

A few minutes later, the scene came in, and she read over it. *I love it. It is very well written. Just remember to keep the main character consistent.*

Good idea. I have a hard time doing that with this character. She does what she wants. Lol

Priscilla laughed. *Tell her to obey you. You are the Author, remember?*

Oops, must have forgotten that. I will remind her, but you know it might not work.

Priscilla again laughed, and they continued to talk like this. By the time Danny got home, she had supper ready, but she was still texting with Ashley.

Danny walked in. "And what is this?"

Priscilla looked up at him with guilt on her face. "I am sorry. I was just talking with Ashley."

Danny shook his head.

"No, it's fine. I was just joking," he took her hand in his. "I will get another cell phone, so just keep this one. Everything will be yours and private."

She nodded. "I would like that. I had such a good time talking to your sister. She is a sweetheart."

"I think so too," he led her to the table. "Let me get your supper on the table."

Priscilla sat but still felt uncomfortable when he served her, or even helped in the kitchen. She looked up at him as he set a plate on the table, and the look in his eyes was so loving that it touched her heart in a way she didn't know a man could ever do. She didn't want to look away as he left to get another dish for the table.

When he sat down, she felt the magic between them. Despite herself, despite the walls in her heart, she was getting worried that she might be falling in love with her husband.

And that was the worst thing possible, because then he could hurt her more than anyone else ever had.

~

Danny was trying to live in his wife's world more, like Paul had suggested.

That meant going to her family's house for supper. He didn't want to go, but he forced himself to go for her. She loved being Amish, and he hated it. He had never told her why.

He wasn't ready for that.

As he tacked up his gelding, he pushed his memories away. Memories are worse than just thoughts about not telling her. After he finished, he pulled up in front of the dawdy house as Priscilla walked out. He hadn't thought he would have to wait long. She was always on time.

Unlike him sometimes.

They worked well together.

He helped her into the buggy, a little surprised when her belly brushed against his arm. Her pregnancy was becoming more noticeable.

"How are you feeling today?"

She smiled down at him. "Honey, I am fine. You worry too much."

"I love you, and so I have the right to worry, my love." He adored saying he loved her.

She never said it back but he was sure she did love him. She showed it in the different things she did for him. Though he longed to hear the words, he was all right with not hearing them for now.

"Well, try not to worry."

He gently slapped the reins on the gelding. "Are you nervous about seeing your parents today?"

She shook her head. "I see them at church."

"But that is not in their home. Where you…" he didn't say it but they both knew his meaning, "where you lived at one time."

With all they had been through he didn't want to go again.

She shrugged. "What happened to me, happens to others. I should be able to handle it."

He rode in silence for a while and then stopped at the end of the street. He turned to look at her, concerned about drawing a wrinkle between his eyebrows. "What do you mean it happens enough?"

She pushed a few wild, stray curls back in her kapp. Not meeting his gaze.

"Let's just say, girls talk and I have heard of different men who are… uh…forceful," she said in her quiet voice.

Not just the quiet voice. The broken one. He hated that tone.

"And some are even family, so the girls have to still live there." She bit her lip, and her hands shook as she held onto her dress.

"It ain't right," he grunted, his hands tightening on the reins.

She shrugged.

"It's what happens here." She paused. "I wonder if it happens with the English."

He frowned. "Sadly, yes. The men don't always get what they deserve. But they do more times than in the Amish. The English get justice."

"Pam told me many English churches try to cover it too."

He nodded. "Yes. Many do."

She looked at him with stronger eyes than he expected, and he wondered what she was thinking? He decided to just ask her.

She looked ahead and pursed her lips. "Seems like the Amish and the English churches have more in common than we think."

He leaned over and kissed her forehead. "That is so. Hopefully we can learn from each other, the bad and the good."

And he meant it. Maybe the Amish had more to offer than he thought, like the Yoders tried to tell him. Maybe their words were getting through his thick head.

About an hour later, he changed his mind. How could a family treat their own family member like this? It wasn't right. He sat next to one of Priscilla's brothers and next to her datt. The women sat on the other side of the table. He hated sitting so far from Priscilla.

His protective side kicked in. He just didn't want to be here.

Well, after all, he was going to be a policeman. He should be protective.

"How do you like being married?" Priscilla's mamm asked.

"Fine," Priscilla answered. She smiled at her mamm and shared a special look between them. Then glanced at her Datt and she stopped smiling. "I like the dawdy house. It's sweet."

"Since you two had been enjoying marriage rights before the ceremony I can see how it would be sweet," her datt commented, and the boys snickered.

Priscilla went white and put down her fork.

"That is none of your concern, sir," Danny said through stiff lips.

Mamm cleared her throat. "Do you enjoy cooking for just one and not all of us?"

Her joke was an obvious distraction from her husband's rudeness.

Priscilla nodded. "I do. I make some great meals, and Danny is even showing me how to cook with healthier foods."

"Oh, like our plain food ain't good enough?" Datt winced.

"No, sir. I love all of Priscilla's plain food, but I enjoy cooking," he wanted to sigh at how hard this meal was. But he wouldn't. He met Priscilla's eyes. "We have fun."

Mamm seemed happy about that. Her face brightened.

"Well, normal men don't cook, unless it's for business," Datt said.

"Well, then, I am glad I am not a normal man," Danny replied.

Priscilla's mouth lifted like she was about to smile. His

heart lifted at the moment shared with her. It was so intimate and personal with her.

Datt huffed at his answer, though.

Since everyone was being rude, Danny thought he would hurry the meal up. "Do you have dessert? I am just dying for something chocolate."

When all their eyes went wide, Priscilla gave a small smile. "We are family, and Danny says some things like that. It took me a bit to get used to it. But he learns it from work."

"Well, where is your work at?" Datt asked.

"I work on a ranch."

"You don't work your datt's land, being his son?"

Danny thanked Priscilla as she dished him some pie. She'd also set a Snickers by the slice. He wanted to wink at her, but he instead let his eyes show how he felt.

"Danny, I asked you a question," Datt said firmly.

Regretful, Danny looked at him. "Pardon me. No, I won't be working the bishop's land. This year or ever."

"Well, that is not good, son." His lips went into a thin line. He put his glass on the table hard.

Danny shrugged. "Well, I ain't ever been a son good enough for the bishop. So, it's no big loss."

"Well, ain't you an arrogant bunch?"

Danny had been called worse, so he didn't reply. Better to say nothing than say too much. All he knew was how proud he was of his bride. She handled the conflict well and didn't let it upset her. When he was done with the pie and his candy bar, he was leaving. He didn't know if he would ever be back.

Maybe, if feeling generous, when his child was ten.

He finished his dessert quickly like the others. There was so much tension in the air you could cut it with a knife. Priscilla said goodbye to her mamm and siblings and walked outside. She patted Missy goodbye, who had followed them with a look of longing in her eyes. Priscilla took Danny's hand and let him help her into the buggy. As they cantered down the road, she leaned her head against his shoulder.

"Well, that went well."

He chuckled.

"You can say that again." Then he sighed. "I am so sorry about what they said."

She let out a small sigh. "I don't expect them to understand. My mamm seems happy with me, and that matters."

He kissed her head. "I am glad. You really want her approval?"

"I do. I don't know why it matters so much, but it does."

"She is your mama, that is why."

She sighed. "My datt was not always that way. He doesn't like rules to be broken, and he was mad when I was first courting you. Of course, mamm backed him."

"That is why he won't let us take Missy?"

"Yes, he doesn't approve of us. Of you," she told him. They both knew animals were for work in the Amish, and not to be pets. Her datt refusing to give them Missy was a big slap in the face.

Danny didn't feel too bothered by losing Missy, though it mattered to Priscilla. However, he didn't like that her datt hated him. He should be used to hatred. He didn't really fit in this life.

"That's why you broke up with me? Because your parents didn't approve?" he asked carefully.

"No, but they wanted me too. You didn't look or act

Amish enough. I finally broke up with you in the barn because of what we almost did," her voice was soft, feeling the shame of that day. But this was a time to be honest with him. "When James asked to court me, I remember seeing you at the singing, and I was feeling so upset we broke up, that I just said yes without thinking."

She looked out into the night as the buggy rolled down the road. "I am not blaming you at all. It was how I was feeling. We had never bed-dated because you didn't want to. He came to see my parents that night and Datt was nice and friendly to him. Like he wasn't to you. And when James left, Datt said he was a good Amish boy and I better not mess it up. He knew with my wild hair I was bad inside and wanted boys..."

She saw in the dusk how hard Danny held the reins.

She was thankful he said nothing and continued, "He didn't come to my room during our first month courting. I often wonder why. Was he trying to make me fall for him? He was nice, but he could be possessive. Then he came to my room after I said no, and he got very physical. It was different from what we did. I didn't want it. I told him to stop, and I thought he would listen. But..."

She could remember that first night like it happened yesterday. The smell of his breath, his kisses on her, the way his hands moved roughly along her body. "But he said I wanted it. I was making him do it, and he couldn't stop."

She folded her arms and leaned over the side of the buggy, about to be sick from the shame of that night.

Danny pulled the reins until the horse stopped and then wrapped Priscilla in his arms. He made it to where she was so close to him, whispering he loved her over and over.

She just trembled. She felt the buggy going again. Then sat up a bit when she noticed they were in their barn and it was raining. She could hear raindrops on the metal roof. It was kind of comforting.

She spoke again, voice raw. She hugged him back and if it was possible she moved closer where she sat in his lap. He just held her. The feeling of shame overtaking her.

"Every weekend, he did it, and then he would leave like nothing happened. One evening he visited with my parents and told them how respectful he was of me," she snorted, feeling anger coursing through her veins. "Then not an hour later he did it again."

She paused, listening to the rain drops, trying to calm down. "When I found out I was pregnant, I was shocked. I had heard of other girls having intimate relations with a man for a long time but they didn't get pregnant. It was my punishment. I kept thinking the child should have been yours, not his. I told my parents. Mamm cried and datt hit the roof."

Suddenly a downpour of rain pounded the roof, so loud they could hardly hear each other. Was God crying for her pain? It sure felt like it.

The rain didn't last long. But they stayed in the buggy, and she couldn't stop the downpour of emotion from her heart.

"Datt said I had to get married to him then," she shuddered. "The bishop was told and then you found me that day." She paused. "I am so glad you did."

He hugged her tight. "Me too, love. Thank you for sharing all that. That was so brave of you. So very brave."

"I thought you should know. I wanted you to know," she said softly.

They sat there a few more minutes, listening to the softening rain. And then it stopped.

"Want to run to the house before the rain starts again?"

She nestled closer into his chest. "Naw, let's sleep here tonight."

He laughed. "I would agree, my love. But we may be sore, come tomorrow."

"We are still young and can get wild," she giggled and kissed his cheek. She almost felt like her old self.

He kissed her forehead and laughed, then took her hand and kissed her hands and fingers. He ran kisses up and down her fingers, lightly nibbling in intoxicating ways.

Priscilla felt so alive and touched by him doing that. There was definitely a connection between them.

But then, suddenly, she remembered those feelings weren't good. She didn't want to be wild and make him lose control and hurt her.

She sat back and moved from his lap. "You're right. We should probably go in before it gets dark."

His brows furrowed, and he frowned but then helped her down. It wasn't raining hard, so he told her to go to the house while he took care of the horse.

At the house, she turned on all the lights and made sure the outside lights were on for him. She loved having lights. She hurried to the kitchen and made hot chocolate and warmed some cookies.

She didn't know why, but she had really felt a breakthrough with Danny. Such a connection and bond with him. She didn't want to break that bond.

He came inside a bit later and took off his jacket, now soaked, putting it on hook by the door. "Oh, that smells good, love."

"I know it's the middle of summer, but I thought something warm would be nice." She poured two cups.

"You read my mind, love." He kissed the top of her head. "As long as there are marshmallows."

She got them out of the cupboard next to him, and he winked at her. She grabbed a couple out and dropped them in both cups.

Danny scooped out his and ate them. "I love these things."

He sat on the counter in front of her.

"No kidding." Impulsively she fed him one. Her fingers touched his lips. He had a hard time swallowing. He touched her kapp and pulled it off. The bun was still there but her curls escaped. She felt those feelings again of loving him and wanting to have fun with him.

She took the hot mugs and set them on the tray. Scooping now cool cookies onto the tray also, she headed to the living room.

After setting the tray on the living room table, she sat down on one end of the couch, and Danny plopped down on the other end.

"I know we covered so much tonight. Some of the things you said aren't true," he said abruptly.

She looked at him, confused.

"No. That came out wrong." He rubbed a hand over his face. "I've thought about it for a bit since you said the same thing in one of your nightmares."

She looked at her hands. She didn't know if she wanted to talk about this.

"You said you had boys fall for you, and you helped them fall. That day in the barn you didn't make me fall. I wasn't leading you the right way, and you had nothing to do with us going too far. My heart was not in the right place. Can you tell me how you felt then?"

She knew he was asking a lot, but she had just told him she got raped every weekend for six months. What could she tell him that was worse? She swallowed hard.

"It's hard to talk about it now because I am so different. I don't want touching now. He took that from me. But that day in the barn..." she paused. "I wanted you. I wanted your touch. And that's why James hurt me. It was wrong of me to want you that way."

Danny worked to relax his hands, which were tightly fisted around the mug he picked up.

"It's hard for me to explain this since I am a man. And men are different than women. But women are made to enjoy marriage and being with a man. What we did physically then wasn't right, but you can and are able to feel it in marriage, if you want to. God designed married people to love each other and desire each other. Ashley doesn't think people, especially Christians, talk about it enough. She may be one to talk to, or our mom," he took a sip of the sweet taste.

Priscilla didn't think she could do that. This was such different thinking. "So, God wasn't punishing me for wanting you?"

"No," Danny had to keep his voice light and not snap like he wanted too. Snap at the people who helped her believe these lies. He sat his cup down before he threw it against the wall. "He doesn't do that. Now we do have consequences for our choices, and if we had gone farther that day, it would have been wrong. God put sex to be in marriage for a reason, and it is good."

She shuddered at the thought. Sex to her meant shame

and feeling disgusted afterwards. "I will think about it. I just wish it hadn't happened, and I don't feel this way now."

"There is nothing wrong with the way you feel. It is very normal," he said.

She might talk to Ashley. She did want to get past it and move on. And she couldn't be as open with Danny. It was just too difficult. She looked at the clock. It wasn't late, but she was tired. All the emotions she had felt today had probably exhausted her.

She leaned back against the couch and took a bite of a cookie. "I will think about it. I am just tired."

He nodded.

"I understand that. You've shared a lot tonight." He moved closer to her. "Come here."

Then he picked her up and carried her to bed.

She put a hand on his chest, touched by his act for her. He laid her gently on the bed but didn't let her go. He just held her there. She put her hands on his shoulders and held him back, feeling cherished. And this time she let herself feel.

It wasn't wrong to have these feelings for her husband.

Then he let go and kissed her forehead.

She knew she had to do something, or she would regret not going to this next step.

She grabbed Danny and pulled him back to her. She could see the outline of his handsome face in the dim light. He was a smart man.

"Are you sure?" he asked, his eyes widening.

She nodded. "I want you to keep holding me."

She knew he wouldn't take it any farther than that. Maybe one day, but not tonight.

He didn't need to be asked twice. He laid down and got his body close to hers, melding them together like their souls were meant to be.

Chapter Sixteen

On the Fourth of July, Danny had taken her on a picnic. His parents had been there the first half of the day, but then they left. The day had been wonderful with Pam and Stan. Priscilla felt accepted. She could be herself with them. Danny's family ate her chicken, potato salad, pie, and cookies gratefully. Sweet tea from McDonalds washed it all down. The best part of her day was being away from the judging eyes of her community.

After a long day, she and Danny were now alone.

Priscilla stood on top of the hill, overlooking the Ohio River. Such a beautiful view with fields, trees, and moonlight shining off the river.

Looking over the mountain top, she was in awe. She turned to Danny, who was watching her closely. "It's so beautiful. I'm in awe."

"I am too." But his gaze didn't leave her face, and his eyes were dark, like freshly melted chocolate.

She looked at him, confused.

He stepped closer until he was inches from her face. "The river is stunning."

His tone was husky, and Priscilla was smart enough to know he wasn't talking about the river. She blushed deep into her hairline. Oh, this man made her feel so alive.

Now sitting across from him on a blanket, she felt so relaxed and happy, more than she had in months.

"Do you like fireworks?" Danny asked.

She nodded. "I watched them once as a kid. They were so much fun, and pretty. I remember how loud they sound. Do you?"

"Very much. I heard them too as a kid, after staying with Pam and Stan for the summer. And I have watched them a lot since then."

"I hope your parents don't mind that we didn't bring them along to this spot."

Danny winked at her. "Oh, they don't mind."

She blushed again.

Priscilla watched the sunset while they enjoyed talking. She noticed how the light changed in Danny's eyes. He looked at her deeper as they spoke, and he moved closer. She leaned into him as he wrapped his arms around her. It was cool up here, but she felt so warm with him. She felt safe.

"I love you, babygirl," he whispered in her ear.

His breath made her tingle. He undid her prayer kapp while his eyes were on hers, as if asking permission. She knew he liked to do this with her hair. It wasn't like it was the first time he had taken off her kapp. He then took her pins out.

He ran his hand through her hair, and she realized how much she had missed this. It was comforting and didn't feel sexual.

He tugged her gently to lie down on the blanket they had brought up. "Let's watch the stars come up."

She was tense at first, but then she calmed into his hold. He wasn't making a move. He was just showing her a good time. She smiled. When the fireworks started, Priscilla jumped. She had been so relaxed in his arms, the bishop himself could have yelled at them, and she wouldn't have moved.

"The fireworks are beautiful," she told Danny.

In the middle of the fireworks, he adjusted his position. Taking her cheek in his hand, he kissed her forehead, her cheeks, her nose.

"Let's make our own fireworks." His voice was husky.

Priscilla closed her eyes, enjoying his every touch. The fireworks were loud, but she hardly heard them. His lips finally found hers, and she touched his chest, wanting to pull him closer. He was so gentle and passionate at the same time. She kissed him back when he deepened the kiss.

After a while, she pulled back, smiling. Danny's face flashed red from the shadow of the fireworks. "That was nice."

He kissed her again.

"I haven't waited this long to do it wrong." He grinned at her. He ran a hand through her hair and she could see he wanted to kiss her again, but he just pulled her close and whispered, "I love you."

She cuddled closer to him. She was glad he had waited. It was worth it.

∼

Priscilla loved sewing circles. They made her feel part of her close-knit community. She liked talking with the ladies, and even gossiping a little. Though she knew some of the gossip lately had been on her.

As she got there, she tried to ignore that fact and just have a good time with them. Annamay even joined her sometimes. But this time she had invited Ashley, and she had agreed to come. She couldn't wait to have her friend there.

Especially since Danny had kissed her.

Since that night, Priscilla had been on edge. Did she want him to kiss her more? Or not? Because that would lead to a place she was terrified to go. Her fear overwhelmed her sometimes. She had spent the last few nights distant from Danny. No more cuddling or kissing. Eventually he would want more. But she was damaged. Broken. And she was growing a baby. She had nothing more to give. But last night, things had changed, she wanted to grow closer to him. She may be starting to trust him again.

Which is why she was looking forward to the sewing circle. She needed to feel normal, somehow.

Ashley knocked on the door, and Priscilla got up to get it. The other women would go straight to Eli's house. She opened the door to see her friend dressed in a fashionable maxi skirt and dark shirt and her hair was even pulled back, though thick curls escaped her bun.

Priscilla grinned. She wasn't sure who this person was.

Ashley crossed her arms.

"Well, that is a nice welcome," she teased.

Priscilla pulled her into a hug and chuckled. "You just look so different."

"I know how to dress to act the part." She shrugged.

"Well, you look beautiful as always," Priscilla walked into where the ladies sat. She introduced Ashley to them and then they sat down to sew the big quilt. Everyone worked on a piece of it. They would be selling it at the farmers' market that weekend.

Ashley fit into the quiet chatter of the ladies and was received like she had lived there for years. Though Priscilla could tell there was something off with her friend. She wasn't sure if she knew her well enough to know if she was right or not. When Priscilla and Ashley gathered lunch together for everyone while everyone kept sewing, she decided to bring it up.

"You seem to fit in so well here."

Ashley nodded. "It's been fun."

But her voice gave away too much.

"What is wrong, Ashley?" Priscilla asked.

Ashley looked up from cutting the bread to make peanut butter sandwiches. Then she looked back at what she was doing.

"Nothin'." She frowned. "It's just harder being back than I thought."

"What do you mean back?" Priscilla felt confused.

"I worked at a bakery as a teenager and was able to keep an eye on Danny. It was a bit stressful because of how they, his adopted family, treated him. And how they treated me sometimes due to Mom's ties to them." She didn't seem bitter. Just a bit thoughtful over some memories.

Priscilla gave her a compassionate look. "Like I tell Danny, not all the communities are the same. Just like families, and even churches, they are all different."

Ashley nodded. "You are right. You're a good wife to him."

Priscilla didn't think so. She wanted to bring up Danny and their talk the other night, but wasn't sure how.

"Now it's my turn, sis. What is on your mind?" Ashley asked.

Priscilla put down the butter knife she was using to spread peanut butter on a slice of bread, and grasped the counter. She wasn't sure where to start.

"I just don't feel good enough for your brother. He deserves better," she put a hand over her stomach. "Not a woman carrying another man's child."

Ashley touched her arm. "He loves you and your child. He has always loved you."

Priscilla met her eyes. "That is another thing. He has always loved me and loved me perfectly, while I have failed him."

"What do you mean?" Ashley asked. Her brows drew together.

She didn't want to say too much.

"I feel things. Before James...touched me. I felt things for Danny, and it was wrong. I wanted more. I do feel a connection with him," she didn't know how to say this without sounding like such a sinner. Her face turned bright red. "Even now I feel emotions, and back then I wanted more than kissing."

Ashley bit her lip and gave a small smile.

Priscilla narrowed her eyes at her friend. "What are you smiling about?"

Ashley tried to turn serious. "I am sorry. I don't mean to, but you are so cute, and I am glad you feel for my brother. It means you two will probably have a great, fulfilling marriage one day."

Priscilla stared at her with wide eyes. *What was this woman talking about?*

"You aren't wrong for what you are feeling." When Priscilla was about to argue, she spoke up. "Now listen, before you were married, you did need to keep those feelings under control and not act on them and even try not to think about them. But God gave you those feelings to help in marriage. It is very normal. Few people talk about women having them, especially Christians."

"So you have them?"

Ashley nodded. "If I let my emotions take control, especially I do, and I have to not let that happen. But in marriage, those emotions and feelings are good and healthy."

Priscilla thought about it for a bit. Then she finished buttering the bread. "I was always told those feelings were bad. Other married women really have them?"

Ashley nodded. "Even my mom can get wild about my dad sometimes. They were always sappy growing up. That was new to Danny since he didn't grow up with outward affection. But that is why he is so open about his feelings now."

Priscilla loved that about Danny. "Do you think Amish women like sex?"

Ashley winked at her. "Well, they got the babies to prove it."

Her mouth dropped open. How could Ashley say something like that, especially in an Amish home?

But then they burst out laughing. And laughed till they had tears in their eyes.

Priscilla turned serious. She shook her head. "It's just all so new."

Ashley nodded. "Also, your feelings had nothing to do with what James did. He was so wrong."

Priscilla looked away. How did Ashley know she felt that way?

Ashley didn't need to be asked. "I know how the

community views God, and that is just not so. He is a loving, kind God, and He doesn't go after His children that way."

Priscilla shuddered. She felt exposed to Ashley, but it didn't feel so bad because she didn't feel a bit of judgment coming from her sister. "I have nothing to give to Danny. He took everything."

Ashley pulled her into a hug and they stood there for some time. Priscilla hugged her back. Pam and Ashley hugged so often. She was learning to like them.

Ashley knew they didn't have much time for this talk. She looked in Priscilla's eyes.

"Again, so many Christians don't talk about this. We talk so much of purity and saving yourself, but when things like this happen, it's so opposite of what they teach. And the church just overlooks it, and that shouldn't be done." She looked back into the room where the ladies were waiting for lunch. "I want to finish this talk. Why don't I send you some stuff to read and listen to since you have your own phone now."

Priscilla felt discomfited. What if Ashley sent sermons? She had a hard enough time listening to them with Danny. Even though the bishop hadn't really hurt her in the past, after their meeting where she lied that Danny was the father, she couldn't bear to hear the bishop teach.

She wasn't even sure why.

Others had been through worse than her and it didn't have this effect. Even when she listened to sermons with Danny, she had a hard time understanding them. The sermons were opposite of what she was taught her whole life.

"Well, that would be fine… are they ser…" she wasn't sure how to ask without sounding rude or offending her.

Ashley shook her head. "No, they aren't sermons. Just testimonies of people who have walked in your shoes."

That must be a terrible thing. She hated walking this life at times. Her hand went to her stomach. Would her baby feel the same way when it came out? Would the baby love her, or be upset that he or she wasn't created in love? Would she even be able to love the baby?

Ashley gave her a side hug. "You've been through so much these past few months. Just take it a day at a time."

"Or an hour at a time." Priscilla rolled her eyes.

Ashley chuckled as they headed back to where the women sat, carrying the sandwiches.

Ashley didn't mention it, but Priscilla knew she had to overcome not feeling good enough for Danny. Especially if she had to leave with him one day. Leave this life. As she looked around her at the ladies she had known her whole life, she hated leaving. Her heart hurt a bit as she thought of it. Maybe she could still make Danny see how good this life could be, especially for their child.

∽

Priscilla wasn't used to riding in so many different kinds of cars. But since marrying Danny, they did it often. It was something new she'd discovered about her husband. He loved to travel and go places. Zack or one of his parents always drove them. She had never been anywhere in the area, so the landscape was unknown to her. She was learning to like their trips. If he would keep kissing her under the fireworks, she would go anywhere with him.

She met Pam at the car and then slid in. She loved Pam's car because it had heated seats. They felt nice against her back. And on this rainy, cooler day, it felt good.

Though she was still thinking about her talk with Ashley at the sewing circle. She had been probably overthinking it.

Pam smiled at her. "You always like the heated seats."

"There are perks to being English," Priscilla said.

Pam chuckled.

"That is for sure. There are a lot of nice things about us English." She winked at her.

Priscilla turned serious. With the talk she had with Ashley, she wasn't sure if she wanted to talk about this issue as well. But she had been avoiding this talk.

"Danny says the church is the best part of being English." She paused. "He wants me to go to an English church."

"How do you feel about that?" Pam asked as she drove to Meijer and some of the bigger stores than what their town had to offer. It was about an hour drive.

Priscilla shrugged. "He is my husband, so I guess I have to go."

"But do you want to go?"

"No. I am afraid." She looked out the window, watching the hills and old barns pass them by. "I feel that if I go, I will be doing something bad. Going is against the teachings of the bishop."

"Well, that is a real concern, and it makes sense why you're nervous."

"Did Danny ever feel this way?"

"No, but he didn't believe what the bishop taught. We took him to church picnics first and then church. But he was also a child, so he didn't understand the differences between the Amish and the English church."

"Ach, I don't know how to make the feeling go away. I feel bad."

"It will take time." She thought about her words as she watched the road. She pushed her hair back from her face. "Time for you to see that the English church doesn't teach wrong things, and it's really what you believe. Do you believe everything the bishops say?"

When Priscilla was about to say yes, Pam added, "And everything they do?"

Priscilla bit her lip. No, she didn't. What they had done to her was wrong. What they did about James's behavior was wrong.

So maybe the bishop didn't have all the answers. She had never considered it before now. "I reckon not. How do I find out the truth?"

"By reading your Bible and by searching it out. It's not easy, especially after so many years of you believing your bishop. God wants you to know Him and serve Him over the bishop. Does that make sense?"

Priscilla frowned in confusion. "Danny talks like this, but it's confusing. Are the bishop's rules not of God?"

Pam shook her head. "No, honey, they are not. You need to search out and see which ones are true and which are not."

"Then how do you know what your pastor says is right?" Priscilla couldn't believe she had asked that, but she felt comfortable with Pam and she expected the truth.

Pam got pink to her cheeks, as if she liked this talk.

"My pastor backs his rules with biblical scripture. He will show you how he came to believe that, and there are still a few things he teaches that I don't agree with. Rarely do you agree with everyone." She smiled. "Even Danny differs with us on stuff."

Priscilla nodded. "The Amish are the same way. Some are more knowledgeable than others."

"Right."

"If I go to an English church in Amish clothes, how will they accept me? They won't want an outsider in their building," Priscilla cried.

"Honey, how do you know they will reject you? Have you been? Do they reject Danny?"

Priscilla shook her head. "But Danny doesn't look or dress Amish."

Pam smiled. "That is the truth. He doesn't. But he is still accepted there. I won't say there will be no one who doesn't see your clothes as strange, but most of the people will accept you and I know they will love you."

She parked the car at Meijer. She faced Priscilla.

Priscilla looked at her hands which lay in her lap. "What if they find out about the baby, and discover what happened to me? It's embarrassing and humiliating."

Pam took her hands. "Honey, they will love you. They know it's not your fault, and they will know how you love their Danny and will love you because of it."

She met Pam's eyes. She wondered how Pam knew so much. Was it because she was close to the Amish or was it something else? She was afraid to ask.

"I will think about it," She sat back to enjoy the heated seat again. "I will have to find a church if we leave anyway,"

She pushed her hair back from her face.

Pam nodded. "Danny will help you with that. You will get through this."

Priscilla didn't agree.

"With a job like Danny's it will also be a rough road," Pam said.

She furrowed her brow. What did Pam mean? He

worked on a ranch. But she was too tired to think about more. She just got her purse and went inside. What would it be like to be English and dress like the world? She wasn't sure she was ready to find out.

Chapter Seventeen

A few days later, Priscilla was getting used to holding Danny's hand in public. She enjoyed it. He often took her hand when they sat on the couch at home too. She didn't mind. She felt safe with him. Though she still had a hard time trusting him, she did always feel safe with him.

Good thing she married him.

As they walked downtown Maysville in the evening, he stayed on the street side of the sidewalk to make her feel safer. He had taken her out to eat, even after all the groceries she got with Pam the day before. Her datt wouldn't have wanted to spend the money. He led her into the bookstore there, he looked down at her.

"Get anything you want and I will pay for it." He touched her face. "I want to do this for you as a gift. Nothing in return."

Her eyes lightened and, for the first time, she didn't feel threatened by his gifts. She remembered a talk with Ashley about how Danny loved to give gifts. It was one of his ways of showing love. He had given Ashley and his loved ones some great gifts.

"Thank you so much." She smiled at him widely. Then she went book shopping. She was a child in a toy room.

Danny got a basket and stood beside her as she looked through the books. Priscilla thought it was so adorable how attentive he was. He looked like a young, sweet Amish husband since he was dressed like one. He dressed Amish when he was out with her since she always did. He didn't want them to get extra attention. If they only knew he wasn't Amish at heart. Maybe she was beginning to like that about him, though.

When she had five books in the basket, she found a couple of more. But she couldn't get them all. It wouldn't be right to spend all his money. "I will get these."

Danny picked up the other books and put them in the basket. "I want you to get all the ones you want."

Her eyes sparkled and giggled. "See, I told you, you wouldn't want to take me shopping for books."

He chuckled.

"Oh, my dear, I will always take you book shopping." He winked at her. "I love seeing you so happy. And books make you happy."

She stepped closer to him and looked up at him through her eyelashes. "Thank you again."

Nodding, he smiled again. "Any time, my dear."

Then he put another book in her basket. She glanced at it and saw it was one on parenting.

She frowned. She had almost forgotten she was pregnant. She wished sometimes they got married without her being pregnant. But then she wouldn't have married him. At least she knew her child would have a great, caring father.

He paid and thanked the cashier.

She smiled at him.

"I can't believe you got me these books. My datt never has. He said it was a waste of money." She paused. "I am sorry. I shouldn't have said that."

"No, it's fine." He squeezed her hand. "You are being honest, and I always want you to be honest with me. I might not always get what you want, but I will always meet your needs. And if I can, I will always get you books."

She let out a small giggle. "I think I might enjoy this part of marriage."

He leaned close.

"Me too." Then they started walking. He held the books like they were heavy. "These might break my arm."

She squeezed his arm. "With those muscles, I highly doubt it."

He smiled. "I will remember that."

She dipped her head and blushed.

In front of the tavern on the street, it got a bit crowded with people. Priscilla stepped closer to him. He took her down a walkway with trees on both sides where it was quiet and no one was around. It was so beautiful. Then Priscilla felt something on her side and she nearly jumped.

A man stood beside her. "Be still and no one will get hurt."

Danny held her tighter and stood against the brick wall.

They both now faced their attacker, who pointed a big knife at them. He couldn't be more than an older teenager.

"Give me all your money," he said quietly. His eyes were wild.

Priscilla wrapped her arms around her stomach, feeling like she may faint.

"Why don't we take a minute to talk here?" Danny paused. "You don't really want to do this."

He was so calm and easy as he spoke.

The boy's hand shook a bit harder. "I just want your money."

"I don't have much," Danny said calmly. "I spent it on my wife's books. See, my wife likes to read a lot, and I make her happy by buying her books. Though they are awfully heavy to carry." He held up the books. "See, books make her happy."

When the boy looked at the books instead of them, Danny used the bag to hit the boy's head and the books scattered over the sidewalk. Danny pushed her against the wall before he tackled the boy. It all happened so fast. Priscilla shuffled along the wall away from them.

Danny had the boy's hands behind his back, and he threw the knife out of reach. He handcuffed the boy, and then looked up at her. "Call the police. Just hit number two, and it will go straight to Zack."

She dug in her small purse for Danny's phone. Her hands shook, her heart beating a mile a minute. She did as he said, and he was right. Zack picked up on the second ring. "Hey Danny, what's up?"

"Hi, Zack," she stuttered. "This is Priscilla... uh, Danny's wife." She sighed, feeling dizzy. Like he wouldn't know who she was. "We got robbed."

"Okay." His voice changed. "Take a deep breath, Priscilla. Where are you? I am on my way right now."

"We are by the tavern in old Maysville by the park..." she talked breathlessly, and she put a hand on her chest. "I don't know the address. I am sorry."

"You are doing just fine, Priscilla. I know where you are. Is anyone hurt? Do you need EMS?"

She shook her head, but then remembered she was on the phone.

"I don't think so. We are fine." She paused. "Just hurry."

"I am pulling up right now," he said.

That was when Priscilla realized the siren and lights of the police car had arrived. She hadn't realized the police station was so close to here. Zack dealt with the robber.

"Thanks." She hung up the phone and dropped down against the wall. A few seconds later, Danny was by her side.

He took her in his arms, guiding her to a grassy area under trees. They sat, and he moved her onto his lap. "Oh honey, you were so brave."

She didn't know what came over her, but she wrapped her arms around his neck and dug her face into his chest. "I was so scared."

"Me too, baby. Me too. Are you all right?" He touched her stomach. "How is the baby?"

She held him tighter. "Good."

Then the tears came and turned into sobs. She could have died. Her baby wouldn't have had a life. She wanted her baby to have a life. A life with her and Danny. What if she had lost Danny? The thought crippled her and caused such an ache in her she thought she might be sick.

Finally, the tears slowed, and she hiccupped. He gave her a napkin from their lunch bag, and then he called Zack for something. She felt a cold water bottle pressed into her hands and he helped her drink. She felt a bit better afterward.

She looked up at Danny. "How did you stay so calm?"

"Stan taught me how to do it."

She whispered, "You are my hero." She paused. "Again."

He just smiled at her, the sun was starting to set now. Then he finally said in a thick voice, "I will always be your hero, my love."

She heard someone approaching, then a shadow fell across the grass. Priscilla looked up to see Stan looming above them. Man, he looked bigger from this angle.

Then he knelt to their level. "How are you, our Priscilla?"

She cleared her throat.

"I am fine now," she said, not sure how to answer. Danny was the only man who had ever cared for her well-being. Having a man care about her was still strange.

"Well, let's get you home," Danny said lightly, standing.

With Stan's help, Danny helped her up.

When they got her settled into the car, Stan handed Priscilla the books.

"You might want these." He had put them in another bag, but had kept one out. He handed her the big hard one that had knocked the boy down. "This one saved your life."

She took it in awe then at looked at Danny. "No, Danny boy did that."

Danny kissed her forehead. "I will be right there. Let me talk to Stan first and then we will leave."

She nodded and held the books to her chest. She was safe.

But then she thought about why Danny was carrying handcuffs. She was afraid to ask though. Though she felt safe she was unsure on how to ask him about it. He was as mysterious as the first time they courted. He wanted her to trust him, but he did things like this that weren't trusting. He wasn't fully honest with her. She was too nervous to ask him. To lose him.

∾

Danny tried to enjoy time with the community, to join his bride's world. He also knew he would be leaving soon, so he knew he could handle it for a few months longer. It did help that he was friends with some of the men from his teenage years and he could always talk to Paul now. They had good deep talks about the Bible and what they believed. He wished Paul would leave the community when he did. But he understood why Paul stayed. He wouldn't judge him for that.

He just knew God wanted him out of the Amish.

As he watched Priscilla get food ready and talk with a couple ladies her age, they stood along the tables all working and knowing what to do as they chatted about everyday life. It smelled so delicious. He wondered if she kinda knew that they needed to leave.

Today was a singing Sunday. After the men ate, they went into the barn. Danny was going to have to sit apart from Priscilla, though he didn't want to. She stood next to him at the door of the barn. He wanted to hug her or kiss her head. But he didn't want to cause more gossip.

So he whispered, "I love you, baby."

She blushed. Her eyes looked at him with such delight. He felt she loved him even though she didn't say the words. He hoped she would say them soon.

And then he might never hear the words again after

she found out what he was training for and what he would do one day and soon. He felt his body stiffen at the reminder of what could destroy their relationship.

Priscilla glanced at him, her eyes turning worried but she kept silent because they had to walk in. She must have noticed his change. How could he keep lying to her?

They sang, and he enjoyed the music despite the guilt bothering him. The voices were beautiful and one could almost notice there weren't instruments. It was some of the most beautiful he had ever heard from a community.

Or maybe Priscilla had opened his eyes to the beauty and the good things of the Amish. He had been blinded by lies and rules before. Now he saw the people in a different light.

He still didn't feel at home here. Not like at his English church. He did feel something new, though. Something he had never felt before. A peace and almost a sense of belonging. But still there was something there he couldn't fully relax.

After the singing was over, young couples played games and the married couples talked. Danny found Paul and enjoyed talking about the ranch, since they worked there part-time.

Then Eli and Joseph came over.

"We wanted to talk to you for a moment, Danny," Eli said.

Danny just nodded and remained silent.

Joseph cleared his throat. "You are still not growing a beard, even though you are married. Amish men grow beards."

Danny didn't feel like talking to these men, but he had to try better. For Priscilla's sake.

And this time was different than the last; he saw them differently. They sadly believed what they said. He had never thought of them that way before. Maybe he could try to change their way of thinking.

"I told you before, my job doesn't allow me to grow beards. I have a question."

Eli nodded rubbed his beard, his legs apart like he was almost ready to fight or argue. They all stood outside the barn.

"Where in the Bible does it say to grow beards? Can you tell me the verses?" he asked with respect.

"That doesn't matter. It is the way we do things. It's what our fathers did. If we break these rules, then we will break God's laws," Joseph said.

"What law of God have I broken?" Danny asked.

"You have been breaking our rules. Don't you see how wrong that is?" Eil tugged at his own sun-bronzed beard, as if frustrated. "We also think you married Priscilla too fast. Many of the church are not happy about that. Some think you forced her to marry you."

Danny grit his teeth. He hadn't heard this rumor yet. How could they think that?

"That is not true. My wife talked to Priscilla before the wedding and it was her choice." Paul spoke up. "Danny and Priscilla are very happy."

"They don't follow the rules anymore. Even Pricilla's hair escapes out of her kapp now. She's only supposed to show an inch to the hairline and she has gotten longer to an inch and a half," Eil said loudly.

Danny didn't know what to say. He had been raised in this his whole life but for once he saw it for what it was: so legalistic. He knew it wouldn't be good if he spoke hastily or in anger.

Just then, Priscilla came up and grabbed hold of his arm. She smiled like nothing was wrong. "I just wanted some time with my husband, and thought I would join your talk, if that is all right?"

Joseph smiled; despite being strict, he was a nice man. He just had rules to follow and make sure others did as well. "Of course. How are you doing Priscilla?"

She touched her stomach. "Very well. Thank you. How is Allie feeling after her sickness last week?"

He answered, and from then on, the talk was light. Danny was so thankful she came over.

As he looked down at his animated, happy wife, he smiled at how she'd kept calm and had helped him.

After the singing, on the way home, Priscilla kept his arm in hers as he drove the buggy. And she even leaned her head against his shoulder. She had seen Danny getting upset and didn't want him to be hurt. It wasn't right the way they talked to him. Again her eyes were opening up to see how wrong the church was.

For some reason, she had gotten protective over him and wanted to hurt anyone that hurt him.

"Can I ask why you walked up when you did?" He paused. "You almost seemed like your old self."

She wished she was the same as before. But that Priscilla might never exist again.

"I don't like how they have attacked you in the past. And I want to protect you from being hurt. Not that I think of you as helpless or something."

He kissed her head.

"You are a treasure. Thank you for doing that. It means so much to me." His eyes watered. "No one but my English family has done something for me like that."

She kissed his cheek.

"I will always be there for you." She frowned. She took a chance and trusted him to answer honestly. "Did you see him there?"

She didn't need to say his name. He normally didn't come to Sunday singings, but this one had been two communities together.

He nodded and sighed. "Yes, I did."

She had felt his eyes on her before the singing, and it felt like he was undressing her with his eyes. And he had undressed her many times. She felt so ashamed.

Then Paul had walked up and stood in front of her to where James couldn't see her anymore. She wasn't sure if Paul had noticed or not. But he was so sweet.

"I can't believe they are allowing him in the community. Oh, I forget he dresses just right," he said sarcastically. "I hear he is courting Mary."

She flinched and finally said, "Of course, he is. She has a younger sister."

"You mean Annie?"

She nodded. "It was the reason I didn't sleep in the same room as Annie after the abuse started. I didn't want him to touch her too."

She shuddered.

He put his arm tightly around her. "I am so sorry, my love."

She pressed into him, loving the feel of his arms around her. She was safe now. She would never again be at the mercy of an abuser.

They rode home in peace, but as they did, both knew it wouldn't last long. Life felt tense, living between two worlds, and something was about to explode. They would be hurt.

Both wished they could keep the happy peace they felt at this moment

∽

"Amish babies are born at home," Priscilla told Danny the following Monday. He had mentioned going to the clinic to see the baby on ultrasound.

She leaned back against the couch, where she had been reading a good book.

"If you want, you can still do it at home. But you haven't had anyone check you since the midwife visited, and I don't want to pressure you, but now it might be time to go in," Danny explained and tried to show her how he was feeling. Concern showed on his face.

She nodded.

"I know, but I am nervous." She bit her lip. Though Christy had visited many times, she still wasn't comfortable. "I wish my mamm was with me."

She wanted her mamm with her but was too afraid of what Mamm would say about the baby. Her mamm knew she didn't want the baby. Her mamm had said nothing of the baby and who the datt was since she had found out and that wasn't normal among their community. Babies were welcome and loved. What if her baby was not ever loved?

He came over to where she sat on the couch and pulled her into his arms. "I know. I am sorry."

She put her hand on his chest and just breathed him in. It felt good to be this close to him. She knew she should go to the clinic. Christy was busy this afternoon and couldn't meet them there. Maybe Pam could meet them there? She'd feel better if she had her around.

She nodded against his chest.

He patted her head. "So you'll go?"

She nodded again. "Yeah. I need to."

"Good. We have an appointment for three today," he told her. "My mom will meet us there."

She sat up and looked at his watch. Thirty minutes until they had to leave.

"Well, I better get ready then." She went to their room. It was still strange to think of it that way. She did her hair nicely and put on the kapp.

She walked out to the living room, and Danny met her by the door.

"You look pretty," he said.

And she knew he meant it. He didn't mind her clothes. Though he wore jeans and a t-shirt nowadays. And she loved the look on him. It was who he was.

She was still learning who she was. God's daughter. What did that mean? It wasn't the same as being Datt's daughter, that was for sure.

Danny opened the car door for her. She liked these car rides with him, whether they hired someone, or whether one of his friends drove them. She loved holding his hand, and even how it rested on her leg sometimes. She didn't mind that. She always felt closer to him then.

They chatted as a friend drove them to the clinic. It was a longer drive than she was used to.

"Why don't we go by the river on the way home?" Danny suggested.

She smiled. "I would love that. Ashley says it's pretty romantic."

"Well, she is the writer, so she should know," he teased.

"Yup. I love talking to her about it. It's so much fun. I feel connected to her."

He nodded. "I am glad, darlin'. You should. She is a pretty special lady like you."

She blushed.

At the clinic, she got out and took his hand as they walked in. There was a bed on the one wall with stuff around it she had never seen before. There was a big screen on the wall. Pam was already in there and she walked over and gave her a hug.

"Hi, my dear. How are you feeling?"

Priscilla tried to smile. "Fine."

Pam smiled. "Don't ever go into acting."

Danny chuckled.

Priscilla looked confused.

Danny touched her shoulder. "I will explain later, dear."

She nodded. A nurse took them back to the room and told her to sit on a large bed. There were wires everywhere and a beeping machine next to her. All of this was overwhelming.

When the nurse asked if she'd be able to access her belly, Priscilla, with Danny's help, showed her how the dress was made to be pulled up. Her cheeks burned. The dress was designed to help mothers easily nurse their babies. The nurse nodded her approval and left them alone.

"We will get to see our baby soon." Danny nearly laughed. He felt so much excitement at this moment. He tapped his boot on the floor.

Pam stood on the other side of her.

Priscilla nodded. "But I don't want to know what it is."

"I agree. I guess we can wait longer," he teased her.

She took his hand as another nurse walked in.

"Hi, my name is Sharon Cooper. I will be taking care of you today." She held out her hand.

Danny shook it and introduced them. The nurse didn't seem taken aback from seeing they were married, since he wasn't dressed Amish. Priscilla was thankful for that.

"Nice to meet you. Now let's see what we have here." She went over to a big black screen on the wall and, using a mouse, clicked some buttons. Then she took a strange looking cream thing out. "This is a transducer. I'll press it against your belly to pick up the radio waves of your baby, which will form an image on the screen. It won't hurt, honey, but I plan to put some warm jelly on your belly to help."

"Jelly is sticky," Priscilla stated.

They all chuckled. And Pam stood next to the bed and explained, "No, honey, that is just what it is called."

Priscilla nodded.

Sharen applied a warm, clear gel to Priscilla's stomach and then moved the transducer over her belly.

Priscilla squeezed Danny's hand as she stared at their baby on the screen. "Look at our baby."

Tears came to her eyes. The baby was moving and so real.

"I know, our baby is beautiful."

She started to cry harder as she watched the baby move.

Danny knew this was more than just emotions, and he knew she wouldn't be happy if the others saw it. Even Pam. "Ms. Cooper, can you give us a minute?"

The nurse nodded and left with Pam.

He took Priscilla in his arms despite the sticky stuff still on her stomach. "What is wrong, Priss?"

She clung to him and cried.

He let her cry, and then when she was ready, she began, "I love how the baby looks, but I am afraid I won't love the baby when it comes out. This baby wasn't made from love. I didn't want that man near me."

"Oh, honey. I thought the same thing for a bit, but I love this child, and this child is a part of you as well. You will love the baby."

"How do you know? You don't know that!" she cried.

He nodded. "You're right, but we need to talk about this or the baby will feel it when he or she is born."

She wailed, "I didn't think of that."

He patted her shoulder. "It's all right. Do you want to see the baby again?"

She shook her head. "No, I just can't right now."

"All right. I will tell the nurse we are ready to leave soon."

She watched the nurse come back and go through the motions this time on what was done, measuring her stomach and everything else.

Back at home, Priscilla felt like the worst mother in the world. What if the baby knew how she felt? Would it damage the baby for life? She went to lay on the bed. She hadn't been laying there long when she heard Danny come in. She felt him get on the bed and then put his arms around her. This time his hands to her belly.

"The baby knows you love him or her," he said softly.

"But what if I don't?"

"You were willing to marry me to keep the baby safe. You could have chosen another way out. But you didn't."

She put a protective hand over his hands.

"So, you do love this child," he continued. "It will just take time to process all of it."

"I am afraid."

"I know," he said softly. "Will you go to counseling with me, or alone, to work it out?"

He had brought it up before and she'd given him a hard *no*. But now that the baby was closer to coming; she could think about it. She would be a mother soon.

"Maybe. I want to heal," she sighed. "I just want to be held."

"I am fine with that, love." He wrapped his arms tighter around her and even wrapped his legs with hers, making her feel both safe and cherished.

∽

He was going to hurt her again. Why wouldn't he just stop? She was scared of him touching her. She could feel his breath on her.

Priscilla jerked awake. She opened her eyes and found Danny's head laying on her chest. His arm over her stomach. She didn't mind him sleeping on her. For some reason, it wasn't a trigger, and she always felt safe with him. But right now, she didn't want to be close to him. She moved him carefully off of her, and she slid over to the other side of the bed. Pulling the blanket over her, she started to cry.

She heard Danny move and knew he was awake. She felt a hand on her shoulder.

"Do you mind if I hold you, love?" he whispered, his voice heavy with sleep.

She turned around and held him tight around the waist. He held her back. She started to talk through the tears. "When he used to come to my room, I used to imagine I was somewhere else. I would imagine the first time meeting you, seeing those mischievous eyes under all that hair. I imagined all the good times we had together. Your laughter, your smile, your touch."

He ran a hand over her hair.

"I feel so guilty for not fighting him. I should have fought him more, and then my child wouldn't have to have a rapist for a father. I froze so often. I couldn't move," she hiccupped. "I wanted to tell my mother, but I was too afraid she would tell my datt and then I would have to go before the bishop. I couldn't imagine going before the church and telling them all I made him do it. I couldn't imagine you knowing my shame."

"Oh, honey, you didn't do anything wrong. Nothing wrong." He ground his teeth, feeling rage. "Dad says many women freeze like that. It's a natural thing to do to keep you safe. It's what the body does to keep you safe."

"I wonder if my mamm really thinks you are the father or she knows?"

"I think she knows. Guilt can make you do crazy things." *He should know.* Even now he thought of how he could tell her about becoming a cop. But he remained silent.

"I am afraid she will see my child as a monster." She wiped her eyes and leaned back where she could see his face in the moonlight from the window.

He touched her face. "Are you afraid you'll think of the child like that?"

She bit her lip, stayed silent, then said, "I am afraid I will think of it as his child and remember what he did to me when I see the baby."

Danny softly said, "I am not saying you won't feel that way. But I know other women haven't, from what they say at the ranch. If you feel that way when the baby is born, then I know families who would take the baby until you are ready to care for it, or they will adopt the baby."

Could she give her child up? She had done too much to keep this baby, but would it be right to keep the baby if she felt something bad? She married Danny to keep this child. Her hand fisted in his shirt. He must have sensed her panic.

"Honey, I am not going anywhere. You have me with no refunds. You and me and this marriage are forever," he said softly.

She felt such relief. Feeling so much love for him and feeling light headed she had to say it, "I love you, Danny boy."

He blinked. "Are you just saying that because it's the wee hours of the morning?"

She chuckled.

"No, I love you. I have always loved you. Even while we broke up, I never stopped loving you." She touched his cheek. "The love is different now, and I love you with everything I have."

He smiled as she spoke. "Oh, how I love you, Priss."

Just then, the baby kicked where Danny was touching her stomach. Danny's eyes got wide as he looked at her stomach in the moonlight. He was in awe.

"Oh my." He kept his hand on her stomach and the baby kicked again. "I think the babe is telling us we need to sleep, love."

She chuckled. "I do love feeling the babe move."

"It must be an amazing feeling," he said.

"It is. I was very surprised when it first happened and tried to ignore it at first. I was feeling so much emotion at the time. But now I let myself feel it."

The baby kicked again, and he smiled. "I got my baby to love me, and my wife told me she loves me too."

She giggled. "Well, then, it may be a good thing I woke you up."

He kissed her forehead and then whispered in her ear, "I love you so much."

She shuddered under his touch. Then she moved to where she could lay her head on his chest where she lay on her side and closed her eyes. "Good night, my love."

"Sweet dreams, love," he said softly as they both drifted off to sleep, the baby safe between them.

Chapter Eighteen

Priscilla woke up, felt for Danny in the bed, and found his place empty. She opened her eyes to see it was late in the day. Much later than she normally slept. She reached for her phone and saw a message from Danny.

> Did I dream you saying you loved me last night. 🩶🩶🩶

She laughed and replied,

> No, my love, you didn't. Just to remind you, I love you.

She got up and stepped in the shower. When she got out, she read the text,

> You can remind me anytime you want, love. 🩶🩶 I woke up to you on my chest and it was the best feeling ever. Your hair was all over my chest. I wanted to stay there all day.

She blushed, though no one was there. She loved the feeling that came over her when he talked like that.

> Aww, I wish you could have as well. Your words mean so much to me. Your words last night meant so much to me.

Danny:

> I am glad. I will remember that, love.

And she would remember he loved physical touch. Though it may be hard for her, she wanted to love him. That meant meeting his needs and making him feel loved.

She wrote:

> I love you.

Danny:

> I love you more. I played with your hair while you slept. I could just love you every day. If love paid the bills, I would be a rich man. Lol

Priscilla:

> You are a rich man. You have me and our baby, don't forget that.

Danny:

> Oh, how could I? I am a very blessed man.

Priscilla knew she had to get ready for the day and

couldn't lie in bed all day dreaming of her man. Though that would be nice.

~

Priscilla decided to attend church with Danny. English church. Since she'd told him she loved him, every day felt beautiful. And since she knew he wanted her to try his church, she told him she'd go. But now that Sunday had arrived, she wasn't sure what to wear. Especially to church. A new church. Danny had gone a few times without her to this church but not often since being married. She didn't feel comfortable not wearing her regular clothes. She put on her pink dress and covered it with a nice apron and then placed her kapp on. She left the room and went into the kitchen where Danny had breakfast ready.

He turned from where he sat at the table and smiled at her. "Morning, my beautiful bride. Are you ready for today?"

She shook her head, being honest with him. "But I am also excited. I've never been to a different church."

"I know, but you will love it," he reassured her. He got up and set a plate down. "Now let's eat some breakfast first."

He pulled out her chair, and she sat down. She loved that when he pulled her chair; he always touched her back in a soft way. Then he sat across from her. Taking her hands, they looked at each other as he prayed. Danny had helped her do that since the bishop and her datt had abused her with prayers. Praying with her eyes open stopped her from dissociating.

"Dear God, thank you for today. Be with us today as

we do what You are calling us to. Give us peace and help understand Your word as Pastor Tony preaches. In Jesus's name, Amen."

She enjoyed how he prayed, but she knew he kept it shorter for her. Though prayer gave her peace, it could also be triggering due to what the church did.

"Amen." Then she dug into his wonderful breakfast of eggs, toast, and coffee. She hadn't been a big breakfast eater until she married him.

After breakfast, they worked on the dishes together. Then he helped her put on her shawl, then looked at her. "Are you sure you are ready for this?"

She nodded. "I want to do it for you."

"Not God?"

"I am not sure if God is asking me to go to another church yet." She placed her hands on his chest. "I try to listen to God's voice but I hear the bishop's voice. It's hard to get through. I hear that going to the church is wrong. And I feel God isn't happy with me."

He touched her hand. "Oh honey, that is a lie. Remember fear is a liar. I always remember that song when I hear lies."

"How do I know what is a lie or not? I believed it my whole life."

"I know, love. Ask people you trust about it like Pam or Ashley or me. That is what I did. But it took a lot to get those lies out of my head."

She nodded. "I will do that. I don't want my baby raised with lies."

He kissed her forehead. "I couldn't agree more."

Danny couldn't believe he was taking his bride to his church. It was like a dream come true. She would get to meet his people, his church family. These people meant so much to him and now they would meet his wife. He felt so proud. He took her hand as they slipped from Zack's car. It shook a little. She felt close to his side. He was glad she was leaning into him, literally, but he wanted her to be relaxed. But then he remembered his first time at an English church. It had been scary for an angry boy.

As they walked inside, he was sure she would come to love it eventually.

Priscilla saw the people, and they dressed conservatively, but not in Amish clothes. Though she wore a long, simple dress with no apron and she still felt out of place. What if the bishop saw her? What would he think? She was sinning.

Then she remembered that was a lie.

Looking around, she wondered what they thought of her. There were couples and families walking inside. The building was big and had a bell on the peak roof. Some said hello as they passed. Would they hate her when they got to know her? She was a pregnant woman married to a man who wasn't her baby's father.

She was almost shaking by the time she got into the church. The pastor greeted them and Danny introduced her.

He smiled wide. He seemed inviting, though not much different how a deacon or bishop would act. They always treated outsiders the best. Too bad they didn't treat their own people like that.

"It's so nice to meet you, Priscilla. I feel like I know you already."

She tried to smile back. This was so hard.

Danny took her arm in his. "Well, we better go in."

She walked beside him. "I am sorry. I embarrassed you."

"No, you didn't. I did the same thing coming here."

"Well, he must be used to mute Amish people then."

He chuckled. "I guess he is, my love."

Then she spotted Pam. She waddled over and hugged her. She always loved how Pam's hugs made her feel. Like she was important to her.

Pam looked at her, she showed so much compassion. Stan stood close to her. The church was like a hometown country one. "It's that bad, huh?"

She shrugged. "It's been a long day."

Even though it wasn't even eleven o'clock yet.

Pam smiled. "It will get easier. Come sit with us."

Priscilla followed her as Danny stayed close. He greeted people, but she didn't talk to them. It was too awkward. Too overwhelming. She slid into the pew next to Pam, and Danny sat on her other side.

Then she heard the piano. As they stood and started to sing, she closed her eyes and let the music take her away. Imagining she was somewhere else where people wouldn't judge her. She didn't think a church would sing together this well, but the sound really moved her. All the voices together was so beautiful. Maybe they weren't as scary as she thought. They had that in common with the Amish. Both knew how to sing. The church seemed pretty close. Maybe like how she had felt her community was until she got raped.

She placed a hand over her belly. Her baby might have this kind of life if Danny made them leave the Amish. The music ended and they all sat. As the sermon began, it was hard to pay attention to. She felt like she was doing something bad. The bishop wouldn't be happy to see her sitting here, listening to an Englisher who taught lies. What if she went to hell for this? She closed her eyes and held tighter to Danny's hand.

He leaned close. "Do you want to leave?"

She shook her head. She would do this for him. But she wasn't sure she was ready to do it for herself yet. Maybe one day. She opened her eyes, but the rest of the sermon was lost to her.

At the end of the sermon, they sang again. She wasn't sure she was ready for singing again. It still moved her but not in the same way. Something had happened during that sermon, and she wasn't sure she was ready to face her fears or the lies she had been taught. Was her whole life a lie? Was the religion she grew up in a lie? It shook her to the core.

They moved to the back of the church after the service ended. This time she felt the courage to greet some of Danny's friends. This was her husband's world, after all.

The drive home was quiet. When they got home, Danny took her in his arms. Then suddenly he picked her up.

She put her arms around his neck. "What are you doing?"

"You are tired. I am bringing you inside to lay down." He carried her inside.

She smiled at him. "But I am getting bigger."

"You are growing for our child, of course you are."

She put her head on his shoulder. He set her on the couch. He got a pillow and blanket. Then he sat down too, at the other end. He put the pillow on his lap and patted it.

She laid down.

"What did you think of the service?"

She met his gaze, though it was a bit awkward from where she laid. "It was alright. I liked it more than I thought. But I can't say it was easy. I felt like I was almost sinning for being there."

He nodded. "You know what, I felt the same way going. When you've been raised in spiritual abuse, it puts blinders on you when you go to other places that speak the truth or just go anywhere where something is taught."

"When will that change?"

"It will take time, love. I will help you with it." He took off her kapp. "We will go through it together."

She blinked, afraid to do that; it sounded almost painful. She knew how hard it was to walk through things. Her man and God would help her. She closed her eyes, growing sleepy.

"Can I take your hair out to make you more comfortable?"

Her eyes were already closed but she nodded. He was gentle as he took out her pins. She fell asleep peacefully while he played with her hair, thinking on all that had occurred that day.

~

Priscilla didn't know the Ark Encounter existed until she met Danny. She sat next to him on a bus that drove them to it. She was amazed by how big the Ark Encounter was —the building was massive. Danny wasn't sure they would walk through the whole thing due to how big she was, but he really wanted to take her to the worship event that evening. She was just happy to be out spending a day with him.

Trust was like love. Sometimes it was painful, and sometimes she enjoyed it. Danny's kisses and snuggles helped. Though she enjoyed their talks more, those snuggles meant so much to her. And she knew he loved them. He loved any time he touched her, and it was never lustful or grabbing, but gentle and patient.

He helped her off the bus and kept holding her hand. He guided her through the opening and into the ark. She hadn't been to many tourist attractions, and this one was overwhelming, but wonderful to see. The hallways were wide and showed different parts of the Bible in different acts. It was so real and life-like. It was big and so large. The woodwork was so beautiful and smooth.

A couple hours later, they bought supper from the cafe and they ate, just enjoying each other's company. She loved this date so much.

"Are you looking forward to the Christian concert tonight?" he asked.

She nodded. "I am. It will differ from the singing in the Amish. Why did you never go to them?"

Danny shrugged. "For some reason, I always felt left out from the rest of the youth. Girls liked to flirt with me, but I knew they weren't serious. And some of it was, I think, how I felt about the Amish. I had a grudge. But I did go to some singings back in Ohio."

"Oh really. How did you like that?"

"About the same. The bishop of that community, not my adopted datt, would pair up couples and send them in the basement to see if they worked well together."

Her eyes went wide. She had heard of communities encouraging that practice. Nothing good came from it, and the couples were sexual with each other even if they remained virgins. She was glad her community hadn't encouraged that. She could only imagine the sexual assaults that went on down there. She was glad James hadn't touched her with others around; it would have been so much harder to bear. To hate it, yet others saw and did nothing. It was hard enough that her own parents knew and hadn't helped.

She shuddered. "I am glad our community doesn't do that."

He nodded. "Me too. I never liked it and always left."

She was proud of the way he went against what people said. "That must have been hard to do, in a way."

He looked thoughtful. "It was. My flesh wanted to. But I could never hurt a woman like that. My English mom and even dad taught me to respect women very well, both their bodies and hearts."

She looked at him with butter-soft eyes. "You do that well. I always feel respected by you."

He met her smile. "I am glad. My parents will be happy."

She chuckled. "I am sure."

Then she looked around quickly, as if they had said something bad. Would it always be in her mind that the Amish were out to get her? While couples talking was normal, the deep talks she and Danny shared were looked down on by her community. Then another thought came to her. For some reason she felt they would leave the community. She was too nervous to tell Danny this just yet. He would probably be so happy leaving. She felt so uncertain.

"Is everything alright, love?" he asked.

She nodded. Unable to share with him one of her deepest fears. She was surprised at herself; she would trust him with what James did so much but not with spiritual issues like this. Was it because God would be mad at her for having the baby in the world? For leaving her parents where she grew up?

He seemed still to be concerned, but he said nothing as he took her hand and gave her a look that said they've done nothing wrong. Sometimes she loved how he read her mind. Other times it was discomforting.

"Let's go in and get good seats."

She nodded and followed him into a huge auditorium room. There was a big crowd already there. Ashley had told her that for conferences, the room could hold up to twenty-five hundred people. Priscilla couldn't imagine that many people in one place, though Amish get-togethers and family reunions could get very large.

Danny led them closer to the front side of the room. She sat next to him and waited for the singer to show up.

Moments later a tall, beautiful blonde woman walked on stage. "Hello, everyone, my name is Rebekah Smith. I didn't think I would be able to make it tonight. So, I wasn't on the plan to be here. Surprise. I feel like I am needed to speak here for someone. Not everyone will understand this or what I am about to tell you. This is my story. I was conceived in rape."

Priscilla's heart stopped. She held Danny's hand tighter. Was she ready to hear this? She wasn't sure if she was.

"I was my mom's fourth child. She was on a trip and was raped. She didn't want to have me, but abortion was illegal in Michigan at the time. I was put up for adoption. I was loved and wanted. I found a wonderful husband and had great kids. Many say, even our President says, people like me shouldn't be here, or aren't wanted. But I am here, and I am grateful for my life."

Priscilla felt dizzy. This was too much. Would her child feel this way? What if her child didn't like knowing how he or she had been conceived? This situation wasn't right.

Danny leaned over. "Do you want to leave, my love? I didn't know she would be here."

She looked on ahead and shook her head. No, she wanted to hear more. She squeezed his hand. She would be fine.

"I have a good relationship with my birth mom, and I have thanked her for giving me life. I am grateful to be here. God planned my life for a reason, and maybe it was to be here tonight. Unplanned, for someone to hear this."

Priscilla pushed her hair away from her face. Was she here to speak to her? She wasn't sure.

"Though my mom went through much pain to have me, I was still a blessing to her and love her to this day. We met later as adults when she started looking for me."

Priscilla started to weep. Would her child say that about her? Or would the child be hurt that it hadn't been created in love? She looked at Danny, who wrapped her in his arms. This child had brought them together. In a way, the child had brought love: a love she had for Danny and the way he cared for her in every way. It had gotten her away from the trauma she was in, and she had found out who God really was. God had brought good out of a bad situation. She felt peace come over her like never before.

Rebeka Smith was right. She had come for a reason, and it was for Priscilla.

Chapter Nineteen

Fall was in the air, leaves were starting to turn, and the air was cooler. It made for a nice day at the Sunday meeting. A few days later, Priscilla looked at Danny across the room. His eyes lightened up, and he winked at her. She blushed to her roots. She loved when he showed her attention at the Sunday meeting and around the Amish. Flirting, even between married couples, wasn't encouraged. Sometimes it was even forbidden. Like most things, Danny didn't care. He did it anyway. She had seen the bishop talk to him about it, but thankfully he hadn't come to her.

She gave him a shy smile as he held her gaze. Oh, how blessed she was to have this man. How different would her life be if she hadn't married him? She would never have found a loving, caring God. She would still know Him as mad and ready to judge her. She felt so free.

Annamay came up behind her as she stood there and whispered in her ear, "Making sheep's eyes at some man."

Priscilla blushed more and turned to face her. She shrugged. "I am. Good thing I married that man."

Annamay laughed. "You sure did, and look at the change in him."

Priscilla loved how he had changed; he was happy and lost so much of his grudge against them all. She even liked him shaved. It made him look different from other married Amish men, and she loved that about him. She grinned at her friend.

"He is so open and honest," she whispered so as not to be heard. "He calls me things like beautiful, sweetie, and all kinds of nicknames."

Annamay bent over in laughter, which was not allowed in church. When she got bad looks, mostly by the elders, she whispered, "Your man sure likes you."

"I am sure glad he does."

Her friend turned serious.

"Look at the change in you. Your hair isn't even pulled back as much, and it shows more in the kapp. You are happy." Annamay touched Priscilla's stomach. "Even knowing this child is not Danny's."

Priscilla looked down at Annamay's hand on her stomach. "He knows and loves my baby. That is all I need."

Annamay's eyes were sad as she met her friend's. "I am sorry for what that monster put you through."

"Me too. But I am not sad about this baby," Priscilla whispered. "I just wish I knew he wouldn't do it to another girl."

A tear slid down her cheek. She wiped it away before anyone saw. Crying was never acceptable in her order. Danny had turned her into a crybaby. She smiled lightly. She didn't mind one bit.

"I need to go outside."

As she was about to step outside, she heard a voice behind her. So close she could feel his breath. She hadn't heard that voice in months, and it sent chills down her spine.

"Hey Priscilla, how is my baby doing? You know it's mine?"

She felt like she was about to pass out. She couldn't breathe. Where was Danny? She couldn't move. She hadn't seen him earlier. Strangely, she had missed him.

"This child is mine, remember that." He stood in front of her and touched her growing stomach. "This child will always be mine."

His touch sent chills through her, but she still couldn't move or tell him to stop. Her voice wouldn't work. Her stomach did a flip, and she felt dizzy. Where was everyone? A few people were around but hadn't noticed them.

He sneered. "You watch, I will come for this child."

Before she could even react, she saw Danny next to her. "What do you think you are doing?"

He grabbed James's shirt, yanked him away from her, and punched him twice. The second blow sent him into the wall, and he slid down to the ground, bleeding but still conscious.

Priscilla moved away from them, and Miriam Yoder's arms came around her.

"Don't you ever talk to my wife like that again. Touch her again and you will wake up next week." Danny's face was red hot, his hands in fists. "And if you ever touch her again, I can't promise where you will end up."

James stayed on the ground with a look of innocence on his face that made Priscilla sick. He acted like he had done nothing.

The bishop walked to them, staring with wide eyes. Deacons stood around him, all glaring at Danny.

"You have hit a brother in anger. You must make

amends, or you will be shunned." The bishop helped James up. "You have offended a brother."

Priscilla looked down. She couldn't face this anymore. Shame came over her. What if Danny apologized? What if he didn't stand up for her? Then, looking at his face, she knew he was still furious. Now pretty much the whole church was watching them. She even saw the young women staring in disbelief. She saw Paul come out from the corner of her eye. Maybe he would help but she also knew this was Danny and her fight. This had to end now.

"I won't apologize." Danny held his red fist in his other hand. "First off, he is not my brother, and second, he is hurting your young girls, and you don't seem to care. What did those women do to cause his abuse? Nothing. He is an evil man that needs to be kicked out of the church!"

The bishop frowned. "James has come before the church and apologized for his ways. We have forgiven him. And those women, your wife included, tempted him. It was not all his fault. Look at your wife's wild hair. She doesn't hide it anymore. She is tempting men with it."

Priscilla felt sick. She knew she should have oiled it like some women did. It was so frizzy, and it showed all the time. But then she looked at Danny and remembered. She had done nothing wrong. She was a child of God. Not a child of the Amish.

Danny shook his head.

"Don't ever talk that way about my wife again. She is made in the image of God. He made her hair that way, and it is beautiful. She is a priceless gift." His eyes blazed. "You are wrong. Those women did nothing wicked. He did. It was all him, and you all let him get away with it. In the real world, he would go to jail for hurting women."

Biting her lip, Priscilla kept her eyes down, but did the bravest thing she ever had done. She stepped next to her husband. She took his sore hand in both of hers. He squeezed her hand. But his gaze didn't leave the bishop's face.

"If you don't repent, then we will shun you and your wife. If you don't repent, you will have to leave the Amish for being prideful and angry," the bishop said, "and for defending a jezebel."

"Don't call her that. My wife is not like that." Danny glared at him. "Oh, you don't have to worry about that. We are leaving this community."

"Then you will go to hell. Only the Amish go to heaven."

Priscilla stared at him, sadly. How sad, he truly believed that of the world. For some reason she felt such pity. Looking around, she saw these people for what they were. Lost people stuck in a religion.

"No! We are going to heaven. Do you know why?" She took off her kapp and threw it on the ground. "I won't go to heaven because I wear a kapp."

The bishop glared at her and then looked to Danny for him to do something.

Priscilla wasn't going to let him talk down to her again. If this was the last time she was to speak to them, she would do it right. "I won't be going to heaven because I'm wearing clips."

She took the clips out and her hair fell around her shoulders in a frizzy, curly mess.

She threw the clips on the kapp. "I won't go to heaven for wearing this apron."

She took it off and put it in the pile.

"Or for wearing this dress or black shoes. Do you know

why I am going to heaven?" She stared in the bishop's face. His cheeks were red with anger. "I am going to heaven because Jesus Christ is my Lord and Savior. He is a loving God who wants the best for his people. Not hurt and hardship."

She held Danny's hand, tight in hers, strong. "Do you know he doesn't like men like James hurting women? All of you know he raped me. And probably other girls in this church. He will continue to do this sin, and he will probably marry and become a deacon and do it to his daughters. His precious children. You are all helping a sinner get away with murder."

Her knees nearly gave out, they were wobbling so hard, but she had to continue. "He is a murderer because he takes things from girls that shouldn't ever be taken. Ever. He kills every girl's heart. God does not put up with men hurting His children and other men allowing it. I can now see why you let James get away with it. Because of all the other abuse that happens in this place. Do you know that the Smith brothers who are now deacons have abused every one of their sisters? Do you know Ben Yoder's family has hurt many girls around?"

The bishop raised his hand like he would hit her but one look at Danny and he put his hand down. "Those things are forgiven!"

Priscilla's hands fisted. "They might be forgiven, but they are not forgotten. I can tell you every one of those victims will forever remember who hurt them. An abuser should never be trusted around a child or woman again. You are helping them get away with it. Not forgiving." She looked around. "We are leaving this community. If anyone chooses to leave, Danny and I will welcome you with open arms. No judgment. If I have learned something from

Danny and his friends, it's that they don't judge me. They welcomed me with open arms. Just like Jesus Christ did. We will help you make a new start. We have English friends who would help in any way. Know that being Amish will not get you to heaven. Only Jesus can. Anyone?"

She looked around at some of the young girls, trying to meet their eyes.

No one came forward. But, as Danny led her out, Annie Miller spoke up. She was a teenager who struggled to fit in.

"Wait." Her father stepped in front of her. She looked down and then moved past him.

"I am leaving," she said softly, crying. She wiped her eyes as she tried to hide her fear. Her back was straight with determination.

Priscilla's eyes softened, and she took Annie's hand. "You are doing the right thing."

As they walked away, she was surprised the bishop said nothing. He seemed shocked they would do this. She didn't care. She had never felt more free.

Annie's parents followed them outside. Her mom was sobbing, and her dad looked livid.

Danny took the horse's rope from Priscilla's younger brother as he looked at them sadly. Ben knew this was the last time he would see his sister or be allowed to talk to her. "I will miss you, sis. Please, don't go."

Danny helped her into the carriage for probably the last time. They would need to sell it. Not that anyone would buy it from them because of the shunning.

Before climbing into the buggy, Annie looked at her parents. Her mom was sobbing and crying. "You can't leave. You will go to hell. God will hate you for leaving.

You will never see your family again. You will never see your sisters."

Priscilla could see Annie's mind changing. She climbed down though it wasn't easy with her big belly and took her hands. "Don't listen to them. They want to keep you trapped. Come now."

Annie's mother grabbed her arm. "You will lose everything, you know. The English are bad."

"Mamm, I can't live in this world any longer. What they did to Priscilla was wrong. What they allow him to do is wrong." Annie pointed at James, who still stood there acting like he did nothing wrong.

"We were doing what was right," her mother cried. "You won't see any of your nieces or cousins again."

Her hands cupped her cheeks, tears trickling down. Fear showed on her face.

Priscilla knew Annie was losing the battle. She was too afraid to leave all she knew to go into the world of so-called evil people. "Annie, we need to go. You can't do anything here. Please, come."

Annie looked at her. "I have to protect my nieces and cousins. They only have me."

Priscilla didn't want to tell her that it didn't matter if she was here or not. They would do what they wanted, anyways. "You can't stop them. Please come."

Annie shook her head. "I can't. I can't leave everything."

Priscilla frowned.

Danny looked down at Annie from where he sat in the driver's seat of the buggy. "Just know any time you want to leave, Priscilla and I will come and get you. We will help in any way, Annie."

His eyes met Paul's, and his friend nodded. They would talk later. This had to stop.

Annie looked at the ground and said nothing.

Priscilla couldn't handle this anymore; the emotions raged inside of her. She climbed into the buggy again.

As they drove away, she felt shock and disbelief. She couldn't believe she was leaving after all.

Though she knew it was the right thing to do, the future ahead of her, a future without her mamm and siblings and church, felt strange and terrifying.

As they got close to their house, she asked Danny to stop. Getting out, she went over to the bushes and threw up. It wasn't morning sickness. For the next few minutes, she kept throwing up while Danny held her hair away from her face. Finally, she had nothing left and sat on the grass and cried.

Danny came over and held her tightly in his arms. She cried until she had no tears left. She sat there in his arms and hiccupped. Danny was silent, content to just sit with her.

They heard leaves crunching under someone's feet as a person came toward them from the woods. Priscilla stood up and fixed her skirts, and she pushed her hair from her eyes.

Danny took her hand and pushed her hair back from her face and kissed her forehead though curls were plastered against her face like she had just run a marathon. Danny led her to the buggy. Then they heard Miriam's voice calling out to them.

She came up and hugged Priscilla, who stayed stiff in her arms. Then she looked at them both.

"I am so very sorry. I couldn't say anything back there, but I have six girls at my house on Saturday nights, and some during the week to help with housework. If I stood up with you, those girls wouldn't be allowed at my house." She bit her lip. "I am so sorry."

Priscilla nodded.

Danny hugged her. "I know why you didn't stand with us. Don't worry about it. Just know when you decide to leave, you have us."

Miriam shrugged. "I believe God may call us to another community to help. We will help you move from the dawdy house. I will be in touch."

She eyed Danny. They both knew Paul would want to talk about Annie and what could be done. Then Miriam touched Priscilla's long hair. "You spoke truth today. God has done much in your life."

Priscilla trembled. "I was so scared, and some of that was said in anger. And that is not good."

Miriam shrugged.

"It was the truth and needed to be said." She smiled. "Stan will love that you got kicked out."

Danny rolled his eyes. "He was surprised I lasted this long."

"You know his English parents?" asked Priscilla.

Miriam nodded. "Pam is one of my closest friends, even more than my Amish friends. She is truly a woman of God."

Priscilla couldn't agree more. She gave her a hug, this time not stiffly.

"I will see you later." She looked at Danny like she wanted to say more, but with Priscilla there, Danny knew she couldn't. It wouldn't be safe for anyone, especially Annie.

There was something more to that story. More personal and deeper.

Chapter Twenty

"You had an apartment picked out?" Priscilla asked. They were sitting at the table that afternoon, talking about their future plans.

"I have some ideas. I had a gut feeling we would leave soon," he told her.

"I felt the same thing."

"Why didn't you tell me?" Danny asked, not upset, more concerned she had hid this from him.

She shrugged. "I don't know. I was afraid to voice the feelings of leaving. I was afraid God would be mad at me for speaking them out loud."

He nodded, understanding very well what she thought. "So, you want to go look at them with me tomorrow?"

They wouldn't be allowed to stay at the dawdy house much longer, that was for sure, because of the shunning they would get from the other Amish. Even seeing Paul and Miriam after it happened could get that couple shunned. She was so close to having the baby and this happened. She wasn't sure if she was relieved it happened now or after the baby came. Her mamm wouldn't be there for any of the baby experiences.

She nodded. "Sure."

She kinda wanted to look at new places. This new place would be Danny and hers together. One they wanted. At times, the dawdy house felt it didn't belong to them because at the time they didn't want to be married. Now so much had changed.

A few hours later, someone knocked at their door. She looked up from where she was almost in Danny's lap.

"I don't wanna move," she muttered.

He kissed her forehead. "Well, I will get it and you stay here."

"All right."

He laughed and dug his face into her neck. Then he gently moved her off his lap. He went to the door in his jeans and t-shirt. She wasn't surprised that he didn't care who saw his clothing. They had already been shunned, though not formally yet, so it didn't matter.

She stayed on the couch but when she heard an Amish accent talking at the door, she stood up. She moved closer to the kitchen but stayed out of sight. She saw several black hats. The men wouldn't all fit inside their small house. She saw her datt among them. Her heart beat a mile a minute as she saw him standing there with the men. It wouldn't end well because she knew Danny wouldn't back down. He wasn't wrong.

"We need to talk to you, Danny," the bishop said. She recognized his voice.

Danny looked behind him at her. He frowned. "All right. It will be a tight fit but you are all welcome to come in."

He backed up and invited them in.

They all found a seat and Danny leaned against the wall. Despite having no place to sit, he felt too tense to sit. After asking if they needed anything to eat or drink, Priscilla went to the bedroom. Since their wives weren't there this time, she wasn't comfortable staying, though she knew Danny wanted her too. She could hear everything from the bedroom. She sat down and started on her knitting, wanting something to do with her hands.

"We want to know why you want to leave?" Joseph, one of the deacons, started out. He was a thin man with a long beard. "Well, besides to wear worldly clothes. Do you like that?"

"Actually, I don't mind these clothes," Danny said in a calm voice. After all that had happened, he felt a peace come over him. It must be God. "Where in the Bible does it say my clothes are wrong? And where does it say we have to wear our hats this size. Where does the Bible say this?"

Joseph's hands nearly crushed his hat. "It's tradition. We have always done these things this way. If we can't follow man's rules, how will we follow God's laws?"

"I agree with that, in a way," Danny said. "We need to have convictions. It is where God leads our hearts. But, don't you see, if our hearts are near to God, we will want to serve Him the way He calls. Those man-made rules are not necessary." He got his Bible from where it sat on the side table. "See where it says here about rules and grace…"

"Your Bible is in English," said the bishop. "It needs to be in German."

"You read and speak English in your homes, and also Pennsylvania Dutch. Do you even know all of the German language?" Danny asked simply.

"That doesn't matter. Reading the Bible in German is

the way we have always done it." Joseph spoke firmly, as if that were the end of the matter.

Danny ran a hand through his hair. He wanted to pull it out. He might have, if he hadn't been raised in this way of thinking. He knew how they got to their way of thinking. And it was wrong. "So you want me to stay in the community, but I have to dress and grow a beard like everyone else?"

"Yes, of course," the bishop said.

He gave a humorless laugh. "And what will you do about protecting Priscilla?"

The men all looked away. They knew what had happened was wrong. He saw it in their eyes, except the bishop's. He wished Paul was here but knew they didn't allow him in meetings like this where shunnings happened since Paul was so against shunnings. It hurt the people so much. Paul just didn't mind the rules. Danny did.

"Staying will only happen if my wife is protected, and what happened today was not protection. And what of our child? Will he or she also have to deal with this spiritual abuse?"

"James follows the rules now and repented from his sins he did with others," the bishop told him. "You need to follow the rules more often, and this bad stuff won't happen."

Danny gritted his teeth.

"So as long as a person has a beard and an Amish haircut, speaks German, they will fit in. They can also hurt others and hate others and still be accepted because they look and dress just right?" He shook his head. "Don't you see how wrong that is?"

None of them would meet his gaze.

Finally, Joseph spoke up. "No one likes what happened to Priscilla. But it did happen. Are you going to be bitter at him for the rest of your life? Unforgiveness is a sin."

"Not bitter." He ran a hand over his jaw where he was supposed to have a beard. "But having boundaries is not wrong. James is an abuser, and he should never be trusted again. Letting the man eat at your table while he hurts others so badly, yet refusing to eat with me because I won't grow a beard, how is that right? Am I sinning for not growing one? Is he sinning by hurting others? What would God say about that?"

Joseph threw up his hands. "Do we do nothing right by your standards?"

No. Danny thought. But held back. He didn't think this meeting would go any better than the others. He just wanted to go to bed and hold his wife all night. But he had to deal with this first.

"There are things I love about Amish ways. I love their animals. I love the way the community is so close-knit. Priscilla has shown me that. It has helped me see the Amish differently. But I can't live by these man-made rules any longer. I want to be able to touch my wife in public without being gossipped about. She is my wife. Where in the Bible does it say it's wrong to hold your wife's hand in public?"

"Why are you always wanting to go back to the Bible? This is the way we do things." This time, Priscilla's father spoke. "How old are you anyway to question the Bible?"

Danny disliked Priscilla's father speaking even more than his own father. That man had ruined Priscilla's life, and he would answer one day for it.

"Because the Bible is what we should base everything

on. If we didn't have the Bible, God's words, then what do we have to go on? We have man's rules to go on, and that is just like the world's condition. It will crumble, and that is why so many young adults leave."

"But they come back," Joseph said.

"Only because you tell them they will go to hell if they don't stay Amish and follow rules." He stood up, feeling trapped by all these men in his living room. "God says the sins are as far from the north and from the south; that is how much He forget our sin. Can't we do that for a brother or sister and not alway think they will go to hell?"

"If we allow rules to be broken, then all of them will be broken. We can stop this to carry on these lies to the young generation," the bishop said.

He wanted to cry out the lies that were behind the door of this church. This religion. But he saw it would do no good. They would have to see it for themselves. And he wasn't the one to show it to them. He looked at his bedroom door, knowing Priscilla could hear every word. He hated that. He wanted to protect her from more hurt.

Joseph stood as well.

"I can see we are getting nowhere here." He patted Danny on the shoulder. "We will be back to talk to you again, though you have been put in the band and will be shunned, since you won't repent from your ways."

Danny nodded and didn't say anything as the men walked out. He heard Priscilla come up, beside him. He took her hand, and she squeezed his even in front of the men.

They followed the men out. At the door, surprisingly, Priscilla called out to her datt to wait.

Priscilla's datt turned around, and she ran to him the

way she'd wanted to as a child, but never had. Tears stung her eyes.

He took her hands in his and held them tightly. Then he put his hands on her shoulders and looked at her, tears in his own eyes. "Please daughter, come back to us. You don't have to follow him."

Tears ran down her face. "I am not leaving because of him. I am leaving because of what they did to me. But I still want to see you. Please say I can see you and the family."

He looked so sorrowful.

"I want to. Cutting you off is worse than cutting off my arm. But I can't have you come when you are sinning and still with him. You will need to repent and shun him as well." He paused, almost waiting for her to answer. "I love you, Priscilla."

She cried harder. She gave him one last hug, and then he patted her head and got in his buggy and rode away.

> She felt Danny's arms come around her as she nearly hit the ground from sobs. Her heart was breaking, and her world coming down, though she knew this world no longer belonged to her.

~

Keeping busy helped with not thinking of leaving her family, probably forever, and the only way of life she had known. The Yoders had come to help pack.

Priscilla had stopped Miriam at the door. "Are sure you won't get shunned for this?"

"My man can talk himself out of anything." She chuckled.

Just then, Stan passed them and winked at his wife. "I sure can, and don't forget it."

Priscilla laughed. It was just so wonderful to have friends like this. Of course, Danny's parents were there, and Zack and a couple other guys. She loved the help, though they didn't have a lot in the house that they owned.

A few hours later, using trucks and trailers, they were on their way to their new home. For a while, at least. The apartment was in a nice neighborhood. A safe and good neighborhood, Danny had told her.

She watched as Danny, his friends, some church people, and Paul and Miriam helped bring in boxes. She brought in a few things but with being so heavy with a baby, she couldn't carry much. As she watched the boxes being brought in, it was like she left a part of herself with them. A part of her life she didn't want to be opened again. After everything was in the apartment and put in places they wanted, Zack left to get pizza.

Eventually, they walked their friends to the door and watched Zack drive Danny's family home. Pam and Stan left in their buggy. Once everyone was out of sight, Danny took her in his arms, and she leaned into him.

When she was about to go in he picked her up. She made a soft cry. "Baby, I am too big for you to do this. My belly."

He snuggled her. "Am I hurting you?"

She moved closer to him.

"No," she said softly.

He carried her into the house and then sat on the sofa, her in his lap. "Well, we are home now. I carried my bride across the threshold."

"What do you mean?" she asked.

He explained it. She looked thoughtful. "There are a lot of things I will have to learn, aren't there?"

He shrugged. "I will be here with you through it."

"What do you want me to know first, Danny boy?"

He smiled and then laughed.

She looked at him with narrowed eyes. "What is it?"

"Well, there is one thing, and it will save a bit of money."

She looked confused.

"You seem to leave the lights on a lot," he said lightly. He didn't seem upset. "Like you do it all the time, and our light bill has gone way up."

Her mouth dropped open. "I didn't know lights cost money."

"That isn't why your family didn't use the electricity?"

She shook her head.

"No, Datt said it was too worldly. That is another reason he didn't like you." She paused. "My mamm didn't do the bills like most Amish households, so I never learned much about doing those things. Since being married you have taken care of the bills. I should have done more to help you."

"Honey, it's fine. I'm just telling you now because we are moving. It never really bothered me before either. I thought it was cute because you like light."

She snuggled into his neck and ran a hand over his hair. "Well, I kinda like dark nights with you."

He moved his head to move closer to her. "There is that positive thinking. So maybe the more conservative Amish have the right idea."

She laughed so hard at that. He joined in.

He picked her up again and carried her into their bedroom. And just as she asked, he did hold her all night.

She realized again that God had blessed her with such a wonderful man.

Danny watched Priscilla sleep the next morning. He thought of all he and she had given up. Though she had agreed to it, it was so hard to watch.

At the end of the month, he would be a police officer. Something he hadn't told her yet. How much longer could he keep that from her?

He ran a finger down her cheek. She was so soft and beautiful. He loved everything about her. He couldn't wait till she was fully his.

Already she had given so much of herself to him. She trusted him, and every time he saw that love and trust enter her eyes, he wanted to come clean about everything.

His past, his upcoming career, and his deepest thoughts and dreams.

But then he visualized her leaving his life—ging back to the Amish, or living a single life without him. Or worse, she would stay, because she didn't believe in divorce. And they would live miserable lives together.

He would lose her joy.

Her laugh.

And, again, it would be his fault. He rested his hand against Priscilla's rounded belly. He felt the baby kick and then kick again. He smiled. He never got tired of feeling the baby move. Was the baby telling him he needed to tell his or her mama the truth? Probably.

Christy, the midwife, said Priscilla had about a month left. But he thought she might go into labor sooner. So they had about a month before their world changed again.

He needed to tell her about his career goals before then. He kissed her forehead, and then kissed her stomach where the baby had kicked him.

"Love you both," he whispered.

He got up and started getting ready for the day.

Soon his job would change, and she wouldn't know about it. Guilt ate at his heart like a dog chewing on a bone.

The guilt was eating his heart away a little at a time.

Chapter Twenty-One

Danny loved driving without having to hide it and, even better, he loved driving with Priscilla beside him. She would often take his hand while driving. He loved holding her small hand in his. When she had found out that he could drive when he drove home the other night, she hadn't seemed that surprised. She had just winked at him and told him he looked good in a jeep with music playing loudly.

Probably because he'd worn English clothes most of their marriage, hadn't grown a beard, and just not acting Amish in general.

So much had happened that him driving was just another thing, and she really didn't care.

Getting out of the car, he grabbed the stuff he had bought for her. Setting it up was almost as fun as buying it for her. Now to go get his bride.

He walked in the house, and found Priscilla in the bedroom. She looked up from putting away clothes. "Oh, you're home early, Danny boy."

She looked away, frustrated.

He nodded, concerned about her response. "What's wrong, love?"

She forced a smile. "Nothing. Since you are home early, we should do something."

Deciding not to press her right now, he said, "I have something planned."

He walked to her and kissed her. Then he took her hand. "I have a surprise for you, dear."

Her eyes widened and she gave a small smile as she followed him. "What is it?"

He chuckled. "Just wait and see."

She smiled. "Well, I reckon I have too."

"Yup." He led her to the front door and told her to close her eyes, which she did right away. He was taken back again on how much she trusted him now. He would never take that for granted.

Closing her eyes, she let Danny lead her outside. She would always go with him. Especially if he kissed her again. Oh, those kisses he gave melted her heart. It made her forget her troubles. The wind was light and the air smelled of fall. She heard him opening the car door.

He let go of her hand and then held her shoulders. "You can open your eyes."

She did, and what she saw made her eyes water. He was so sweet. How was she blessed with such a man? On the passenger seat lay a soft, pink blanket, a book, a box of chocolates, cute glitter sunglasses, flip flops, and a little stuffed animal. She leaned into his arms. "Danny, you really bought all this for me?"

"Yes. I did," he said softly. "It's my way to show I love you."

"I don't know what to say." She was still in awe of this.

"Your face says it all." He stood a few minutes, giving

her time to process. "Do you wanna go on a drive with me?"

She nodded.

"I love you so much." Hugging him, she kissed his cheek. "I will go anywhere with you."

Then she moved some of the things to the back seat and hopped in.

He shut her door and walked around to the other side. He started the car.

She looked through all the stuff, and even put on the flip flops. They matched her peach maxi dress. Putting on the sunglasses, she sat back and looked at him. "So, what do you think?"

He winked at her. "You look like a hot mama."

She smiled. "What does that mean?"

He pulled out of the drive. "It means you look pretty. Hot mama can mean you look a bit wild, but you're really not."

She grinned and winked at him, "Well, I am wild about you. So, I guess I can be."

"What's not to be wild about. I am just the best."

Despite her big belly, she leaned over and kissed him again on the cheek. "Yes. You are."

He laughed. "You are going to make me drive off the road."

She took his hand. "No, you won't. I trust you."

She leaned back as he turned up the country music. He had picked some great love songs to play. How beautiful their love story was turning out to be.

He parked in front of the Beehive restaurant set along the Ohio river. She hadn't been there yet. He opened the door and took her hand. "Let's have a magical night."

"It already is." She winked at him.

They walked into the restaurant. She held his arm. It felt so right being here with him. The waiter led them to a porch overlooking the river. There were two trees beside the porch and one flanking by the river bank.

They sat at the table, across from each other.

"This is so beautiful. I can't believe you planned this." She took his hand as he reached for her.

"Almost as beautiful as you."

She blushed. "You're too sweet. Have you ever been here before?"

"On a date no," he said. "But Mom brought me and Ashley here a couple times growing up."

She leaned back but still held his hand. "I never asked you before, but have you ever courted anyone but me before?"

"I am glad you asked." He paused. "No. I haven't. It's not because I haven't wanted to get married. I did. I just wanted to do my job more. And I had to decide what to do about being Amish."

She wanted to ask why he had joined when he knew he would leave, but she didn't want to pry. "I guess I am a bit different. I didn't want to get married for a while. I really wanted to do something else…"

"Do you mean that you'd like to be a nurse, love?"

She nodded, slightly. She wasn't ready to talk in depth about that right now. Instead, she looked at the menu. "What do you recommend here?"

Danny gave her hand a squeeze and then picked up the menu like her avoiding the question was no big deal.

She was glad he wasn't bothered by her not answering. Maybe one day they could talk more about it.

"I like their hamburgers. They are good," he said.

She looked over her menu. Hamburgers sounded good. She hadn't eaten much lunch today.

The waiter came and took their orders. When he left, they talked about light topics.

Then Danny asked, "Can I ask what was bothering you today?"

She took a sip of her sweet tea. "I am having a hard time adjusting to apartment life. The dawdy house I knew I would live in, but the apartment is not what I planned."

"I am sorry. Maybe we can find a house to rent," he suggested.

She shook her head. "No, I will be fine. I am also struggling with not seeing my family. I really want a relationship with my mamm. I wasn't ready to be cut off from them, but then again, I probably wouldn't ever be ready."

"I am so sorry about that. I wanted to wait till the baby was born to leave. But you weren't safe anymore…"

"I know this. And I feel we had to leave too. But to leave everyone at once is so hard. It's nice talking to the Yoders, but they aren't family."

"I understand that." He gave her a sympathetic look. "My family is everything to me, and you are the best part of it. Then our baby."

She smiled. Their food came and the topic changed again. The evening remained pleasant.

A dream date.

Like Danny said, it was magical.

～

Priscilla didn't want to go shopping, but she had to get food and some things for the baby. She wore a long maxi dress that was big enough to fit two of her. She liked how the dress fit on her and still felt modest. She tried to not think of what the bishop would think of her wearing it.

God's opinion is what mattered, she reminded herself.

Pam had agreed to take her shopping while she was running errands. Priscilla walked down the aisle to get spices Danny wanted, and that's when she saw the bishop's wife. Ruth Ann Miller was a plump woman with graying hair. She hadn't wanted to be a bishop's wife and had actually mourned her husband going into that position, so she didn't do much to help the community. She got worse after taking Danny in, many said. She made it clear she hadn't wanted him.

Priscilla wasn't sure if she should talk to her or not.

The decision was taken from her when Ruth Ann walked up to her. She looked her up and down, and then stared at her middle as if the baby might pop out right in the middle of the store.

"I can see you are dressing like the world," Ruth Ann stated.

Priscilla shrugged. "I dress how I feel the Lord and my husband want me too."

Ruth Ann snorted at that. "Your husband. How can you respect him when he is sinning by taking you from the community?"

Priscilla's eyes narrowed. But then felt a check in her spirit, only a few months earlier she had felt the same way. "Danny serves the Lord, and I freely left with him."

"That is the lie he has told you," she replied.

"Can I ask you something?" Priscilla asked.

Ruth Ann shrugged.

"You raised Danny from a boy. Did you ever love him?"

She looked down.

"When he came to me, he was an angry little boy. He never liked how we raised him." She met Priscilla's eyes. "Our children don't need love. They need structure and discipline."

Priscilla blinked. She knew that was what so many believed, but it wasn't true. She placed her hands on her stomach. Her child would know love.

"I agree they need structure, which Danny didn't get. His whole world was one chaos to another until he became an adult. But you are missing so much. My child will know love and yes, discipline. But unconditional love is the greatest of those things."

She shook her head. "You think you know so much. Wait till life hits you, and you can't breathe. When your husband becomes a bishop, and you hate it, and then he takes in an angry boy."

"Because he wasn't wanted, and he knew it. A child knows when they are being controlled and not loved. And Danny wasn't loved at all. You should have let him live with the Taylors."

"We couldn't," Ruth Ann said angrily, her face red.

"Why? They loved him unconditionally."

Ruth Ann backed up. "He was born Amish so he had to stay Amish. It was in his blood."

Priscilla shook her head. "You're wrong. God was in control of his life and wanted him in His family. Especially since he was rejected by his own people."

She leaned against the cart, feeling suddenly drained.

"You will see after he grows tired of you and your way of life, that I am right. He is a runner, and he will just run from you."

Priscilla shook her head. "No, he won't. I know he won't."

She started trembling, and Ruth Ann noticed it. She looked even more smug.

"We have been through a lot of crap, as Danny would put it. And we made it through. So no, he won't leave, because he loves me and is loyal. He has shown me more love in the last few months than my whole life. He loves me like God loves everyone."

Her lips went into a thin line and she shook her head. "I can see what Danny has done to you and your head."

Just then Priscilla felt someone by her side and knew it was Pam.

"So what, now she comes to your rescue like she did to Danny all the time?" Ruth Ann stared at Pam.

"No, I am just protecting my child, like I always have done. And Priscilla is my child too now. You can't hurt her with words any longer. Or actions."

Ruth Ann actually glared at Pam. "I am done with this conversation anyway."

With that, she walked away.

Priscilla was out of breath. "Can we go now?"

Pam nodded. And they left the empty cart there and just walked out. In the front seat, Priscilla turned on the heated seat and just focused on breathing. After a few minutes she sighed.

"How was Danny raised by her? And I know the bishop is worse. Danny is such a gentle man."

"Danny knows what they both don't. He knows God's grace. They don't see grace anywhere in life. And we all need it. But they only see justice and judgment. It can be generational sin or just how they are taught their whole lives."

Priscilla bit her lip. "I am glad we don't have to live

like that anymore. I am so tired of judgment. Especially judgment for doing nothing wrong."

Pam nodded. "Do you want to get something to eat or go home?"

Priscilla looked at her phone. Danny would be home soon. She wanted to talk with him. She loved his wisdom. Though she knew some of what happened today would hurt him. Despite not liking where he came from, he did care for the people who gave him a room and food for six years.

"I just wanna go home."

Pam nodded and started the car. She turned on some music. As always, it calmed Priscilla. Sometimes she wasn't into talking, and Pam was wise enough to remain silent when she needed it.

Danny walked inside to a home smelling of amazing bread. Oh, his wife was such a good cook. He didn't see her in the kitchen, but he spotted the cinnamon rolls and took a bite of one. Then she walked into the kitchen. She crossed her arms over her belly nad smirked at him.

"What do you have here? I hope your wife knows you go into houses and just eat food before supper."

He straightened and looked at her with such adoration. He decided to play along. "Oh, she does and since I am so cute, she lets me."

Priscilla burst out laughing. "Well, you are a bit prideful, mister."

"Well, my wise wife is the one that tells me these things so they must be true." He winked at her.

She cringed at the word wise. "Well, then get over here and see how much she likes you."

It was all he needed for him to take her in his arms. She ran her hands up his neck and into his hair. It didn't take long for him to respond and kiss her. She tasted of sugar and cinnamon. And her kiss was almost as hungry as his. She had become so alive in their marriage. He hated hiding his upcoming job from her. As he ran his hands through her hair, he felt pure bliss.

By the time they came up for air, they were both breathless. She pulled him for another kiss. Then she gave him a sassy look.

"You do that really well, Danny boy."

"I was thinking the same thing about you. About how blessed I am to have you in my life." He walked with her in his arms to the sofa. They had learned how to do that well now. He sat her in his lap. He could tell something was up. "How was your day?"

She snuggled into his chest. "It wasn't the greatest."

She told him about seeing his Amish mamm.

He was glad she couldn't see his face and see his anger and hurt: his anger at his parents, at the bishop especially, and even at James.

Then he sat back and let out a breath.

She sat up and looked at him. "I am sorry. Maybe I shouldn't have asked her all that. I just wanted answers."

"I am not surprised," he said. "That is how they have always been. I felt like a servant and never a part of their family. At first, I even ate at a different table than the family. Like a shunned person. But then we moved, and I ate with them again. Though it wasn't much better, at least I didn't feel so alone all the time."

She touched his arm. "I am so sorry you were treated that way. It's a terrible way to treat someone, especially a child."

Danny agreed.

"But I moved on from it and wanted to do better." He touched her stomach. "Our child will grow up different."

She nodded. "Just because the bishop treated you that way doesn't mean all Amish do that."

"I am working on believing that. It's not easy after so long of seeing the wrong they do. I do struggle to see the good in the mess of the wrong."

"We all do that from time to time. But I hope I can teach our child the good that came from our past too."

He kissed her forehead. "You are so good for me, my love."

She smiled at him.

"Someone has to keep you on track." She kissed his cheek. "I love you."

He chuckled. Then he thought of how he needed to tell her about his career. How would she react? He was so afraid she wouldn't understand. Would she go back to her parents? She had run once, and her family was still the closest people to her. Fear ate at him.

She played with his hair. "Hey, honey, what is wrong? You look like you ate sour pickles."

He looked at her and tried to hide what he was feeling. "I must be just hungry, that is all. It was a long day at work."

She didn't look convinced but got up and set supper on the table.

Chapter Twenty-Two

A few days later, Priscilla made a big salad and some fancy bread she had wanted to try. She was getting used to making lighter meals. Danny liked them. And in her fancy kitchen, as she called the apartment kitchen, tasks were easier to do. Though she really enjoyed cooking with Danny more than cooking alone. He would flirt and play with her. And she would forget she was pregnant. She would even try to flirt back, though she was terrible at it.

Tonight, Danny stopped by the door of the kitchen like he normally did, and waited for her to come hug him. Sometimes he would go find her if she wasn't in the kitchen.

She started towards him, ready for her hug, but then stopped. Her eyes went wide as she looked at his hair.

It was cut short. A little longer on the top, but all his curls were gone. How could he cut his hair without telling her? She knew it might be silly, but it stung her heart.

"What is this?" She finally made the question out.

He smiled, a little reserved. "I got my hair cut. My job required it."

"Oh," was all she said.

He hugged her, but she didn't hug him back. "What is wrong, love?"

"Nothing," she said.

"Honey, I know something is wrong." He looked down at her. "Do you not like my haircut?"

She shrugged.

"It's fine." She tried to pull away. "Now let's eat."

He let her go. He never kept holding her when she tried to pull away, even gently.

She set everything on the table and then sat down. She tried to hold her emotions in. But this hurt badly. When he sat across from her, she didn't meet his gaze. She still held out her hands so he could pray.

He took her hands. "Honey, I won't be able to eat anything till I know what is wrong."

She looked at him and saw pain in his eyes. Was she hurting him by doing this? She didn't want to do that.

"I am sorry." She stood and crossed her arms around her rounded belly. "I just wasn't told you were doing this, and I know you don't have to tell me. But you tell me everything under the sun, and you keep this a secret."

She looked down. "Maybe I am being selfish but I like your hair and…"

She couldn't tell him she loved to run her hand through his curls while he slept or when he laid in her lap. She loved how it felt between her fingers. It was silly. Was she naughty for playing with his hair? She didn't want to be.

Danny walked up to her.

"I am sorry. I honestly didn't think you would care that much. That was wrong of me. I would care too if you cut your beautiful hair." He sighed. "Sometimes it's hard to remember to tell you everything, but I am trying. Will you forgive me?"

"Of course." She met his gaze. "I am probably overthinking it."

"No, you are right. I should have talked it over with you." He put his hands on her shoulders. "And anytime you want to play with my hair, you can."

Her eyes widened with surprise. "That would be naughty of me."

He leaned close. "No. It would be a bride having fun with her husband. I like it when you do it."

She softened under his gaze. "Really?"

He nodded. "You better believe it. You are not doing anything wrong."

She put her head on his chest, and they pulled each other close. "I am working on getting the bishop's lies out of my head."

She felt him nod. "I know that feeling well. It will take time."

She had to believe that. But how long would it take?

~

Danny looked in the mirror, making sure his dress blues were perfect. He should be happy today. He had been training for years with Stan and with Zack in the last couple of months. He had been in college the last months to do it. Now the day had come: he was becoming a police officer.

And Priscilla wasn't here.

It wasn't right. She should be here. But he still hadn't

told her he was becoming a cop. He had excuses and now they'd left the Amish, and telling her still felt too hard.

Would she go back to that way of life? Was he the only reason she had left? Maybe not, but he was so afraid she would leave him.

And she wouldn't trust him anymore.

Not many people had wanted him growing up and now, if he lost her, he would lose everything. He knew it was him, why they left, and losing her would be the worst.

Straightening his dress jacket, he walked out to the crowd of people in the hall. It would start soon. He had watched so many people become cops, and now it was his turn. The last graduation had been when Zack had become an officer. Now it was his turn. He saw his parents in the crowd, and his sister. But no wife. Priscilla should be here.

Guilt ate at him.

Ashley came up and gave him a big hug.

"Hey, Danny, where is Priscilla?" she asked innocently enough. She looked around him. "I wanted to see what she was wearing."

His sister, the fashion queen.

Even now she was dressed in a formal long, blue dress, with black high heels, and her hair scooped up high on her head. Her neck and ears shone with bright jewelry that glittered in the bright lights of the room.

The hole in his chest got bigger.

"She wasn't feeling well and couldn't make it," he said simply.

It wasn't a lie. She had gotten a slight cold after leaving the Amish, probably due to stress. She had been through so much. He should be home taking care of her, but he was here, lying to his family.

He was a dirtbag. His stomach churned.

Ashley frowned. "Well, that is rough. It's probably stress, poor thing."

She smiled at her parents, who had just walked up, and asked for a picture to remember the day.

Danny smiled and went through the motions. He felt like the biggest liar in the room. It should have been the happiest day of his life, but it wasn't. He missed Priscilla with him. She would hang on his arm and probably hate the crowd but she would try to enjoy the event. She always tried for him. He loved that about her. Oh, how he wanted her here.

He took pictures with his parents and friends to remember this day. One that would change his life forever.

Then the ceremony started, and when he was called on stage, everyone clapped. He felt such pride. This was a dream come true. He would be a good officer. As he looked over the people, he saw his family and friends, so happy for him. The tears in his mom and sister's eyes. The pride on his dad's face. It was priceless.

A day he would never forget, and the most important person to him was missing. She should be here.

On stage, he repeated the words he had memorized. "I, Daniel Taylor, do solemnly swear that I will support the Constitution of the United States of America and the Constitution of this Commonwealth, and be faithful and true to the Commonwealth of Kentucky, and that I will faithfully execute, to the best of my ability, the office of police officer for the people of Kentucky. I serve the City of Maysville, Kentucky."

As he said the words, he thought of what a liar he was at home. He was wrong for hiding this. He wasn't being honest with the best person in his life.

He walked off stage as a police officer of Kentucky, and again, his family hugged him.

He had done it.

He was finally an officer. Despite his conflicted feelings, it was a great day. One that he had dreamed of since ten years old.

But what would happen when Priscilla found out?

Chapter Twenty-Three

Priscilla sighed. She was really going to do this. She was going with Danny to his church again.

She had gotten up Sunday morning and readied for the day. But instead of doing up her hair, she let it down. Now she wished she owned mousse, like what Ashley wore in her hair, but even if she did, she didn't know how to use it. So, she brushed her hair and wet it down a little to keep the curls under some control. She even parted it to the side. She wasn't sure if that was how it was supposed to be done, but to her, it looked good. She dressed in a long, blue maxi dress. It was the only thing conformable with as big as she was now. She couldn't believe how relaxed she felt in forbidden English clothes.

Priscilla went to the kitchen to get breakfast. She started the coffee machine.

He walked closer to her. "Oh, you look so beautiful. I don't know what to say."

He put a hand on her shoulder, touching her hair. It was so silky and soft in his hands. He could get used to this.

"Thanks." She dipped her eyes. "I have something to tell you."

He raised an eyebrow. "Is this why you let your hair down for me?"

She shrugged and blushed. "I knew you would like it." She touched his cheek.

He was getting distracted by her touch. It was like all his thoughts went out of his mind. He groaned.

She smiled, enjoying the effect she had on him. "I am very excited to try church, this time without feeling pulled between both worlds."

He pulled her into his arms for a tight hug. His face going into her hair. The guilt that claimed him was too big. She was doing what was hard for her because she loved him. And he was here being a liar and not telling her about his achievement. He was a rookie now. There was no hiding it from the public, but his own wife didn't know. As he held her, tears came to his eyes. He couldn't do this any longer.

He pulled away and let her see him.

"What is it, Danny boy?" Her breath caught. She wanted to comfort him and make it all better. What was wrong?

He should tell her. He imagined how she might stiffen in his arms, and how her eyes would be filled with pain at his lies. Then he saw her walking out the door and taking his whole heart with her. He couldn't handle that.

"I am just so thankful you are going with me," he finally told her.

She eyed him, her eyes showing disbelief. But then she smiled. "I am happy to go."

She kissed his cheek.

He couldn't resist any more, and he ran his fingers through her hair. It felt wonderful between his fingers. She must have liked it because she turned into putty in his arms. She even dipped her head a little and moaned in pleasure. He didn't kiss her, but he didn't need to because this connection was beyond a kiss. It was like their souls were one. He was giving to her, and she was giving to him.

He felt a bond like no other with her.

His own heart would break when he found the courage to tell her he was a cop.

As she finished getting ready for church, she remembered how wonderful it felt to have Danny's hands in her hair. It was pure bliss. She had never felt so connected to someone before.

She straightened her maxi dress and then fixed her hair again.

As she rode to the church, she knew she had to bring up to Danny about what she felt about the church and some of her fears. She bit her nail. Ashley wanted to paint them soon. But she wasn't sure about it. It would be toxic for the baby. She touched her stomach. She wouldn't want to do that.

"Do you think I will hear more of the service? Last time, I only really heard the music."

Danny took her hand. "It depends. Just don't put a lot of pressure on yourself. I used to pray a lot if I struggled with listening. Can we pray and listen to music along the way and see if that helps you?"

She squished his hand. "I don't mind."

He prayed out loud and then the music played the rest of the way. It did relax her. By the time she walked in the church, she was pretty excited. And she didn't feel the shame with her hair showing in a church building. God was already releasing her from the lies, even one this small. It gave her hope.

Priscilla laughed at something Ashley typed.

Leaning against Danny, she snapped a selfie and sent it to his sister.

"Hey, don't tell my sis all our secrets," Danny teased her, though he didn't really care.

"She likes to know things." Priscilla sighed.

She looked to see Ashley's reply.

Why don't you get closer, cause you don't look close enough.

Priscilla laughed so hard.

Danny glanced at it and read it. "Well, I agree with her. Come here, love."

He took her and moved her to his lap.

She giggled. "Danny, please."

She wasn't really offended.

He snapped another picture and sent it with the message *this is much better, sis.*

Then he took Priscilla's in his hands.

"You don't tell her everything, right?" He kissed her neck. "Like how much I like kissing you."

He kissed her again.

She tingled under his touch.

"I tell her that..." she whispered.

He laughed when she couldn't continue.

Priscilla heard the phone ding. She let Danny kiss her a few more times, then he picked up the phone and held it so they could read it together.

Much better. The three of you look great together. Talk later, girl. Love you.

Danny sat back. "Did you hear the sermon this time?"

She turned serious, biting her lip.

"A little bit of it," she shook her head. "But not most of it. I wonder when I will be able to."

"Well, it took my mom six years to hear a sermon," Danny said.

Her mouth dropped open. "Six years. What happened?"

He shrugged. "A lot. She was raised kinda like us."

She frowned. "How sad. I can't imagine that."

He nodded. "You may talk to mom about it one day."

"I'm not sure." She bit her nail. "I'm afraid of what she will say."

Though she had never judged her before. It was still a deep fear.

"You can trust her, my love."

Though why trust his mom when he wasn't being honest with her? He needed to tell her the truth and soon before it was all ruined.

∽

Priscilla walked into the library one peaceful afternoon after her second church attendance. Pam had dropped her off while she was doing errands. Priscilla loved it here. She loved the quiet and peaceful feeling she got from just looking at the books. She got one of her favorites from the shelf and decided to sit back and read. She knew she could at home but sometimes she felt too cooped up. And this was better. She sat in the chair by the window, the sun bathing her.

After about thirty minutes, she got into the book. Then the baby kicked hard, and she put her hand over where the baby kicked. Then she spotted her mother and Annie. Her eyes widened as she met her mother's gaze. She wasn't sure what to do. But she wanted to talk to her so badly. Putting the book down, she got up, though it wasn't as easy now, and walked over to her mamm.

"Hi, Mamm," she said.

"Hi, Priscilla. Are you ready to come back to us?"

The question stung, but she shouldn't be surprised. She just shook her head. "I want you at my birth, Mamm. Like we planned."

"You are still using Christy?"

She nodded. "She is not Amish and decided to keep me on."

She didn't tell her mamm that is why Danny wanted her to go with an English midwife. So she wouldn't be left alone if they left the Amish early, and so that the midwife would not make her feel shame for being pregnant before marriage, something a midwife should not judge.

"Well, I can't be there. But I will if you come back to the community. Do you know how much you have hurt us by leaving?" Mamm said harshly.

Tears came to Priscilla's eyes. She said nothing.

"You know you will go to hell if you don't come back to the Amish."

"That is not true," Priscilla said with passion. "I will go to heaven because I am a child of God."

"Well, I can't be at your birth, and your child will be born into sin. Sin of this world," Mamm bit back. Annie stood next to her.

Priscilla was shocked her mamm would talk to her this

way. This wasn't like her. She stood there, looking at her shoes.

"So, if my child was born Amish, they wouldn't be born in sin?"

She knew what they believed. She had been a bit afraid of it, though she knew it wasn't true.

"Right." Mamm nodded like she knew.

Priscilla stepped back, shaking her head. Blinking back tears. "My child will be born into a loving home, no matter what you say."

"Fine. Anytime you want to come home, you are welcome. Even that husband of yours is, though he will have to grow a beard."

Priscilla crossed her arms. "No way. I like my husband without a beard and in jeans. He has a heart for God. He has a real relationship with Him. And he has shown me more love from God than you or our community ever could. I now know who God is because of my beardless husband and his Christian family."

Mamm glared at her. "Fine. You go the way of the world. They will leave you one day."

"Like my own family has? No, they won't, because they actually love me." Priscilla blinked. "Can I ask you something, Mamm?"

Mamm looked reluctant but she nodded.

"Do you really believe Danny is the father or do you know the truth?" She paused when her mamm's eyes widened. "Do you know I was raped for months?"

She couldn't believe she said that. She looked around making sure no one had heard her admit that.

Mamm's hand went to her mouth. She shook her head, but her eyes showed so much regret and sorrow. She didn't say anything and then just left.

Priscilla's own eyes watered as she watched her mamm leave. She hadn't asked in anger. She just wanted to know the truth. She held her stomach. She was getting too emotional. It wasn't good for the baby. She went to the bathroom and was glad it was a one room where she could be alone and just breathe. She sighed. That had not gone well. She hadn't thought it would, but it still hurt.

She got her phone and texted Pam. Then she sent a message to Ashley telling her what happened. She knew it might take her friend a bit to get back.

A few hours later, Pam dropped her off at home. Priscilla hadn't felt comfortable telling Pam about seeing her mom. And she was thankful Pam didn't push. Instead, Priscilla had a good talk with Ashley about it. But she still felt so drained. She made a simple supper, too tired to make something big. She just wanted to lay down and forget it happened.

Danny had texted he would be a bit late, so she ate without him and then went to the closet. She knew it was strange but she liked to sit in there. It was pretty big and made her feel safe. Amish didn't build closets since they had just plain things. She wished she had one so she could have hid in it before James came over. She held her legs to her chest, as much as her belly would allow. Pulling a blanket over her, she felt like she really needed Danny right now but he was working. She didn't mean to be spoiled but that was probably how she sounded. She wanted her husband there to hold her. To comfort her.

I have you in My hands, she heard a voice say.

Did He really have her in His hands? Then why had she been hurt? Why hadn't He stopped her from being raped? He could have. Her heart hurt at the thought of God watching her be hurt and not doing anything about it.

"Why, God? Why did it have to happen?"

She felt the baby kick her legs, which pressed against her belly. Was it to bring this baby into the world, or was the baby a product of that sin? She remembered what Rebecca Kissling said, "I was a blessing to my mother. We love each other."

Would Priscilla's child love her?

She looked around the closet and felt like God was watching her. Did she believe everything she told her mother today? Or was she still trying to perform and be the perfect wife? Could she trust God with everything? Even her body and her baby?

"God, I don't know what you want from me. I am so tired of trying to be good for You… for Danny. For everyone."

All I want is your heart, My beloved Daughter.

Tears ran down her face. Was she ready to give Him it all? Even those bad months? The terrible memories ran through her head like the movies she had watched with Danny. Was God there when she was hurting?

I cried every time you did, My child. I was there with you. I sent you Danny.

The baby kicked again. And He had sent her baby. She held her stomach with both hands as she wept for the woman she would never be again.

"God…" she cried out, just letting her pain out. He was listening as she let it out. Finally, the tears eased. "Jesus, take it all. My heart. I can't do it on my own anymore. I am tired of performing, of trying to be perfect. Just take my heart and heal it. I give you…"

She stopped. Could she do it? Could she trust Him with what meant the world to her? "I give you Danny and what he means to me. And…"

Again the tears came in anew. They shook her whole body as she wrapped her arms around her belly, holding her baby.

I love you, my beloved daughter. Before I formed you in the womb, I knew the hairs on your head.

Just like He knew the hairs on her baby's head. She felt a peace come over her. She could do this.

"I give You my body." Leaning her head against the wall, she let herself grieve what James took from her. Something she would never get back. But then the tears dried up like a well in the desert. She felt a peace come over her and knew God was holding her in His strong hands. Even stronger than Danny's. She was His daughter.

Pulling the blanket closer she let her eyes close as she thought of how she was God's child, like the baby was hers.

Someone gently shook Priscilla. She blinked and saw Danny kneeling by her. Her eyes felt like sandpaper and were a bit blurry.

He smiled. "You look beautiful, sleepy head."

She rolled her eyes at him. "You are blind."

She lay her head on his shoulder. And he tucked her in, just sitting down there with her. He never pressed her for more. She softly told him what happened with Mamm and then she told him about what God had done for her.

After she was done, he picked her up and carried her to the bed. He sat against the headboard and held her in his lap. He met her eyes. He was silent for a while.

Then he said, "I have no words for what happened. I am glad you see yourself the way God does, and the way I alway have."

She rested her head against his shoulder. "You always saw what I was blinded to. Our child was a gift to us."

He reached down to touch her stomach. "Yes, the babe is."

"I want to know it all. All God has to show me. Will reading the Bible be easier and going to church not feel like a struggle?" she asked with excitement.

He nodded, but looked thoughtful.

"You made a huge step here, and I am so proud of you, love," he ran a hand down her cheek. "though overcoming spiritual abuse is a journey. You will probably still have to fight what the bishop has said in your head. It may take a long time. You've lived your whole life in lies and man-made rules. You have to think differently and know what God wants of you. I believe counseling may help."

Her back went stiff. She wasn't sure she was ready to be judged by a person. That person would look at her and see... Then she stopped herself. She was already thinking everyone was out there to judge her. God wanted her to be fully His and that meant healing.

"We don't have to decide now, love. But it may help one day. I want us to be healthy parents and be the best couple ever." He smiled slyly. "And that means be better at something than kissing." He kissed her forehead. "Though we are pretty good at that."

She blushed.

"That is true." She loved kissing him. "I love you so much, Danny boy."

He held her tight against him. "I love you more."

The baby kicked him as if needing more room, due to how close his parents were. He chuckled but didn't let Priscilla go.

"God, thank you so much for what You did today. You have brought your daughter to You. You brought us together. Thank you for this baby, who is kicking me." The baby kicked him again. "Thank you, Father," he said through a thick voice full of emotion.

"Amen," Priscilla said against his chest, feeling safe in the arms of her man and just as safe in the arms of her Father.

Chapter Twenty-Four

A few days later, Priscilla enjoyed shopping with Pam. It helped her to not think about her family.

She missed them so much. It helped that she loved Danny. She loved thinking about him and wondering when she would see him next. Of course, being married to him helped, but still she felt like a young bride waiting for her man to come to court her. She had gotten used to waking up in his arms. They were always gentle and never grabbing at her. She remembered even that first morning, waking up in his arms and having him watch her as she slept. She felt no fear, but smiled as he gazed at her.

"You are so beautiful, my precious," he had said.

She had just lied there, enjoying his touch and words. They melted her so much. As she looked at the vegetables in the grocery store now, she softly smiled.

"What is that smile for?" Pam smiled. "I don't think vegetables are that interesting."

Priscilla blushed to her roots.

"They aren't. I was thinking of..." she bit her lip, "of Danny."

Pam smiled broadly. "Somehow, I knew that. How is loving my boy and being loved by him?"

Priscilla's eyes softened. "Wonderful. He loves me so much. I actually feel it. Last night, we went to the 606 rodeo in Ewing. It was great. We saw other Amish there, but none from my community. It was just a great time."

"I love that, sweetie. I hear that rodeo is a great one."

"It is." She crossed her arms. She thought "Things aren't perfect, and sometimes I wish he talked to me more about things. I feel like he is hiding something from me. Especially since leaving the community. When we were in the community I didn't feel that as much. Maybe it is just a bad feeling."

Or was it because so many Amish husbands kept things from their wives?

After they had left the Amish, she had that feeling, and she wasn't sure why. He had hidden a cell phone. He had handcuffs that she'd been too afraid to ask about. And then he'd told her he could drive and owned a jeep. What else could he be hiding? Maybe she was wrong. What did she know about men?

Well, she couldn't stand here at the vegetables thinking about it all day. She had stuff to do. After they finished shopping, they headed to Ross's to shop for clothes. She wasn't too sure about English clothes just yet, but she was getting used to some of them. She wore them with just Danny around. He had even ordered some through the mail, and she had loved the styles he picked.

As Pam drove towards Ross while still in the parking lot, Priscilla felt the car jerk and her body swung forward, then ricocheted backward. A car hit them from behind. Glass shattered. She held onto the dash as she put a hand on her stomach. She looked behind her to see the back window had broken.

She felt her belly, looking down at her belly. Was the baby all right? This wasn't good. She should see Christy soon to make sure, or go to a doctor. She looked over at Pam, who looked shaken up but fine.

"Are you all right?" she asked in German, going back to her native language.

Pam nodded and answered back in German. "Yes. What about you?"

Priscilla stared at her. "The accident caused you to speak German?"

Pam looked over at her and smiled. "I will explain later, sweetie. Let me go see the damage and then call someone. I think you should go to the clinic."

Priscilla shook her head.

"No, I will just see Christy today." She looked for her phone and found it in her purse and pulled it out. "I will message her now."

Pam nodded. "Good. Stay in here."

Priscilla nodded. Her heart was still beating a mile a minute. But as she messaged Christy, she started to calm down. She used some of the ideas Ashley had taught her to calm down. Getting overworked wasn't good for the baby. When she was done texting, she got out, needing to stretch her legs. They were still wobbly. She leaned against the car in the large parking lot. It was nearly empty, which was common for the afternoon. There was a beat-up car behind the,m but the driver looked to be all right.

Then she saw a cop car pull up. Had they done something wrong? She got nervous, but then she saw Danny get out of the passenger side of the car. He wore a uniform, right down to his shoes. Shock wracked her body. What was happening? Danny couldn't be a cop. That wasn't his job. He worked on a ranch, not a police station. But when he saw her, his eyes went wide.

He nearly ran over to her. "Are you all right? Were you hurt?"

Her mouth went dry. He was really a cop, and no one had told her. She felt like a fool. How had he lied to her this long? She bent over, almost shaking. What was wrong with her? The shock was too much after the accident.

Pam was by her side then and held her. "Honey, what's wrong?"

Priscilla's eyes came to meet hers. Hard.

"Why didn't you tell me?" The words came out breathless. She couldn't believe he would lie to her. She had never felt so betrayed. "You aren't really a cop, are you?"

She wouldn't believe it.

Pam looked confused. "What do you mean?"

Danny looked so guilty; it showed all over his face. "Priss, I am so sorry. I planned to tell you. I didn't want you to find out this way."

She stood up, feeling stronger. "And how did you plan for me to find out? When you get shot by a bad guy?"

She yelled at him in German, knowing he understood her.

He took off his hat and ran a hand through his hair, messing it up.

"I am so sorry, honey," he said in English.

"Don't," she cried. "Don't call me that. How could you keep this from me? What does this marriage look like to you? A joke! I love you."

The hurt on his face showed all the confirmation she needed to see.

"I did plan to tell you." His face paled the color of a

sheet of paper. His legs set apart. He was going to lose everything; he knew it. "Please. I love our marriage. It is the best thing that has ever happened to me."

"Better than being a cop?" she hissed back.

When he didn't reply right away, she turned her back and walked away from the car, but there weren't many places to go, so she stopped.

"Yes, I love you. I want us to make this marriage work." He walked beside her.

She didn't believe him, he had lied to her too many times. She had been such a fool to let herself love him.

"Well, the life we did have has been broken," she said in defeat.

"No, please," Danny almost begged her.

She shook her head as tears came. Oh, how she had been such a fool. This wasn't happening. Her life wasn't about to fall apart again. She had married a man she hadn't wanted to at first. She had left her only way of life, her family, and now this. She held her stomach. She was so close to having the baby, and now this happened. Her heart was breaking.

Pam came next to her. She seemed to take in the situation well and sent a disappointed look to Danny. "We need to get you out of here, honey. When will Christy come over?"

Priscilla glanced at her phone.

"In two hours," she said softly. She looked at the car. It was smashed in the back and the windshield was broken.

"I can drop you off with my car, Mom," Danny offered. "Or will Dad come to pick you up?"

Priscilla glared at him. She wanted to tell him what he could do with that offer.

"I am having Stan pick us up. He is off soon," Pam said

as she patted his chest. She seemed to have sympathy for him.

Well, Priscilla was out of that for him. How could he lie to her again? When Stan pulled up, Priscilla got in the back and said nothing to Danny.

He stopped her from shutting the door. "I will be home in a few hours, Priscilla. We can talk then, my love."

She glared at him.

"I am glad you remember where you live at least." Her eyes were hard against him. "About talking, I don't know if I can, Daniel."

She used his formal name, knowing he didn't like it, but she wanted to hurt him like he had hurt her. She knew she shouldn't. She was beyond hurt though. She shut the door and put her head in her hands and leaned forward. Pam and Stan stayed silent in front, and she was glad for that. She wasn't up to talking. Not even to them.

When they pulled into the apartment complex, she wanted to go hide at the library or maybe just hide in the closet. But Christy would come over soon, and she had no way to get there. She didn't want to have to ask Zack to take her. He might be working. Working, apparently, with her husband.

Pam walked in the house with her, and Stan carried in the groceries. Though it took him a couple of trips, he didn't complain. Priscilla was in a daze as she sat on the sofa. She really wanted to talk to her mother. This was so hard to process. She just wanted her mamm to hug her and take this all away. Could she do that? She knew a few people from Danny's church now that could take her to her mother's house. But to go back...

And they would tell Danny, who wouldn't like that.

Not that she cared about what he thought right now. This was all too much.

"Honey, I think I should stay here with you." Pam sat beside her.

Priscilla shook her head. "No. I will be all right. I will just rest till Christy gets here."

Pam hugged her. "I am praying for you."

"Did you know he didn't tell me?" Priscilla had to know.

"No. I thought you knew by now." Pam kissed her forehead. "I pray you will give him a chance to hear him out."

After Christy came over and checked her out, she was relieved to see she and the baby were fine. Priscilla looked at her hands. She really didn't care to do that, and she felt like telling Pam so, but she didn't. She wasn't comfortable enough yet. But she would let Danny hear what she thought. Her eyes grew heavy as she laid down. Maybe if she went to sleep, all of this would be a bad dream.

Chapter Twenty-Five

Though this time he didn't have to take the uniform off, Danny didn't want to remind her what he was. He walked in wearing jeans and a t-shirt, like normal. He found Priscilla on the sofa. Where was his bride greeting him at the door for a hug and sweet words? The sight of her stung his heart. Her eyes were red, but she wasn't crying. Her hair was a bit messed up. She didn't look happy to see him. Her eyes came up to meet his, then she went back to staring into space.

He sat on the other chair. "Are you all right, my love?"

She glared at him. "No, I'm not."

He clasped his hands together. He wasn't sure what he had expected from her when she found out, but this was not it. This wasn't like his sweet Priscilla.

Her eyes were hard. "When did you plan to tell me you were a cop? When the baby was born? Ten years old? Or maybe grown?"

"No. I planned to tell you soon. But I was afraid." He paused. "I am so sorry for not telling you."

She stood up and crossed her arms over her belly. "I

just don't understand how you can grow up Amish and be okay carrying a gun."

"It's because I grew up Amish that I am a cop," Danny told her.

She threw up her hands.

"I just gave up my home, my family, everything I know, to live this life with you." She knew she might be wrong on this. She had agreed to leave, but it was so much all at once. "And now I find out this! How could you keep this from me?"

She respected law enforcement but she didn't trust them. And she didn't want to be married to one of them.

He stood in front of her. "I am so sorry. Will you forgive me?"

She frowned.

"I do love you, Danny. But I can't trust you now." She shook her head. "I don't know where to go from here. I have just lost so much. Maybe you haven't, because you wanted to leave the Amish sooner. Is this why you joined the church, so you could marry me?"

"No." This was not going well. She was talking crazy. Though from how she saw things, it looked like he joined just for her. "No, I joined the church because I had a falling out with my English family and was angry. I love you with my whole heart. There is nothing I wouldn't do for you."

She glared at him. Those eyes that were always kind or afraid, now so hard on him. "Will you give up your job for me and the baby?"

His eyes got wide. Was he willing to give up what he loved for her? He wasn't sure if he was. What was he supposed to say?

Tears came to her eyes. "I didn't think so."

He came close to her. "I love you. That will never change, my dear."

She sat in the chair.

"I don't want to talk about this anymore." She met his eyes this time. Softer, the way he was used to. "I don't want to hurt you. I am upset, and I don't want to say something I can't unsay." She shook her head. "I probably already did."

Tears came to his eyes. He had hurt her so much. How had this gone so bad?

"All right. Did you eat something?"

She shook her head.

He went to get the bag he left in the kitchen. "I didn't think so. I brought you some Chinese food."

She got up and walked over to the table. She sat down.

He knew she must be upset, because she didn't protest when he dished out the meal and got her a soda from the fridge. They both ate in awkward silence.

That night, Priscilla felt overwhelmed. She wasn't sure what to think of this newest lie. So, she had tried to stop thinking about it. She got ready for bed and lay next to Danny. Normally, he would reach out and hold her by now, but she knew he was giving her space. She wasn't sure what to do.

She laid still, trying to decide if she should reach out to him or not. She wanted this marriage to work. She didn't believe in divorce. Was it wrong to go back to the Amish and raise this child alone? Leave this marriage? No, she wanted to make it work. Though she didn't trust him, she still loved him so much it ached. She loved him so much, and she couldn't change that.

If she wanted this marriage to work and last that meant

reaching out to her husband, but how? She was still so angry at him.

My daughter, I have forgiven you.

Was that God talking to her? She wasn't sure. But she knew she couldn't just let this go so soon.

My daughter, Danny was a gift to you.

She felt the baby kick within. Was the baby upset that she wasn't cuddling with his or her dad? Then it hit her. She had never thought of Danny as her child's father, but now she did. When did that change? She felt a strange lightness at that thought. He was the father; he had been there since she told him she was pregnant. He had done so much for her.

But he had lied to her for so long.

And about many English things.

The battle of what he had done in the past was like a war within her, but she wanted this marriage to work, and that meant even when she didn't feel like working it. It was as if her body overtook her, and she moved to where she leaned against his back. She felt him jerk at first and it made her flinch, but then she wrapped her arm around his waist. Her hand intertwined in his hands. He squeezed back. She didn't have to say she loved him like they normally did every night before going to bed. Tonight, she had shown what love was, even when she didn't feel like showing it.

With that, she let her body relax and fell peacefully asleep.

~

Priscilla got up the next morning alone. She hadn't even heard Danny get up. She must have been more tired than she thought. Not a surprise, based on the night before. She didn't know what she wanted, but she wanted to talk to her mamm so bad. She would do anything to just talk to her right now.

She got dressed and made sure her Amish dress was proper and followed every rule. Every foolish rule. She shook her head. No, that was something Danny would say or think, not her. She was a good Amish girl. Then she looked around her apartment. Right, like most Amish people lived in apartments.

Again, she shook off the feeling of guilt of leaving, and after eating something light, she headed to the door. With Maysville being so small, it thankfully did have buses. She walked to the bus stop and when the bus came, she got on. Sitting down, she thought of how Danny would be upset that she was traveling alone like this. He would worry. Did he worry because he cared for her or because he was a cop? She didn't know now. She just wanted to go hide in her barn and dream she wasn't pregnant or married and was a single girl again.

Dream of when she had fun with Amish cousins and friends.

The bus stopped where it was close enough to walk to her old home. As she walked down the street, she thought of how she looked Amish, but now had a cell phone in her pocket. And then it hit her as she walked.

She wasn't really Amish anymore. She didn't feel that community belonged to her anymore. She was Danny Taylor's wife, and she loved that. The thought saddened her that she wasn't Amish anymore, but then she remembered she was a child of God. She believed and knew God loved her. She had never believed or felt that in the Amish.

What would she rather have her family and the tight community, or God and a man who loved her?

She knew she would pick Danny any day. She loved him too much to walk away now. Even if that's what it felt like going back home. But she just needed advice from her mamm.

She got to the door; the flowers were starting to die now that it was fall. It reminded her of her once beautiful marriage, now dying like the flowers. She saw Missy laying by the steps. She patted her for a bit, and even gave her a hug. How she missed the dog. Maybe Missy gave her enough strength to face her mamm. She kissed her soft head. She finally stood and knocked. She was so nervous that she couldn't just walk in anymore like before.

Her mamm came to the door. Her green eyes went wide. "Priscilla."

"Hi, Mamm, can I come in? I need to talk."

Since the shunning had just started, her mamm might bend the rules by letting her in. As long as her datt didn't find out, her mamm would be fine. Though even if he did, mamm did what she wanted most of the time. She had for a long time. It made Priscilla wonder why she was so different from her mamm. Maybe by inviting her in, she was accepting her for what she had asked last time she saw her. Maybe her mom did know who the father was or had come to realize it. She felt better now that her mamm had accepted her despite the hard truth.

Her mamm gave a curt nod and opened the door.

She walked in and enjoyed the smells she had missed from this old house. Mamm led her into the kitchen and then put some coffee on. If she had been at her house, she would have used her espresso. Though she kinda liked coffee this way. Plain and simple.

The way she used to be.

Mamm then sat at the table and asked for Priscilla to do the same.

She did, feeling nervous, though better than she thought she would. This wasn't where she was supposed to be.

"Did you decide to come back to Amish life?" Mamm asked, not harshly but very direct.

Priscilla shook her head. "No, Mamm, I didn't. But I found out some things about Danny that I don't know what to do with."

Mum's eyes got wide. "What? Did he hurt you?"

Priscilla wanted to almost laugh at that. Why be so afraid Danny would hurt her when her parents had been about to marry her to a rapist? The hypocrisy of that made her sick. "No. He is a wonderful husband."

"Well then, what?" Mamm tried again.

"We have a great life. I am really happy. I love him so much. I didn't think it was possible to love someone that much." She shook her head. "It's probably the only thing keeping me from running back to the Amish." She paused. "I found out Danny works as a cop." Tears came to her eyes as she looked at the table. "How could he hide that from me?"

Mamm stood up and poured the coffee. She sat back down and handed Priscilla her cup.

Priscilla finally looked at her mamm, who looked shocked.

"A cop carries a gun," her mamm finally said.

Priscilla nodded. "I know. That is wrong. What am I to do?"

Mamm put her hands around the mug and looked at her coffee for a few moments, and then met her gaze. "I'll tell you what. You come back to the Amish and live here. Raise the child here."

Priscilla stared at her. Raise a child alone? She would never be able to be married again. Not that it mattered; no man could match up to the love Danny had shown her. And she loved him too. She knew she could never love another the same way.

She wiped her eyes as more tears came. "I don't want to leave him, Mamm."

"But he is serving the devil by being a cop. He is a bad man."

Priscilla's eyes narrowed.

"Because he does what he believes is right is bad?" She didn't know what overcame her, but she crossed her arms. "Danny and his family have shown me more love than I have ever felt. He respects me. He always thinks of me first. He loves our child more than anyone could. He is one of the best men alive. He just has a thing for keeping secrets. And I don't know what to do. I wanted some help, Mamm. I didn't want to hear you say he is serving the devil, when I know he is not."

Her Mamm sat back. "What do you want me to say? Has he ever shot a man? Killed a man? That is what your husband will be one day: a killer. Is that what you want?"

Priscilla gasped. Was it true? Would Danny sin against God and kill a man one day? Stan probably had shot someone, but he was older and had been a policeman longer. It was possible that when Danny became that age, he might have killed someone.

Would he come home covered in someone else's blood? Her mind kept going places. It wouldn't stop. She stood up without drinking a sip of coffee.

"I have to go, Mamm."

Mamm stood with her and didn't reach out to hug her.

Priscilla wanted to reach out to her but was too afraid of rejection. Her mother had never been much on touch. She could only remember a few hugs she ever got growing up from her mamm, and never any from her datt. She walked out without trying.

"You will see that I am right, Priscilla, and you will be back," her mother said from behind door frame. "Because this is who you are."

The tears came harder. She wasn't sure where to go, but she wasn't waiting for the bus. She didn't want to see Pam. Danny was her son, and she would defend him. The only other person she had was Ashley. She hated that her bestie lived out of town most of the time. Maybe she was in town this week. She walked to the end of the driveway and carefully sat down by a big tree. Her body was getting worn out with all this sobbing. It was bad for the baby.

She hit Ashley's name and hoped she would come and get her. If not, she worried Ashley would call Pam. She closed her eyes and waited for her to pick up.

"Hey, Priss, what's up?" Ashley answered lightly.

So, no one had told her Priscilla had found out about Danny.

"Are you in town today?" she asked through tears.

"Yeah. I just got into town this morning," Ashley said with worry. "What's wrong? Where are you? Is the baby hurt?"

"I am at my parents' house. Can you pick me up, and I can't talk right now."

"I am on my way right now. It's on Pleasant street, right?" Ashley asked in a rush.

"Yes. It is," she sighed. "I need to go."

Chapter Twenty-Six

"No. You need to stay on the phone."

"Please, I just need time alone right now," Priscilla told her. She leaned against the tree.

"Fine. But I will be there soon."

"Thanks." Priscilla hung up. Her eyes were dry for the moment. How could this happen? How could the man she loved be a cop? And to keep that from her? She was now pregnant with a child from a man she hated, and in a marriage with a man she loved beyond belief but she didn't trust.

He couldn't be trusted.

Could life get any worse?

Randomly, a song started playing on her phone. She wasn't sure why it was playing; maybe her finger had accidentally opened an app, but instead of turning it off, she closed her eyes and listened to the words.

"In the eye of the storm," the artist sang.

Well, she was in a storm. But was God here? She let tears come again. Her world was coming down. How much more could she take?

I am here for you, my daughter. I am here. I have not left you in the eye of the storm.

But God, I do not want to go through this. Not again.

She remembered laying under this same tree when she found out she was with child. She discovered the pregnancy after she started throwing up a lot and her period did not show up. She hadn't even known her period had to do with pregnancy. She knew her mamm got sick with kids, and so she'd started to be suspicious. She could still remember how she felt when she looked at a pregnancy test she had bought from Dollar General: fear and such despair.

Now that she had grown more in her faith, she knew she wouldn't despair this time. God was with her, even if she didn't always feel him. As the song ended, she wept hard.

Then she softly said, "God I trust you. I gave you my child and…" It was hard to say, and she almost didn't, but she knew she had to. "I will give you my marriage. I give you everything. Even my pain and what happened. Make this better."

As she said the words, she felt such a release. She was still in pain but it was different. She did what she had been fighting, what she needed to do.

Just then Ashley pulled up and jumped out of her car. "Oh, my dear."

She ran over to her and wrapped her in a tight hug.

Priscilla hugged her back and cried more on her. Finally, she stopped, and Ashley helped her to the car. When she settled Priscilla in the front seat, she looked at her. "Do you want to talk here or some other place?"

Priscilla shook her head. "Not here. There are too many good and bad memories here already."

She didn't want to add more. She sat back as Ashley drove. They both said nothing as she drove. No music played.

Then Ashley pulled into a parking lot in front of the Ohio River. Though it didn't have the setting old historical Augusta had, it was beautiful and gave her peace again.

Ashley turned to face her and handed her a water bottle. She acted so much like Danny at that moment. It made Priscilla's eyes water. Even if they weren't blood, one could tell they were siblings.

She took a long drink and then looked out at the river. She finally sighed and said, "I am shocked. Did you all know that I didn't know what Danny did for a living? Were you fooling me?"

"No, my dear. We didn't," Ashley answered quickly. "We knew when you first got married that you didn't know. You were still living with the Amish. But when you left, we thought he told you. I guess we all assumed he told you. We honestly didn't know."

Priscilla didn't say anything. Then she finally looked at Ashley. "What am I to do? I love Danny more than I thought I ever could. But I don't really know him. And I can't trust him."

Ashley nodded. "I know. I guess you have to decide if you want to make the marriage work. To stay in the marriage."

"Do you think I should leave?"

Ashley looked troubled. "If I say no, you'll think I am doing it because I love my brother. If I say yes, I may be encouraging you to leave. I don't know. This choice is yours and yours alone. What you need to think about is can you live with a policeman? Because that is what Danny is. He is a cop through and through."

Priscilla trembled. "I don't like guns and killings. I have come to care for Stan, though he is a cop, but I didn't marry him. I don't want to be married to a cop. How can I be now?"

Ashley crossed her arms, unoffended, but thoughtful. "I don't know. I have been around them my whole life. I see the good and even the bad. I have loved a cop most of my life."

"Zack?" Priscilla asked, surprised.

She nodded. "Yes. I would choose to be a cop wife if he would just ask me. But that is my choice. You need to be able to make that decision too."

Priscilla leaned her head back on the car seat. She didn't know if she could love him despite the fact that he had lied to her, love him despite the fact he carried a gun for a living. She had too much to think about.

It felt like her brain would explode and her heart was breaking.

∽

That evening, opening the door, Danny walked in the kitchen to find Priscilla on her hands and knees, head in the oven. She had changed into her work dress. Her hair fell around her shoulders, just the way he liked it.

When she looked up at him, he winced. Maybe she wasn't too happy to see him. But she was showing him how she felt, or at least he thought she was. He sat down on the floor, his back to a cupboard, so they could be eye level.

Priscilla eyed Danny sitting on the floor across from her. She felt like glaring at him, but instead she kept her feelings from him. He held out his hand. She crossed her arms and sat cross-legged as she leaned against the cupboards. He just shrugged. He wore a white t-shirt and jeans like every other night he came home. The kitchen was so small their knees touched as they sat across from her.

"Again, I am sorry for not telling you. That was a mistake."

She frowned and said nothing.

"Can you talk to me, honey?"

She looked defeated. "What else don't I know about you? Have your feelings been a lie too?"

"No, I love you, Priscilla, and you know that. I would marry you again a dozen times over." He ran a hand over his head. "I should have told you the truth. It was wrong of me. What do you want to know? I will never lie to you."

"Really?" she said angrily. She looked at the ground. Her face crumbled. "Have you really been a cop for a while?"

He nodded. "Yes, I have been."

"And you knew you were going to be one when we married?"

He took a minute to answer, but then he nodded. "Yes. I have been training for many years with Stan. So, I am ahead of most cops."

She met his gaze. "Does that make me feel better? You carry a gun!"

His jaw popped. "I help people."

"Why did you become a cop?" Her eyes didn't leave his face, so when his face fell, she noticed. She regretted asking so harshly. He looked down and was silent for so long.

"It ain't a fun story," he muttered, not meeting her gaze.

She had guessed that. She took his hand in hers.

"I am listening, baby," she said out of habit, or maybe she meant it.

When he said nothing, she scooted closer, and knelt in front of him. Taking his face in her hands, she met his look.

"No matter what you tell me, I will always choose you. You have shown me what it is like to love. To feel loved by you. You helped me feel again." She kissed his nose.

She leaned her head against his, closing her eyes. She had repeated some of the words he had told her, but it was still true. Even though it was so hard for her to say those words. He knew how hard it was for her to open up. She knew she had said the right thing when she felt wetness on her cheek.

Opening her eyes, she was shocked to see her strong, kind husband crying. Men didn't cry where she was from. It was still strange for her.

He cleared his throat. "Thank you for those words, love."

He took her hand in his and stared at them.

She moved to sit next to him as she stayed silent. That was never hard for her unless she was with Danny. She wanted to joke and tease him, but knew she had to be quiet, for he had yet to say a word.

He finally spoke, strained and unlike him.

"You know I am not the bishop's son. I was the oldest of my parents. I had a sister, three years younger than me. For an Amish family, we were small, and that made my pa mad. But for some reason, my mamm never got pregnant again after she had my sister." He squeezed her hands. "I think God was protecting more babies."

Priscilla didn't want to hear more. Her heart hurt so bad for the look on his face. The look of a boy.

"My datt started beating me and my sister when I was around seven. I thought it was my fault. I became so afraid of him. None of the other Amish saw it. They didn't see the bruises or how my mamm looked." He swore. "Or they didn't want to know. I was ten when my datt broke my arm. I couldn't handle it anymore. My mamm would tell me my datt didn't mean to do it. The bishop was talking to me one day about how to be a good boy when I ended up telling him about my datt. He looked at me and said I should never lie about my datt again. Said I was being a bad son." He paused. "I couldn't believe it. The Amish always said the English were bad. I kept thinking maybe they are worse than my datt, so I should be grateful. Though I didn't know how the world could be worse. I was ten when the beatings got so bad I thought death would be better. But I couldn't let him win. I had a sister and my mamm to think about. Then he started to threaten that he would kill us." He stopped and wiped a tear away. "I didn't believe him. No one could be that evil."

Priscilla gasped. She didn't want to hear more.

"One day I came in from chores to find my datt in a rage. I stopped at the door. There was more blood than I had ever seen before. I will never forget the smell, the blood everywhere. My mamm and little sister lay in their own blood, and his hands held a wooden stick with blood all over it. I knew he had done it. He had killed them." His shoulders shook as tears ran down his face. He hung his head and sobbed.

Priscilla wasn't sure what to do. She had never seen a man shed a tear, let alone sob. If she hugged him, would he feel shame?

She didn't care.

She wrapped his big form in her arms and let him lean

into her. He sobbed into her chest. Priscilla held him and cried with him. Cried for the little boy she heard in his voice.

Finally, he wiped his eyes and laid his head in her lap though her stomach made it hard. She ran a hand over his short hair as he started to talk again. "I ran out. I could see he was going to go after me. I believe it was a miracle, because for some reason, out in the middle of nowhere, a cop car passed by. I ran after it and the officer stopped the car. I don't know what I told him. I was hysterical, but he got the message and put me in the back of his police car. I had never been in a car. Then he parked where it couldn't be seen. He told me not to move and to lay on the back of the seat. Of course, as a boy, I didn't listen. After calling for backup, the cop went after my datt. I watched through the trees as the cop bravely went into the house. He arrested my father and protected me at the same time. I was in awe of that. I decided on that day, I would be a police officer. I remember thinking I would be a good one, too. No one would get hurt while I was on the job." He paused. "What happened next wasn't so fun. It was confusing what the bishop did, but I moved in with him right away."

She kissed his head. "Why didn't your kin take you in?"

"The bishop said they didn't want me." He frowned. "I wondered if that was true or not. But I haven't seen them in years. I moved in with the bishop, not because he wanted me, but he wanted me silent about what happened. He wanted to hide what happened to us; it would make the community look bad. Well, my datt still had to go to prison, and I was a witness. The cop, Stan, and Pam helped me through the whole trial. They encouraged me and the cop even fought the bishop to let me testify. I did, and my datt is still in prison." He paused. "I still lived with the bishop, and that's when we started moving. Every two to three years, we moved. Stan would keep track of me since we never moved far from the last place. I hated it. I knew it was another way for him to help me forget, and I might have if it had not been for the cop who visited every holiday and birthday. They took me out and loved me for who I was. Then I moved to Kentucky. I was older and knew I wasn't moving again. Everyone knew I wasn't going to stay in the church, but I joined because I had a fight with Stan and Pam, and the bishop kept pushing it. I regret joining. I knew God didn't want me to. He wanted me to serve Him, not a man or a church. Stan and Pam moved close by, and I started training to be a cop, along with being a better Christian. I was going to leave the Amish for good when I met you and I couldn't leave." He looked up at her. "Meeting you was the best thing in my life. You have to know that?"

She put her hands around his face and nodded. "I do."

Leaning down to kiss him, he met her halfway. He ran a hand freely through her hair, and his lips tasted of tears. She moved closer to him and kissed him back. Feeling his passion and emotions, she put her hands in his hair, wishing it was long again.

Finally, she pulled back, her back hurt from sitting on the floor for so long.

He ran a hand to her face, and then he caught her hand in his and intertwined their hands as he laid his head back on her lap. He was thinking of their future now that they had uncovered all their deep secrets.

Chapter Twenty-Seven

Was she ready for this baby? All Priscilla knew was she was getting bigger and bigger. Maybe she would be the size of her datt's draft horse soon. Danny had laughed at her with that joke and took her in his arms. Though she hardly fit anymore. Not that either of them cared.

Danny had told her he would get parental leave from work after the baby was born. That was different. Amish men didn't do that, and sometimes women were not respected. Though she had heard and seen that changing among the Amish men. She was glad to hear it for their wives' and children's sake.

Though she had accepted his past, she never thought she would be that tragic. She still struggled with his lies though. It was something they talked about often over the last few days since she found out. There were times when she just couldn't talk about him being a cop. It was too much with the baby coming soon, and now this. She just wanted to close her eyes and forget and go back to before she knew he was a cop.

Before the lies. Before the betrayal.

But she knew she couldn't. She had to grow up and deal with her emotions.

She pulled bread out of the oven just as Danny came in and stood by the door, looking so adorable in his t-shirt and boots. She had married such a handsome man. The way he looked at her made her melt. Like she was the best thing in his world. Which he told her often.

She finally asked, "What are you looking at?"

"My beautiful wife. Thinking how blessed I am to have you in my life." He smiled and held out his arms. "I have a surprise for you, my love."

She went into his arms. "Is it a book?"

He chuckled. "Really, love. It's better than that."

"Five new books." She gave a little jump.

He kissed her.

"Nope. Come stand over here, and I will show you." He took her into the living room. She let him. "Now close your eyes."

She looked surprised and gave him a pouty lip. "Then you owe me another kiss."

He complied. "All right. Happy now?"

She chuckled and brought his head down to her mouth and kissed him again, long and hard. It didn't take long for him to take her back in his arms and return the kiss. He deepened it, and her legs went weak. But he held her tight. By the time she pulled away, she was breathless.

"I am happy now." She gave him a sheepish grin.

He laughed.

"I love you so much, baby." He kissed her forehead. "Now close your eyes like a good wife."

She pursed her lips but did as he said. She heard some noise as he went back out the door, but she made sure she didn't peek. She loved his surprises almost as much as his kisses. Then her face reddened. What was wrong with her? She felt like a young bride. Not a woman ready to have her first child. She rubbed her stomach. *Come on out soon. Mama's ready to meet you.*

Then she heard something on the floor. Danny touched her shoulders and guided her over to something. "Now sit here, baby."

She looked confused, but sat down in a pretty comfortable chair. Was she sitting in the other chair in the living room? She wasn't sure.

"You can open your eyes, love."

She did, and looked down at what she sat in. It was a beautiful, old wooden rocking chair. Just like her mamm's. It was comfortable too. Oh, he had given her a piece of her past.

"You did this," she whispered through much emotion. "Why?"

"I love you." He knelt in front of her. "I got it from the Yoders. I don't want to take your past from you. I want to accept it. I want our child to grow up knowing the Yoders and how they give and love and have community. And maybe one day we will have the love of our Amish parents. Even mine."

Her eyes watered. "You don't know what that means to me. You have really accepted me for who I am."

She touched his face. When he did stuff like this, she could almost forget the lies. She was going to try, though, to trust him again.

He touched her face. "I love you so much."

She looked into his eyes and felt peace wash over her. But she also had to pee, which was her life now. He helped her stand up. She walked into the bathroom. He was always careful not to go in with her, but he stayed outside the door like he thought the baby would pop out any minute.

Before she got to the toilet, liquid gushed all over the floor, and it wasn't urine. She screamed, and she heard Danny come in.

He took one look at the floor and then got his phone out. He had the midwife on speed dial. She wanted to laugh about that, but suddenly her stomach spasmed. Was this normal? She heard Danny on the phone with Christy as another pain hit. Leaning against the bathroom sink, she thought she might throw up her breakfast. The pain was that intense.

Danny finally hung up after what seemed forever and asked her if she wanted to go to the bedroom. She groaned. She might as well. She didn't want to have the baby on the bathroom floor.

As she settled back in the pillows, she sighed. "When will Christy get here?"

"Well, she is two hours out, but she says you won't have the baby that fast." Danny tried to calm her.

"I could." She settled back and a few minutes later muttered as another pain hit. "Man, these are intense."

Danny sat by her side. "Do you want to change into something more comfortable?"

She wasn't sure what the Amish wore, but it had to be a lot to still be modest. She wanted to be modest too, especially with Danny here. The most he had seen her in was a tank top she had used as an undershirt. And her trust in him wasn't what it was like a week ago. She wanted to cry for that. Could she trust him again? Her mind said yes but her heart... then another contraction hit.

"No, I am fine. This dress is big. But I don't want to get it bloody."

"Don't worry. I will buy you another one," he told her.

She leaned back and practiced breathing calmly through the contraction pains. About an hour and half later, which felt like a year to her, a contraction ripped through her, and suddenly, she felt so much pressure. Maybe she should push. But it was too soon, and she still had her underwear on. She didn't know if she could take them off by herself and asking Danny was beyond embarrassing.

But the choice was taken from her. She made herself start pushing.

Danny was at her side. "Are you pushing so soon?"

She just moaned.

"I don't think you should just yet," he told her.

"You try to keep this child in me," she cried as she bore down again.

"All right... but..." He ran a hand over his hair. "Shouldn't you have... um..."

Then it hit her what the poor man was trying to say. She closed her eyes. She might as well help him before he choked on the words. "Yes. I need help to get my underwear off. But don't look down there."

"Of course not. I won't." He sure wished he had more training as a cop. He had only been one for less than a month and he hadn't delivered any babies yet. He had to go to an area where he could help with more births so he would be ready. Though he had taken some classes, delivering his own child was different. This was the woman and child he loved.

Awkwardly they got the underwear off. She sighed and lay back down, putting her legs up. That gave her some relief. She stopped pushing for now.

Half an hour later, Christy was still not there. Great, she was going to have this baby alone.

Well, not alone. With Danny, but he was a man who hadn't even been intimate with her yet. She was sweaty and felt gross.

Danny's hair was messed up, this was way and that. His face was red.

She closed her eyes against the fears. What if the baby looked like James? She hadn't let herself think about that, but now that the thought was here, she let her mind wander, and it was going to dangerous places. What if the baby didn't like her? What if the baby felt like he or she wasn't wanted?

She didn't know how to feel; all she knew she wanted this child out.

And not just to get rid of the pain. but to hold the baby and to tell the baby it was loved. Tears ran down her face as she pushed again. This time, she felt something different. Was she dying? Was her body falling out? Then she got nauseous and a burning feeling flamed below.

Why had she been made to go through this? Where was God in it? Was He with her now? She wiped her eyes.

Beloved child, I am here for you. The same way I was there the night James came to you. I hurt for you and wept with you.

She cried. Was God there then? Then why hadn't he stopped it? Because of free will. James had a choice not to do that, and he'd chosen wrong. But where was her choice? Would she have run away if she knew James could get her pregnant? He had not cared for her or the child.

But what was she to do in the English world, knowing no one? She wouldn't have no help? She let the tears come more as she pushed again.

I loved you through it all. I gave you a beautiful gift.

She believed that now. She was a gift to Danny and to his family. They loved her very much. Was all the pain worth it?

Beads of sweat beat down her face. Was it worth it?

Danny went to the end of the bed, her dress was pulled up to her knees. At this point she didn't seem to care. "Okay, baby, I need you to relax. I can see our child's head."

She screamed as he said that. Was he serious? She couldn't do this. She wasn't ready to be a mama. "But I am not ready to be a mamm."

"Well, the child is coming." Danny grabbed a clean towel they had bought for the baby to be wrapped in. "Now I need you to give one big last push, love. Now."

She cried as she pushed like her life depended on it. Or the life of her child. As she pushed, she felt such a love for this child. It overcame her. *God, help her,* she prayed. The worst pain she had ever felt overcame her. She was sure it was one of the worst things she had ever felt.

Just then she heard a cry, and Danny wrapped the baby in the blanket. "He's a boy."

She didn't know what overcame her, but she reached for the baby. He came over and put the baby in her arms. She laid the baby against her chest and looked down at his beautiful face. Christy had told her to keep the umbilical cord as long as possible.

Though she really wanted Christy to get here now.

He looked nothing like James. But even if he did one day, his father would always be Danny. She looked in his beautiful blue eyes and felt a love so deep for him.

"Oh, thank you God for my son," she whispered. She lay kisses on his head over and over, as more tears ran down her face. Then another pain hit her. Christy had told her this would happen.

"Amen," Danny said. "You did so well, my love. How strong you are."

She looked at him. "I am not strong. God gave me the strength to do it. How I love the boys in my life."

Danny kissed her forehead. "How I love my little family."

Just then, Christy walked in. The look of shock on her face was priceless. "Well, looks like I wasn't needed here."

She smiled and then went over to see how everyone was.

Chapter Twenty-Eight

Danny walked out of the room as Christy took over the medical care. He felt like he was on top of the world. He called his parents. Something he had forgotten to do. His mom answered.

"Hello, grandma," he said.

She didn't say anything.

"Are you serious? How is Priscilla doing?" she asked quickly. "What did she have?" Then she spoke to Stan. "You are a grandpa."

He heard his dad get on the other phone. "Congrats, son. We are so happy."

"A baby." He laughed. "A boy." He laughed again. "It was so amazing to watch, and so overwhelming."

His mom laughed. "Oh, my goodness. Can we come over? I am sure you need something to eat. Let me bring you some food."

He laughed at her reaction.

"Sure Mom, you can come." Priscilla and he had talked about having them come over after the baby was born. "Can you call Ashley?"

"Of course. I will call her right now. Love you, my dear. I am so proud of you."

"Love you too, mom." He hung up.

He texted Ashley, knowing she was probably writing right now, but she wouldn't mind. *Congrats you are an aunt.*

A few sections later, he read the reply. *Are you serious?*

Danny: *Yup. You have a healthy nephew.*

Ashely: *Oh my word!!!! I am dying right now. I will be there tomorrow to meet the little guy. How is my sis doing? And you too? How long did it take?*

He laughed at her reply. That was his sister all right.

Danny: *I will explain tomorrow. Mom is calling you.*

Ashley: *Yup. She just did, and we are screaming together.*

He laughed again and closed his eyes. He knew he should clean up the bathroom since that was where her water broke, but he was thinking of all that had happened. His bride was safe, and his son was perfect. He was a father. That was a big change to get used to. But he was ready for it too. He knew he would be a father the moment he had proposed to Priscilla.

When she had pushed out the baby and he had caught him, it was the greatest and most fearful feeling he had ever experienced. And he was a cop. He had felt a lot of things. But nothing like this. God had blessed him so much. Though he didn't like what Priscilla had to go through to marry him, God had brought good from it. And he had felt that stronger today than any other time.

He knelt down in front of the couch and thanked God for all that happened and for keeping them all safe. Especially Priscilla and the baby. He praised the Lord for all he had been given.

Priscilla couldn't believe how much she loved her baby. She was in awe of him. She didn't even let him sleep alone. He was always sleeping on her or Danny. He loved the baby just as much as her. Right now, the baby laid on her chest. They still had yet to name him, though he was a couple days old. They called him Baby. But then sometimes they called each other baby, so it could get confusing, but they just laughed when it happened.

Danny came in and brought in groceries like he normally did. He was always getting her something. He sat next to her. "How are my babies?"

She smiled. "Very well, but we do need to name this baby."

He smiled and kissed her head. He had a worried look about him. His body was tense.

"What's wrong, Danny boy?" she asked gently.

He frowned. He touched her hair. "How did you learn me so well?"

"I love you, that is how." She leaned into his hand.

He sighed. "Stan just told me about a case and, with everything that just happened, it hit a little close to home."

"Can you tell me what it is?" She figured he couldn't always, but she wanted him to tell her if he could.

"Do you remember the lady we heard at the Ark?"

She nodded. "Of course."

"Well, she is a lawyer and has been fighting a case where a rapist is getting custody of his kids."

She bit her lip. "Are you serious? How can that happen?"

"I don't know, but it makes me sick."

She agreed. And said what he was thinking. "That will never happen to our baby."

"No, it won't. Stan and I were talking about what we can do to help."

"Will it be dangerous?" She was still worried about him.

He shook his head.

"No, honey. Stan knows how to do this kind of stuff." He kissed her forehead. And they sat in comfortable silence for a while. "So, do you think we should name our baby, baby?"

She chuckled at how he asked it. "I have an idea."

"And what is that, my love?"

"What about Charlie Sammy?"

He looked at her stunned. "Really?"

She nodded.

His eyes watered.

"I think Sammy would have loved that." He paused. "How did you know my sister's name?"

"Ashley told me your sister's name." She moved Charlie over and she let his head rest against her as well. She was right where she belonged.

Chapter Twenty-Nine

Danny didn't know he could love a little guy so much. But he loved Charlie. It was such a protective love. No one was going to hurt his baby. His son.

He walked over to the crib when he heard the baby fuss. Priscilla was asleep on the bed. He changed him and went into the living room.

He wrapped the baby like Priscilla had taught him to do. And then he laid him on the couch and just watched him. His big blue eyes scanned around. He semblance looked nothing like his birth dad. Would he ever look like him? Would Danny be able to handle it?

Yes, because he loved his son, no matter.

Charlie wiggled and got his hand out of the wrap. Danny handed him his finger, and the baby's little hand wrapped around it with such strength. *Oh, my sweet boy. Daddy loves you.*

As he watched Charlie, he thought of how this all came about. Though he didn't struggle the same way Priscilla did, it didn't mean he didn't hate the man who hurt his wife. The scars might always be on Priscilla, and he couldn't take it from her.

But God said not to hate. He knew that. He had struggled with it before with his biological father, the bishop, and the Amish.

But James would never get justice. Even he knew that. The Amish would always stand behind him.

Revenge is mine, said the Lord.

But would God judge the man one day? Would he get what he deserved for this? Yes, he knew that answer. God would judge him on judgment day and that would be harsh.

As he looked at Charlie, he thought about how he hated a man that gave him this little miracle. Though that evil man didn't see the blessing he had been given, Danny would cherish that gift.

"Huh, little man, is daddy a hard head sometimes?"

Charlie cooed like he agreed.

Danny chuckled. "I know you're right, my man."

As he watched the baby, he silently prayed, *Lord, I have been a fool. I have been so angry at James. It has eaten me up. God, take this anger from me. Help me forgive James. I can't do it alone. I need you.*

He let a tear run down his face. He felt such a relief. Still feeling so much emotion, he closed his eyes as he held his son.

Priscilla came in and found both of her men sleeping. It was so adorable how Danny had a hand on Charlie's back and on one shoulder. She was beyond blessed. She went over and touched Danny's shoulder.

He looked up at her with sleepy brown eyes. He smiled.

"Hi, sweetie." He opened his arms and moved Charlie to the side.

She didn't need to be asked twice. She hadn't sat in his lap since before the birth. It felt so good to be in his arms again, though she was careful how she sat. "What have my boys been doing while I was sleeping?"

"Charlie was showing me where I was wrong," he said.

She looked confused then said, "Well, you know how our son is so wise."

He chuckled. "God got ahold of me, and I let go of my anger against many people…"

He didn't say who.

But she knew it was against James.

She blinked. "Wow, I am not sure what to say. But I am glad."

He nodded and remained silent.

She sighed. "I guess I didn't hold a grudge against him. Or anger. It was just what some men do…"

"No, it is not. Christians and many people I know would never do that."

"I am learning that. But it's hard to change my mindset so soon."

He kissed her cheek. "It will take time, but I believe you are seeing the truth."

She nodded.

"I am. You are helping me do things differently." She paused. She felt like she could tell him again of her dream and could pursue it again. "I want to be a nurse or go into some kind of nursing one day. I knew living Amish, I would never be able to. And now, with Charlie, I am not sure if I want to try."

"I can see you as a nurse," he said gently. "If you really want to do it, I will support you in it."

His words touched her. A new career was too much to think about with an infant to take care of and with learning the English world. Though she had lived it halfway at the beginning of their marriage, living in it fully now was very different. She couldn't even drive yet. But to know she had his support meant the world to her. How was she so blessed to have a man like him? A few hours later, Danny lay his head in her lap as she ran her fingers through his hair. They talked of light subjects, and then Danny chuckled.

"What?" Priscilla looked down at him.

"Just thinking of the times you did this before, and I was pretending to be asleep."

"What?" Priscilla sounded shocked. "How could you not tell me you were awake?" She pursed her lips out in the most adorable way. "I said some personal things, Danny boy."

He lightly smiled.

"I know, baby, but I felt I couldn't tell you, or you would get scared. Also…" He paused. "Also, if you knew I was awake, I would do what you weren't ready for."

He winked.

She smiled lightly, blushing. "And what were you wanting to do?"

He sat up and dug his hands through her smooth curls as he pulled her close and kissed those soft lips. She melted under his touch.

When he pulled away, he smiled. "So that is what I wanted to do, but you weren't ready."

She winked at him. "Well, I could have taken a kiss or two, but I was just waiting and feeling like I was gonna get old and gray."

He laughed.

"Well, you are far from old and gray, hot mama." He touched her face. "You were worth the wait."

She leaned into his hand. "You're right. By waiting, you told me you cared and respected me, Danny boy."

Chapter Thirty

A couple days later, when Annamay showed up at her door wearing a white tank top and jeans, she hugged Priscilla like no time had passed. In a way, Priscilla felt the same way. She had missed her friend. She was close to Ashley, but she had known Annamay since childhood and they had grown up the same. So, there was a bit of a difference in their friendship.

"Come on in." She turned the coffee machine on, knowing how Annemay loved fancy coffee. "You won't get in trouble for being here?"

She picked up Charlie, who lay in his bassinet.

Annamay shook her head.

"No, I haven't joined the church. And I know Miriam has visited." She sat at the table like she belonged there and had been many times. "And everyone knows the Yoders visit and bring goodies with them."

Priscilla smiled. So not much had changed. She sat down. "The gossip pool is the same."

Annemay chuckled. "Yup. You are happier now. Your

eyes shine now. Can I ask who put that sparkle into them?"

Priscilla blushed. "Danny is wonderful. I never thought I could love someone so much."

Annamay looked at Charlie. Priscilla asked if she wanted to hold him, and Annemay did take him. She held him like he was a doll. She looked like she may break him. It seemed to touch her.

Annemay smiled. "I am glad. Though I've heard he's a cop. How are y'all doing with that?"

She kissed the sleeping baby.

Priscilla shrugged. "It's been a rough patch. I just can't believe he hid it for so long in training. But we are so much more open now and we tell each other everything."

"Everything?" Annemay asked pointedly.

Priscilla saw she walked into that one.

"I have told him my dreams of the future." She pointed to Charlie. "It doesn't matter now that I have a baby. I can't do it."

"That is not true. I know Danny; he will help you live your dream."

Priscilla got up to get the coffee. "But I would need a GED, and I haven't done any high school."

She poured them both coffee and sat back down.

"Well, I think you can, and Danny will help you."

Priscila looked thoughtful. "I want to heal more before going into a profession."

"You mean counseling?" Annamay looked surprised.

Priscilla nodded. "I think so. Danny has been in the past. I want to be the best mom and wife I can be, and that means going through some painful parts to get there."

"Wow, you have changed."

"What, you don't think I would have before?"

"You just seem open to it. Our community ain't big on therapy. If you follow the rules, you won't need it," Annamay said it sarcastically as she rolled her eyes at the thought.

Priscilla snorted at the thought. That was not true. "The Sugar Creek Amish support therapy and counseling."

Annamay nodded.

"I hear that." She crossed her arms. "I am getting my GED."

Priscilla's eyes widened. "Why?"

"Because if something bad happens, I want an education to fall back on. I want more education than I have. I feel stupid."

Priscilla understood that. If she could have gotten a job easily and stayed in the church, maybe she wouldn't have had to marry Danny, and she would be raising her child alone. She knew other women did it single. But then she wouldn't have Danny, and he was the best thing to her.

"But what if the church finds out, Annamay?" Priscilla asked.

Some of her old fears surfaced.

She shrugged. "I haven't decided if I plan to join or not."

Priscilla looked at her friend, dressed more like the world than Priscilla was while still living with the Amish. "Can I ask why?"

"I am sick of the hypocrisy of it. So sick of religion." Annamay took a sip of coffee. "What they did to you. What you were forced to do."

Priscilla flinched but nodded. "It was wrong. I shouldn't have had to marry someone I didn't want too. But just so you know, Danny is the best thing that happened to me."

"But you shouldn't have been forced to get married. It was wrong. Neither of you wanted it."

Priscilla had to agree, though she was tired of this conversation. She didn't want to remember those first fearful days, weeks, and even months.

Annamay frowned. "Annie left the church."

Priscilla's mouth dropped open. "Really? Why?"

Annamay swore angrily. "Your father-in-law helped her and probably the Yoders too."

Priscilla nodded. "Stan is not allowed to tell me all he does, but I am not surprised. Why did she leave?"

She wasn't sure if she wanted to know the answer to it.

"James hurt her," Annamay said just above a whisper.

Tears came to Priscilla's eyes. She knew that pain. Not another victim. Not another child.

"She didn't get pregnant, but it really messed her up. She doesn't talk anymore. Her parents didn't know what to do with her. So the Yoders stepped in, and they actually have full guardianship because of the state she was in."

"A judge got involved?" Priscilla was shocked.

"Enough to do that to save her."

"But not to get James." Priscilla didn't need an answer. She knew they didn't go after him.

"Annie is of age."

"She is hardly eighteen!" Priscilla spat out.

"I know. And her life is ruined, just in a different way," Annamay said sadly.

"My life isn't ruined." She took her baby back and held him close, needing to feel him against her. He was safe. He would never be touched by an abuser.

"I love my baby so much, and I do love my life," Priscilla said simply. "If you don't join the church and want to move out, without going to Stan, you can come here."

Annamay smiled.

"Thanks. I do appreciate that. Though I am probably more worldly than you." She looked at Priscilla's long dress and hair in a ponytail. "You left but you still dress like a good girl."

Priscilla chuckled. "I just dress like I feel like, and Danny likes my clothes. What you wear shows your heart."

"You mean I am a rebel." She looked at pictures on the wall. "Your hubby is still cute, even without the hair."

Priscilla laughed again. "Yes, he is."

She took out her phone and showed Annamay the pictures they had taken over the months. Danny loved pictures, and she was learning to love them too.

By the time Danny walked in, the two friends were laughing on the sofa, and Charlie was in the bassinet again. Danny smiled at them, his eyes sparkling.

"Well, what brings Annamay to our house?" He picked up Charlie. "Is it this cute baby boy?"

"Of course," she responded. "And I needed time with my friend."

Sitting on the couch, Danny wrapped his other arm around Priscilla. "Well, that is great. You are welcome here anytime."

He kissed Priscilla's head.

Annamay spoke to Priscilla, "Do you want some more time alone? I can go get takeout for us later."

"No, you're fine here. I have supper in the oven." She looked to Annamay. "Do you wanna stay for supper?"

She shrugged. "Sure. If you are a better cook now."

Priscilla stood up.

"Well, maybe I won't feed you then." She went to check on dinner. "I will be right back."

Danny wanted to slap her backside, but with Annemay there, he didn't. He just watched her leave, loving the smile on her face.

"She is truly happy," Annemay commented. "I love seeing that."

Danny looked at her and rocked Charlie when he started to fuss. "Yes, she is. It's been a long time coming, but we have made it through so much."

She eyed his uniform. "Yeah, I say so. I am just glad she is safe."

Danny nodded. "I try. Only God can help me do it."

She looked at him unblinking, and, like many Amish women, she had no understanding of that kind of relationship.

As Priscilla got supper on the table, Annamay told her she had a surprise for her. They walked outside, Danny holding Charlie.

"Whose car is that?" Priscilla asked.

"My English boyfriend's," Annamay answered. "It's nice."

She went to the back door.

Priscilla eyed her and wondered if her friend was right to have an English boyfriend. But Annamay's choices were her own, and she would have to live with that.

Annemay opened the back door and out jumped Missy.

Priscilla's mouth dropped open. She couldn't believe it. The dog jumped on her and she hugged her. Her datt had actually given her and Danny her favorite dog. That meant he accepted Danny or was trying too. She giggled in delight as the dog jumped all over.

"Do you see her?" she asked Danny.

Though of course he did.

He laughed and patted the dog. "I do. I am so happy for you."

Maybe one day her parents would even visit her.

∽

That night, Priscilla sat on the bed in her nightie. They had put Missy in the other room for now. The dog was house trained. Priscilla was so excited to have her here. She had gotten lots of kisses from the dog. But it also made her feel more homesick.

She had just fed Charlie and laid him down. She was feeling discouraged from what had happened with Annie.

Danny came in. He wore a t-shirt and shorts, which he normally slept in. He sat next to her and took her in his arms. "What's wrong, my love? Do you just need snuggles?"

She leaned into him, glad he was there and not afraid to talk about the hard issues with him. But she had never really talked of James often. "Annamay told me Annie left."

Danny nodded. "I know. Paul and Stan helped her."

"You've seen her then?"

"Once, when we were taking her to a safe house." He held her tighter.

"She's not good."

"No, she's a shell of herself. We did a blood test. She is not with the child, but the doctors said the damage was bad," he said with a heavy voice. "Physically, and not just emotionally."

Priscilla shuddered and moved to where she was closer to him, her knees up. She didn't cry, just started shaking.

"I am so sorry. This is too much for you."

She shook her head. She knew they couldn't press charges. The chances of James getting time was slim, even with the state going after him. "It's just that he will do it again. Until when? How many women will he have destroyed, and how many babies will he bring into the world?"

"I don't know, but he moved to another community in Ohio."

She sat up and shook her head.

"So he can hurt more girls there?" She leaned against his chest. "He will get married one day."

"Probably will."

"And he may do it to his daughters and granddaughters," Priscilla bit out.

Danny didn't have to agree. He knew it was true. It had happened before. Incest was common with the Amish. Some said they were too close, and many were related. It was how some men got away with doing it. And within the community, there were always lots of babies and kids. He used to think they only had them to use in that way or for work. But now he knew that wasn't true. Many families did love and cherish their children.

"Holding onto bitterness against them, against him, doesn't help anyone," he said.

She nodded.

"I know. I am not. I have you." She held onto him tighter. "And they don't have that rock in their life."

"We have God, and that is the only reason we made it this far." He paused. "Remember, we haven't had it the easiest either, but we have God. And so does Annie and the others."

She let that sink in and sighed. She thought of Missy. "What do you think of having Missy here? Do you think my datt is accepting you?"

He shrugged. "I don't think so. They came to me at work today."

She eyed him. "Why didn't you tell me?"

"I didn't have time till now, dear. Just like before, they came and tried to change my mind. We talked, and they left mad. I don't think they will be back. Especially now that Charlie is here. They were more concerned about that. Because that child was not born Amish."

Pricilla snorted rudely. How dare they say something like that about her baby. But then she knew how blinded they were, and how at one point she had been like that. She leaned against the headboard and looked Danny in the eyes.

She spoke softly like it was wrong to say this, but it had to be said, "My datt is blinded by spiritual lies. Anyone can be blinded by it, even in the Christian church of pastors, deacons, and bishops." She shook her head. But Danny remained silent and she continued, "Spiritual abuse is probably one of the worst abuses out there, and believe me, I've been abused a lot now. Because the spiritual abuse takes the blood and life from someone, where a person is supposed to be loved and cared for. Spiritual abuse views a God of condemnation and judgment. Not one of mercy and grace. It made me people pleaser, made me perform, and made me suffer months of abuse."

Her face crumbled as she thought of the months of abuse in her own father's house and in the community and safety of her church. She should have been protected. Annie should have been protected. She was taught that if she submitted enough to her parents and the church, then she would be protected by them. But they had let her be raped and blamed her for it. She had tried the same with Danny: if she was a good enough wife, he may not hurt her. But that was not love. Not unconditional love.

"It is the worst form of abuse that can be done to a person because it is done by His church and to His own people. They are gambling with people's souls because they don't want to face the issues."

Danny watched her as she spoke, remaining silent and thoughtful. For his wife, this was a lot to say. She wasn't talkative like he was.

"You have so much wisdom on it, my dear. It took me much longer to figure all that out. You are very right about what you said. It says in Romans 8, There is therefore now no condemnation to them which are in Christ Jesus, who walk not after the flesh, but after the Spirit. For the law of the Spirit of life in Christ Jesus hath made me free from the law of sin and death." He paused. "I have been careful not to use Bible verses, though I do believe there is healing in the Word. It can be triggering, and I didn't want you to think I was using the Bible against you. I knew one day, you would know what God and His Word can do for you, my love."

She nodded. "It had been a long time coming here. And I don't want to go through it again. But there is light at the end of the journey."

Danny took her in his arms and she went willingly. "Yes, there is."

He knew enough that they would fight the demons

they had been raised to believe were true again, but for now, spiritual awakening was a breakthrough. One that was healing and amazing to see. Only God could bring good from so many mistakes.

Chapter Thirty-One

A week later, Danny chased Priscilla into the bedroom as she giggled. He gently grabbed her. Lay next to her. She could get used to evenings like this.

For some reason, she loved the feeling of his chest; it made her feel a little wild. At her response. His eyes showed surprise.

"What are you doing, lovely?"

She didn't know how to answer, so she leaned in and kissed him. And he didn't need to be asked twice. His hands intertwined in her hair, and he deepened the kiss, making her feel so wanted and so cherished. But he had always stopped himself before. He never went far, but now she wanted him to.

She did something she had never done before. She put her hands on him.

He still didn't take it farther. She pulled back and looked at him. Her hand was still on his chest. He looked dazed. She smiled just for him, loving this control she had over him.

"Are you sure you want to do this, Priscilla?" He put his hand over hers on his chest.

She nodded. "I do. I am ready. I want to know all of you. I want to love you and to have you love me."

He nodded.

"I want to love you as well." He paused. "But promise me something."

She looked down. She nodded.

He touched her chin and brought her head up to look at him.

"If you feel like you are leaving your body or feel any shame, stop me." When her eyes widened, he continued, "Promise me. I know it will be hard, but I don't want you to feel used. I want you to feel cherished by me. Loved fully and completely. If you feel any shame or if you are leaving, stop me, please. Trust me."

She met his eyes. She didn't want to do that. She wasn't even sure if she could, but he was right. For them to have a good relationship, she needed to do it. She nodded.

He smiled at her.

"Trust me, my love." He winked at her. "Are you sure you want to do this?"

She whispered she loved him over and over.

He didn't need to be asked twice, and he laughed deeply. Gently taking her into his arms, he kissed her neck. She closed her eyes. She didn't know something could feel so good. His touch made her feel alive and loved. He whispered in her ear that he loved her. She giggled, feeling precious and cherished. She let him take control and trusted him with her heart and soul and even her body. For the first time, she experienced a man loving her.

It wasn't scary or painful, but pure bliss.

Danny ran a hand along Priscilla's cheek as she slept.

He wasn't totally sure if he had dreamed last night, but no, it was very real. He had never seen Priscilla act like that. So maybe his wife was outspoken in something, and he finally found out what it was. And he would love helping her find her voice in that area again.

He knew after months, almost a year, of loving her, that she might come to love him, but to now know she really desired him the way he did her was a powerful feeling. She looked like a delicate flower as she lay there...

Just then, he heard the baby. Knowing Priscilla needed her sleep, he picked Charlie up and he got a diaper and wipes. After changing him, he wrapped him in a blanket the way Priscilla had shown him the baby liked. Then they walked to the kitchen, and he got the coffeemaker going before sitting at the table.

"Hey, how is the little man doing?" He smiled down at the baby and kissed him on the head. "I got the day off, so I thought we would have some fun today. How about we throw a ball around? Huh." He paused. "Well, one day, you will be able to soon and you will be the best."

He continued softly talking to Charlie.

Priscilla came in and found them like this. She softly smiled. Her white robe went to her feet, and her pink toes stuck out. Her hair was this way and that. Well, he shouldn't be surprised. They had both been a bit wild last night, and he loved that woman's hair. She looked so adorable. He could stare at her all day.

"Good morning, sexy."

She smiled at him. This time sappy, and in her own kind of drunk way. "Morning, handsome."

"Did you leave your body at all last night, my love?" He was serious as he asked.

She shook her head.

"Not once." She winked at him. "Though you kinda put me into a coma."

He laughed deeply. "Good."

She swatted his shoulder playfully.

"Naughty boy." Then she walked over to the coffee pot. Pouring herself a cup, she muttered, "I am going to need this, this morning."

He got up and put the baby in the swing. Walking over, he whispered to her, "I am sure you will. You know, we could always go to bed with the chickens and wake up like this."

She turned around, her eyes wide and her mouth dropped open.

"Ashley showed you that song?" She chuckled in shock.

Ashley had sent her the song, "Going to bed with the chickens." Ashley had told her this would be Priscilla and Danny soon. She hadn't believed her, but now she did. She wanted to be like that.

Well, maybe she already was.

Danny shrugged. "I have seen it before, but I like the idea. How about you, my love?"

He kissed her and then took her in his arms as she melted against him. She was like putty in his hands.

Pulling back, he said, "I thought the kiss would help my cause."

She winked at him. "Chickens."

Then nibbled on his ear.

"I like how you did the neck kissing," she whispered breathlessly. Then she moved her head to where it would be easy to kiss her neck. It was sensual and so inviting. "I think you could use more practice."

He didn't need to be asked twice, and he gently laid

kisses on her. He was going to enjoy this side of his bride. The way he did when he first courted her so long ago. But now it was different and even better. If she let him practice, he would get better.

⁓

Priscilla laid on the couch that afternoon after Danny went to work and Charlie was napping. Grabbing her phone, she didn't know how to tell Ashley what she did last night, so she decided to just call her. Missy sat on the floor next to the coach. She was always by Priscilla's side or Charlie's. Priscilla was so happy to have her, and Danny never minded the dog inside. Actually, he was the one who always called the dog in for the evening. He was such a softy. She chuckled. Oh, he sure was.

Ashley answered in her cheerful voice, "Howdy, girl."

Priscilla was quiet, suddenly nervous.

"What's wrong, Priscilla?" she asked, concerned.

"Nothing." Priscilla giggled. "I have something to tell you."

She paused.

"Well?" Ashley asked.

"I went to bed with the chickens last night." She chuckled. She wasn't sure what she expected from Ashley, but a piercing scream was not it.

"Oh, my word, girl!" She then chuckled and Priscilla joined in. "I am so happy for you, Priscilla."

Priscilla laughed. "I can't tell. You might get another niece or nephew in the future."

"I already have the best nephew in the world," she said softly. "I just want you and Danny happy."

"Thanks." She giggled.

Chapter Thirty-Two

Priscilla laid by the river, closing her eyes against the warm sun. It was cool today but still pleasant. She loved these times with Danny and Charlie. After having the baby, she never expected to have this much love for someone. Someone so little and beautiful, and her love took over her.

Missy laid by the baby. She was such a calm dog, and she loved Charlie.

Danny softly sung to her like he had in the past, and even while Charlie was in her belly.

He sang a lullaby, and it was soft and sweet. He may not sing in tune, but it was beautiful none of the less.

Suddenly she felt a bundle of emotion, and she turned her head to the river, away from him.

It didn't take long for him to stop singing, and he came over to her and laid behind her. He wrapped her in his arms tightly. "What's wrong, my love?"

She didn't cry, but she felt an ache in her heart. Finally, she was able to speak.

"I feel such a loss. I never learned or sang a lullaby. I

know it may feel childish, but I've never even heard my parents tell me that they love me. I know they do in ways, but I never heard the words. It's why it was so hard to tell you I love you and to believe you loved me. I've never been told that."

He nodded against her back.

"I was raised the same way, and I can't imagine never telling you or the baby how much I love you. My parents did teach me to accept and say I love you, but it's not the same." He paused. "It's never too late to learn a lullaby."

"I want to learn." And they lay there like that as the baby slept, just listening to the sound of the river. Something changed between them. Something powerful. It was also about God. As she listened to the river, it was like she was hearing how much God loved her. It was still hard for her after all the judgment she had been taught to believe about Him. She still had such a great deal of fear of Him at times.

Especially in her nightmares.

But for now, she was being loved by her man and her God.

∼

"How was your day?" Ashley asked the day after their river trip.

Priscilla looked at her phone and thought about the question. She had always been honest with Ashley. She still wondered how they became friends so fast. Danny said it was meant to be by God.

"Good. We had a picnic by the river and some strange things happened."

"What do you mean? Your family showed up?"

"No. Thank goodness." She checked on the baby and then settled into the living room rocking chair Danny had given her. She pulled her legs up to her chest. "But it was still strange and powerful. I felt such love by Danny, and even God. But this time, I felt reassured that God loves me. There are still times where I have difficulty believing it. Especially when the lies creep in. Today was definitely a turn around for me."

Ashley was quiet for a minute. "You don't know how much I love hearing you say that. I knew it was true, but to know you believe it. What did Danny say?"

"He is happy, but I haven't explained what happened yet. I am in awe over it, I guess. So much has happened, and I still miss my family a lot."

"How are you doing with that?"

"I don't know. Lonely. I've never known a time without someone around all the time. I did at the dawdy house, but this is very different. The Yoders have been great and they help with the loneliness, but it's not the same."

"No, it's not. I know even Danny misses that life."

"He does. I think he is finally realizing what he lost and appreciating some things the Amish do."

"Everything has some good. I have tried to show him that before, but before you came into his life, he didn't see how great that could be to his life."

"I agree. It's been a growing period for both of us."

"Ain't life always."

"You don't always have to point that out, girl."

"Sorry. Habit, and I am always right."

"Always, huh. Now to get as wise as you are."

"One can only dream."

Priscilla laughed at that. She loved these talks with her friend. She didn't realize how rich a friendship could be with someone English. Of course, it was different from her relationship with Danny. But still as rich.

"So how is your dreaming going? How's the book? Did you see the new picture of Charlie?"

"Oh, he is so sweet. The book is all right. I am working on the climax right now. I need more pics of my little muffin."

Priscilla always melted when Ashley called him that. She was so blessed to have a family who cared for her and her little family. When Charlie cried, Priscilla said goodbye.

A few hours later, Danny came home from a short shift. He had filled in for someone. Priscilla was happy to have him home early. Even if she just saw him a few hours before, he was still her favorite person to be with. He stood by the door and opened his arms to her. She walked into them and put her hands on his chest as he wrapped her in a hug. He kissed her head.

Looking down at her, his eyes narrowed. "Something is different. What is it?"

"Come sit." She led him to the sofa, and he sat down. She went to check on the baby and then came over. Without being asked, she sat on his lap and he gladly held her.

"Now what is up, my love?"

She told him what happened at the river. "I just had to process it all."

Danny took her in his arms and held her tight. "Oh, my love. I am so happy for you."

She hugged him back and smiled. She felt his joy.

Then Charlie started to fuss.

"Oh, he is hungry." She got up and went to go get him. She got a blanket. She still wasn't comfortable nursing in front of Danny, even if they had fully learned to love each other. She settled into the chair. "So, what are your thoughts?"

"I am just so happy you realized that. I know how hard it is to come to that."

"Did it take you longer?"

He nodded. "But I was angry and fought God much longer. You wanted Him. You just didn't know who He was."

"No, I didn't. I am glad I am learning now." She paused. "Do you think I should write to my family? Tell them about Charlie?"

He seemed to think about it.

"Well, I am sure they have heard about the baby. The Yoders said they know." He paused. "I think it's a good idea, if you want. But don't expect a response."

"Oh, I won't. You know I grew up there too."

He nodded. "I thought I would bring this up, but before the baby was born. You wanted to be a nurse or do some training, right?"

She nodded. "Yeah, but I didn't finish school."

"With the baby, it may be a bit harder, but what do you think about finishing school and getting your GED, and then seeing where you can go from there? I want you to live your dreams and that may be being a wife and mother, but it may be something in nursing."

Her eyebrows rose. "Are you serious?"

"Of course, my love."

She looked down at the baby. "You know Amish women don't have much of a say about what happens in their life and having an education and careers is not an option for them besides baking and sewing."

"I know this, and I feel that is wrong. Our future

daughter will do and be whatever she wants to be. Just like our boy."

Her eyes watered.

"Thank you. You don't know how much that means to me." She wiped her eyes. "I haven't given it much thought with everything going on. I want to give it a try, but I want to wait till he gets a bit older. I want to heal more."

His eyes sparkled. "All right. I agree with that. I will go with you and also help you study."

She smiled. "If I get an A, can my tutor give me a kiss?"

He laughed loudly and winked at her. "If you get an A, I will give you a hug with it."

"Oh, I think I will like my lessons." She chuckled. "And if I get a B, I get to hold you down and tickle you."

He shook his head in laughter. "Sure. Just get all A's and you will get lots of kisses."

She laughed loudly. "Don't forget the hugs."

She was right where she belonged after traveling such a long road. She hadn't been sure she would get here, but God's plan was better than her own.

Acknowledgments

This story came from my heart and soul. How I enjoyed writing it and changing it into the story it is now. I had a lot of help along the way. I've really found my community with this story. And it's not just because it was written and published in six months like my last story. Lol

First Sarah McNerney, she gave me the courage and support to try this new genre. Writing it without her wouldn't have been the same. No one will know what scenes are real and not from our friendship. All the late night talks and planning the publishing has been great. I will always have those memories with her and treasure them. Laughing over how perfect Danny is and so much more.

My wonderful editor, Jessica Ham, did such a great job. She has taught me so much about writing. You are the best.

Crystal Caudill was a great help with the plot. I've enjoyed getting to know her through this story. She is a great friend and also a fellow Kentuckian.

My cover designer, Hannah Linder, did such a good job. This story wouldn't be the same without this beautiful cover. It makes the story. She has such exceptional talent.

Anne Perreault, for always being an inspiration to me. She does such great work, and I love seeing what more she will do.

To David, who answered all my questions about cops

at the end part of the edits. It was very helpful and the future talks we've had with you telling me so many great stories of your years as a police officer.

Last but not least, to my Jesus. I always said I wouldn't write Amish fiction but You had other ideas. You laid this story on my heart. You helped show me what sometimes the church does and how You can heal that. How you never meant for it to happen to Your children.

Self help

If you are ever in a situation like Priscilla, she could have gone to the police but many times the police won't touch the Amish because of their religious beliefs. There have been times where they have been tried for what they did.

Every situation is different, I don't think any decision you make is a wrong one; many times in the situation it's the only decision you can make at the time.

Priscilla, in her situation, went to trusted friends, Miriam and Paul Yoder. They were going to help where they could. And I do believe they would have saved her from marrying James, but she and maybe even they would be shunned by the community. Though other churches may not be the same, many are not trained in abuse like this. There people can help but as a church. When Danny mentions counseling. it was not through his church. Some churches can counsel but sadly most I don't believe can. Priscilla was so afraid of being hurt again by her own people. She married her first love, knowing she trusted him. She knew he could take care of her deep down. It just took her a bit to let her heart believe it.

There are places to go in situations that are abusive.

Almost every town, even small ones, has a safe place for women.

Here are some resources I have followed while researching. While I don't agree with everyone, they advocate for women and children so much. Sarah McDugal, wildren to wild and Heather Elizabeth, (Held and Healed: Christian rebuilding after abuse) and Patrick Waever are huge supporters for women and children and even men because men can be survivors too.

Human trafficking hotline: 888-373-7888

National domestic abuse hotline: 800-799-7233